dj. **1.** marked by the ability

› creating [the ~ impulse]

ething created rather than

rts] *n.* **1.** one who is creative;

:reation of advertisement

aterial produced by it esp.

CREATIVE COUPLES

COLLABORATIONS THAT CHANGED HISTORY

To David, my partner and my biggest supporter

“Lovers don’t finally meet somewhere.
They’re in each other all along.”

Rumi

ANGELLA M. NAZARIAN

CREATIVE COUPLES

COLLABORATIONS THAT CHANGED HISTORY

ASSOULINE

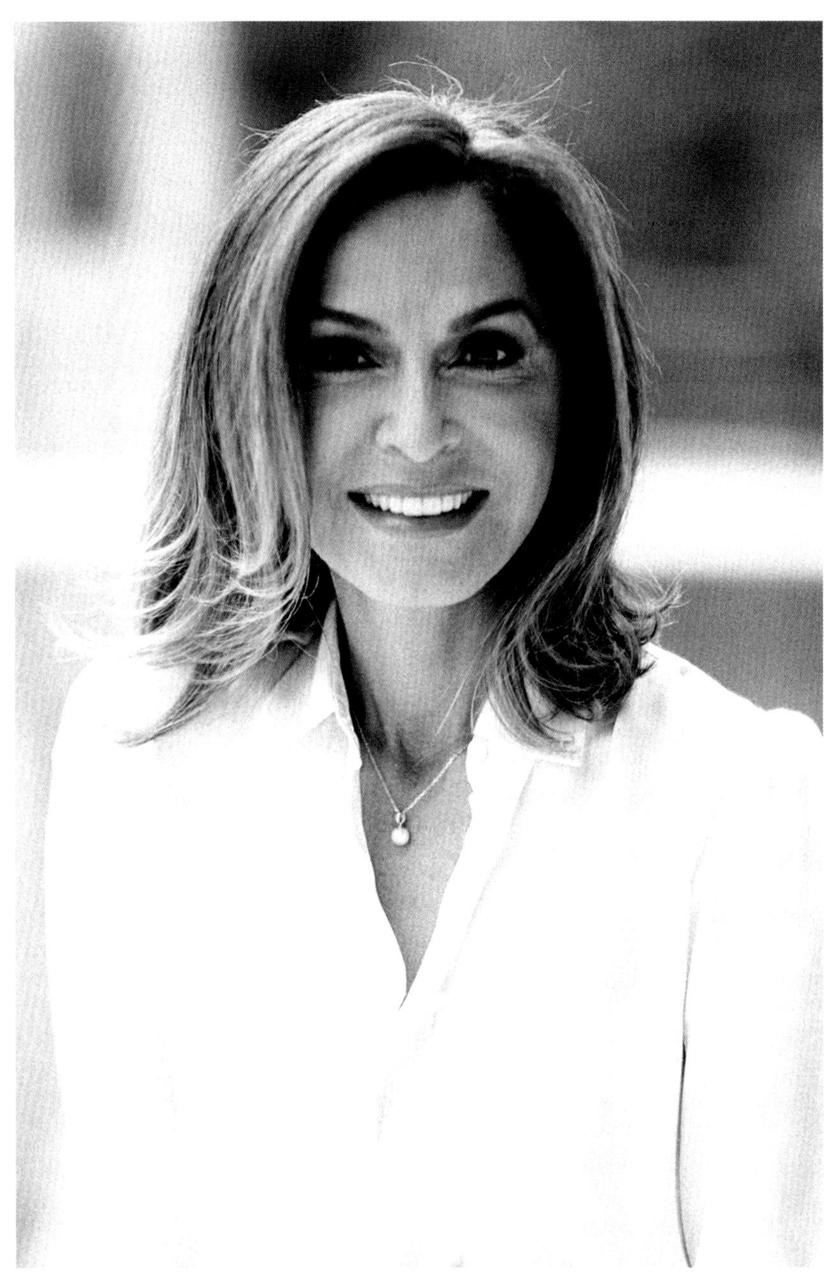

Portrait of the author by Katie Levine.

Contents

The Power of Partnerships: 15 Couples Who Changed History

By Angella M. Nazarian

I'm a big believer in the ability to tell stories through people. So for me, the profile is not just a means to get to know and understand a notable couple; it can also teach us something about human nature or our cultural values. Even before finishing my last book, *Visionary Women,* I knew that another volume was waiting to be born. In my decade-long research on women's leadership, I came to the realization that many of the pioneering women I had featured in *Visionary Women*—such as Sandra Day O'Connor, Shirin Neshat, Leymah Gbowee, Marina Abramović, Amelia Earhart, Miuccia Prada, and Marie Curie—had spouses, partners, or male allies who steadfastly supported their work.

I also found that many of the significant innovations of the twentieth century had come about through the joint efforts of men and women working together synergistically. When we think about it, it makes complete sense: Life, work, and gender are often intertwined and inseparable, especially in today's climate, where an unprecedented number of women have entered the workforce.

This strong cultural shift toward greater participation by women has created a much-needed sense of urgency to discuss the ways in which men can become (and, indeed, many already are) potential allies and supporters in women's growth. In fact, in 2014, the United Nations Entity for Gender Equality and the Empowerment of Women (known as UN Women) launched a new initiative called HeForShe, which aimed to get men to pledge to promote gender equality. So great was the reception of this campaign that the UN Women website crashed in the aftermath of the media blitz that followed. Secretary-General Ban Ki-moon became the first person to officially sign on to HeForShe, and soon many other high-profile men such as actors Hugh Jackman, Jared Leto, and Russell Crowe aligned themselves with the initiative.

Only a few years later, while I was in the midst of writing this book, the cultural wildfire of the #MeToo movement spread from coast to coast. More than a year has passed, and we are still finding the right language and the best ways to foster genuine, open, and coed conversations about the subject. How do our stereotypical perceptions of masculinity and femininity limit our range of experiences and growth? How do our very first experiences with our parents, siblings, and the men and women who raised and taught us affect the way we relate to the opposite sex? How can we begin the process of deconstructing and redefining age-old beliefs about manhood and womanhood? One thing seems clear: Women can't make progress alone. As the celebrated Supreme Court justice Ruth Bader Ginsburg, who is known for her groundbreaking arguments on women's rights, has aptly said, "I always thought that there was nothing an anti-feminist would want more than to have women only in women's organizations, in their own little corner empathizing with each other and not touching a man's world. If you're going to change things, you have to be with the people who hold the levers."[1] By working with men, we can elevate the conversation to a plane where we build a sense of trust and respect for the work men and women do together and separately.

Considering this momentum, it would be interesting to step back and take a closer look at the dynamics of some of the world's most prolific partnerships through time. I wanted to better comprehend the underlying factors of two people coming together—as a couple, as well as partners in work—and to examine how personal relationships affect a couple's working relationship. Furthermore, I wanted to explore what makes a gratifying and productive partnership. A broader understanding can only come about by allowing for context and history, and by recognizing a wide spectrum of relationships that fall under the heading of partnerships.

> “Love does not consist of gazing at each other, but in looking outward together in the same direction.”
>
> Antoine de Saint-Exupéry

We have always been fascinated by love stories, and throughout time various cultures and myths have attempted to explain the mysteries surrounding men and women. Take, for example, Adam and Eve. They are considered to be the world's first couple, according to the Bible. Through their story, we encounter the power dynamics of the sexes; the importance of connection; the nature of love, seduction, passion, and temptation; and even the fall from grace, and the ensuing efforts to recover the "Eden" state of mind. Adam and Eve may have given us the first blueprint of a complicated love relationship. Both the Persian and Talmudic mythologies discuss how God first made a two-sexed being—a male and a female together—and then, later, divided it into two. As the story goes, the feminine and the masculine halves strive to come together in a heat of attraction, love, friendship, and intimacy. Similarly, the Chinese book of meditation, the T'ai I Chin Hua Tsung Chih *(The Secret of the Golden Flower)*, tells us that in each man and woman there are two psychic poles that are eternally seeking to merge into one. Just as electricity flows between a positive and negative terminal, so does psychic energy flow between two poles that have been called "masculine" and "feminine." These early writings may have been the first explanations of the laws of attraction between the sexes.

Ancient cultures have also attempted to examine the enigmatic relationship between men and women through storytelling. In ancient Greek texts, the feminine element brought inspiration, a sense of aliveness, intuition, and clarity to the male counterpart. For example, Ariadne, the maiden in Greek mythology, enabled Theseus to find his way out of the dark labyrinth after he slayed the Minotaur. She ensured his safe return to light by supplying him with a spool of thread to lead him out again. Sometimes, stories warn us of the danger of falling under the influence of the female force. Such was the case with Mark Antony, who at the time of meeting Cleopatra stood at the pinnacle of his power. Cleopatra was the queen of Egypt, yet her country was one of the Roman Empire's dependent provinces that Antony oversaw. Legend has it that Cleopatra's magnetic personality and seductive powers cast such a spell on the lovestruck general that he lost his abilities of sound judgment and was duly defeated in the civil war. Their love story is a cautionary tale of losing oneself in the gravitational pull of passionate emotions.

But perhaps the most comprehensive explanation of attraction and relationship dynamics has come from the writings of the pioneering twentieth-century psychologist Carl Gustav Jung. He and his research assistant, lover, and partner, Toni Wolff, happen to be one of the couples that I have showcased in this tome. Their profound and intimate working relationship gave rise to some of the most prominent psychological theories to date. Jung and Wolff foraged through ancient alchemical texts from shamanistic and indigenous cultures and came upon the idea that each person is a combination of male and female polarities. Jung went on to coin the terms *anima,* which refers to the feminine component in a man's personality, and *animus*—the masculine side of a woman's self. The anima and animus, he believed, had far-reaching implications in the dynamics between the sexes and in every person's search for individual wholeness. He believed that men, identifying with their masculinity, typically project their feminine sides onto women; women, meanwhile, do the opposite. Thus, the law of attraction is one in which a man finds himself drawn to a woman who embodies his own, unrecognized female side, and vice versa. In Jung's view, relationships serve as the primary vehicle for self-exploration, and the integration of our own undervalued characteristics. It is usually when the initial high of attraction wears thin that couples face the difficult task of sorting through their expectations and projections, and reconciling them with reality. The point that Jung and other psychologists make is that, through grappling with and understanding the other, each partner's consciousness is expanded and personality enriched.

This book is an invitation to take a closer look at our complex relationships with the opposite sex in love, life, and work. While reading the chapters, it is worthwhile to ask ourselves the following questions: What was the value and the larger mission of each relationship, and how did each person serve the other in their partnership? Where did the couples' source of attraction lie, and how did they respond to conflict?

In the following chapters, I have profiled fifteen couples that have operated as forces in each other's lives and in the world at large. This compilation of profiles is not just a celebration but also an investigation into the different forms by which men and women relate to one another in partnership—as muses, mentors, lovers, colleagues, and life partners. Each couple seems to have its own unique relationship style and ensuing dynamics; there is no magic formula for success that fits all partnerships. Some of these duos have worked together in the same field, while others have empowered one another's work through their support and encouragement. In some cases it was the man and in others it was the woman who became the more notable of the two. However, in all of these pairings, as you will note, the partnership has fostered a far greater impact than either of the individuals could have made on his or her own.

I hope these profiles surprise and inspire us toward a deeper understanding of gender dynamics—and ultimately guide us toward a fluid and more fruitful range of interrelations.

“Coming together is a beginning; staying together is progress; and working together is success.”

Henry Ford, *founder, Ford Motor Company*

“The great marriages are partnerships. It can’t be a great marriage without being a partnership.”

Helen Mirren, *actor*

“In all the world, there is no heart for me like yours. In all the world, there is no love for you like mine.”

Maya Angelou, *poet*

“It takes two flints to make a fire.”

Louisa May Alcott, *novelist*

“Enchanted partnership begins with the conscious understanding, on the part of two people, that the purpose of their relationship is not so much material as spiritual, and the internal skills demanded by it are prodigious.”

Marianne Williamson,
author, lecturer, and activist

“Any good marriage is secret territory, a necessary white space on society’s map. What others don’t know about it is what makes it yours.”

Stephen King, *author*

Lou Andreas-Salomé & Rainer Maria Rilke

The Intellectual Trailblazers

Lou Andreas-Salomé was the intellectual femme fatale of her time. She was not a beauty by today's standards—she dressed like a nun, some said, in the high-collared habit of a scholar, and she wore her hair pulled back—but this radical Russian feminist had a charm and brilliance that captured the hearts of the philosophers Friedrich Nietzsche and Paul Rée, as well as a host of other prominent thinkers of the era. And, as she walked into a friend's apartment in Munich on a spring day in 1897, wearing a loose dress with cottony layers, her hair tied in a tousled knot atop her head, she was soon to do the same to Rainer Maria Rilke, who would become one of the most important lyric poets published in the twentieth century. At the time, Andreas-Salomé was thirty-six years old, married, and had written several scholarly books and essays. Rilke was an aspiring poet, fifteen years her junior.

Rilke felt that he already knew Andreas-Salomé from reading an essay of hers, titled "Jesus the Jew." (Incidentally, her portrayal of Jesus corresponded with a cycle of Rilke's poems called "Visions of Christ.") Andreas-Salomé's work captivated Rilke, but her magnetic presence also sparked an unusual relationship that would last for nearly three decades. Andreas-Salomé was first his lover, then his guide and mentor. It took more than a decade for them to fully realize their highest needs in the relationship; they would become equals and kindred spirits who supported and nurtured one another's efforts and work. The day after meeting Andreas-Salomé, Rilke wandered the Munich streets with a handful of roses, too scared to appear at her doorstep. Never mind the torrent of poems he had anonymously sent her prior to that fateful meeting. Andreas-Salomé, who was by now used to this kind of adoring attention, only claimed that she wished he would "go completely away."[1]

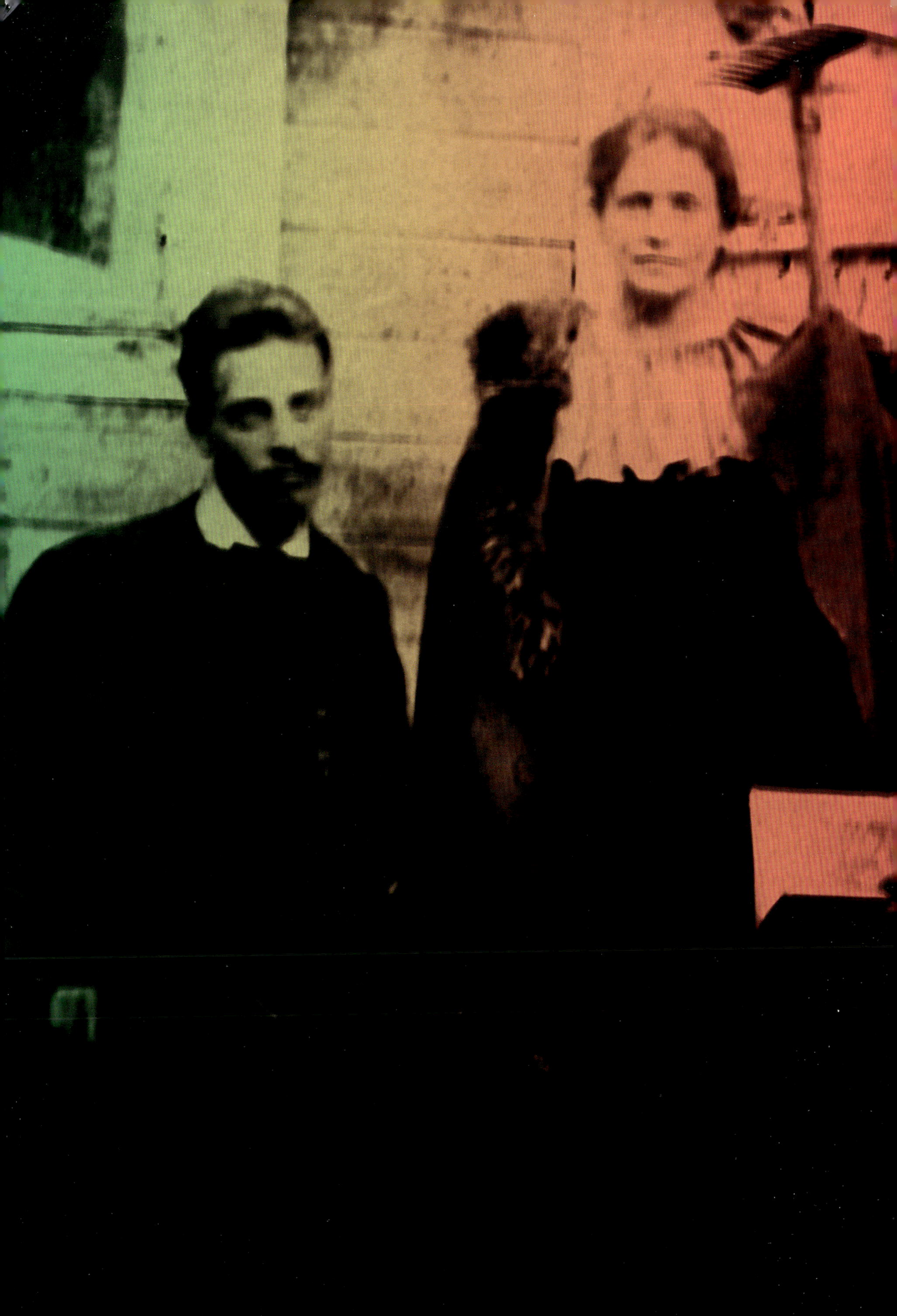

She had been through this pattern of relationships before, and at each turn, she had to assert her will to avoid becoming consumed by the identity or needs of a partner. From an early age, Andreas-Salomé wanted to be free to pursue her own intellectual quests—an anomaly for a young, upper-class woman raised in the restrictive Victorian era—and in 1880, she left her home city of Saint Petersburg for Zurich, to enroll in one of the few universities in Europe that had opened its doors to women. By age twenty-one, Andreas-Salomé was embroiled in a love triangle with Nietzsche and his friend Rée. Both men proposed to marry her, but she had a proposition of her own: to form an intellectual trinity. The three of them would live and study together, but their relationship would remain strictly platonic; Andreas-Salomé feared that sexual relations would distract her from her true quest and shackle her to a man. Her mother was outraged by her daughter's plans. That bold refusal of limitations, however, would become a hallmark of Andreas-Salomé's character. "I can neither live according to models, nor will I serve as a model for anyone else; but I will structure my life in accordance of myself, no matter what the consequences," she said.[2]

One can only imagine the tensions that arose between two friends vying for the attention of this elusive woman. Before long, ulterior motives and misunderstandings drove a wedge between Andreas-Salomé, Rée, and Nietzsche, and plans for their intellectual ménage à trois were aborted. However, Andreas-Salomé had left a dark and powerful mark on Nietzsche's life. In 1886, he summed up his experience with her in a scathing verdict about women. "When a woman has scholarly tendencies," he wrote in his work *Beyond Good and Evil,* "there is usually something wrong with her sexually."[3] Andreas-Salomé did display a fear of sexual intimacy, but Nietzsche's sweeping remarks indicated a limited, one-dimensional view of women. In the following years, Andreas-Salomé would refute Nietzsche's views in a variety of books and essays that focused on women's sexuality and independence, placing her at the forefront of feminine theory at the turn of the century.

Legend has it that Friedrich Carl Andreas, Andreas-Salomé's future husband, sought her out with similar passion after reading her first novel, *Struggling for God.* A professor of Iranian and western Asiatic culture who was well versed in literature, history, and art, Andreas had an intellectual curiosity that Andreas-Salomé found appealing. Although they married in 1887, their relationship did not conform with traditional gender roles or common marital practices. For one, they never consummated their union. Andreas-Salomé only agreed to marry Andreas on the condition that Rée, who at this point had given up on wooing her, would continue to be a part of her life. Rée would be one of the many admirers with whom she spent time during her forty-plus-year marriage to Andreas.

> “I hold this to be the highest task of a bond between two people: that each should stand guard over the solitude of the other.”
>
> Rainer Maria Rilke

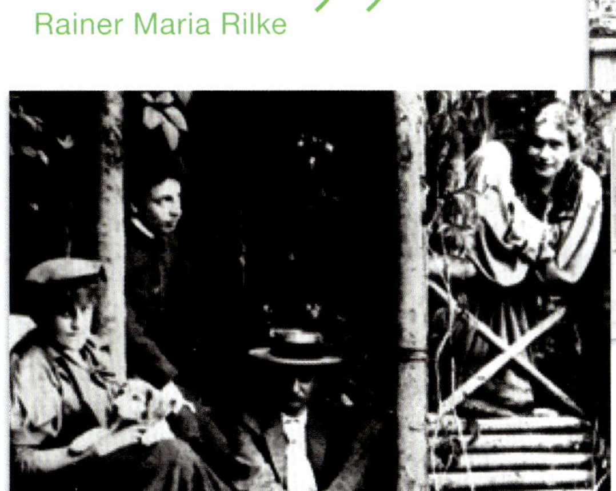

From left: Lou Andreas-Salomé, 1897; Lou Andreas-Salomé posing for her portrait.

It was against the backdrop of such storied and colorful relationships that the besotted Rilke pursued Andreas-Salomé. Little did she know that she would soon give more of herself to this young, sensitive man than to any other man in her life. Perhaps it was because his poems had made an impression on her, but less than a month after their first meeting, Andreas-Salomé and Rilke took a two-day trip to Wolfratshausen, Germany, where they became lovers. Many scholars believe that it may have been Andreas-Salomé's first sexual experience.

“You come toward me in everything that's beautiful,” Rilke wrote after their consummation of love.[4] Andreas-Salomé later reflected on their relationship in her memoirs. “We were not two halves seeking the other,” she wrote. “We were a whole which confronted that inconceivable wholeness with a shiver of recognition.”[5]

Despite the deep romance of their words, their relationship was not always on equal ground. In Andreas-Salomé's presence, Rilke acted unsure and needy—more like an adoring protégé than a self-possessed adult. Painstakingly, Andreas-Salomé guided and edited his work, served as his mentor, and introduced him to important literary figures in Berlin. She taught him Russian, advised him to copy her courtly style of handwriting, and urged him to cultivate his masculinity. She even suggested that he change his first name, René, to the more masculine, German version. Thus, Rainer Maria Rilke, one the greatest poets in the modern world, was born.

Andreas-Salomé became the center of Rilke's universe, even though he had to live on the periphery of hers. She continued traveling to visit friends and maintained an intense writing schedule, which made Rilke cling to her all the more. Andreas-Salomé may have been ambivalent about their relationship at the time; in 1898, she published a short novel called *Deviations,* which chronicles a woman's conflicted desire to be subservient to the man she loves while also feeling a need for autonomy. In what may have been an attempt to keep Rilke at a comfortable distance, Andreas-Salomé decided to take a trip to Russia accompanied by both him and her husband, Andreas. There, they met the great author Leo Tolstoy, and Andreas-Salomé introduced Rilke to all that she loved about her homeland. In a burst of creativity following the trip, Rilke produced a breakthrough cycle of poems that would become the first part of *The Book of Hours: Love Poems to God.* When published, it bore a dedication to Andreas-Salomé.

In the fall of 1900, Andreas-Salomé and Rilke set out to visit Russia again, but this time as a couple. The trip proved to be emotionally exhausting for Andreas-Salomé, for Rilke was overly dependent on her. The strain led her to break off relations with him after their travels ended. On New Year's Eve of 1900, she confessed in her diary the reason for the split: "What I expect from the coming year, what I need is almost only silence," she wrote. "I need to be more by myself."[6]

The separation devastated Rilke, but he needed to do some growing up on his own; only after he'd achieved that would he and Andreas-Salomé be able to come together as friends and literary allies in later years. Shortly after his split from Andreas-Salomé, Rilke met a sculptor by the name of Clara Westhoff during a stay in an artist colony. That he didn't idolize her was part of the appeal of the relationship. In fact, this time Rilke was on the receiving end of his partner's admiration. He then made an abrupt decision and proposed to marry Westhoff. Andreas-Salomé showed her disapproval by warning Rilke that, should he marry, she would no longer be available to him.

Rilke resisted contacting his estranged friend for two and a half years, until he began to suffer from a terrible depression and became desperate for Andreas-Salomé's guidance. He had been living in poverty in Paris and had fathered a child, though he rarely shared a home with his wife or daughter. When he reached out to Andreas-Salomé, she didn't push him away, and although she didn't offer to meet, she wrote him a letter full of kindness and warmth. Possessing a special understanding of the young artist's temperament and sensitivity, she encouraged him to write more letters, as she thought this would serve his art and simultaneously lift his spirits. Thus began a lifelong correspondence between the two, in which they poured out their innermost thoughts and feelings to one another. Some two hundred of these exchanges are compiled in the book *Rilke and Andreas-Salomé: A Love Story in Letters.* Their messages were not only a monument to their capacity for friendship and intimacy, but also a sign of Rilke's need to impart his fears, desires, and the life around him to his trusted confidant.

Although Andreas-Salomé wouldn't train as a psychoanalyst until 1912, it was her natural instinct to help Rilke develop his sensitive nature in service to his art. How, he asked Andreas-Salomé, would he learn to channel his feelings into poetry? Her validating response was that he was already doing it through his letters. Indeed, Rilke incorporated the scenes

> "For one human being to love another: that is perhaps the most difficult of all our tasks, the ultimate, the last test and proof, the work for which all other work is but preparation."
>
> Rainer Maria Rilke

and images he described to Andreas-Salomé in their correspondence almost word for word in his moving novel, *The Notebooks of Malte Laurids Brigge.* Interestingly, Andreas-Salomé also made references to specific characters from Rilke's letters in her own novel, titled *Marriage,* at the time. A shift in psychic orientation was taking shape: Rilke had become a formidable partner in this artistic interchange.

When Rilke sent Andreas-Salomé a copy of a small book he had written about the sculptor Auguste Rodin, who had become his mentor in Paris, she wrote back to say that it was his best published work. "From now on you can depend on me," Andreas-Salomé promised,[7] and she soon invited Rilke to visit her at her home in Göttingen, Germany. Their visit did not rekindle the spark of physical attraction but rather a creative connection that fanned both of their intellectual fires. Subsequently, Rilke invited Andreas-Salomé to Paris to meet two of the most important people in his life: Westhoff and Rodin. By that time, Rilke had become Rodin's most trusted assistant. The two artists could not have been more different from one another. Physically, the sculptor was imposing, big, and sensual, while the young poet was slight, narrow-shouldered, and spiritual. Both men were attracted to ambitious, independent women, but they had divergent views of womanhood. Rodin, a known womanizer, thought women were manipulators who wanted to trap men into marriage. Rilke, impacted by the depth of his relationship with Andreas-Salomé, accepted that men had the ability to sustain

“The closer two people stand to each other inwardly, the more readily they become for each other the condition under which alone their two beings find expression.”

Lou Andreas-Salomé

meaningful relationships with women without sex. As the journalist Rachel Corbett explained in her book *You Must Change Your Life: The Story of Rainer Maria Rilke and Auguste Rodin,* Rilke believed that "[t]o think of women purely in terms of pleasure and consumption was to think like a child."[8]

It wouldn't be long before Rilke would leave Rodin's studio and draw wide acclaim for his writing. His prose poem *The Lay of the Love and Death of Cornet Christoph Rilke,* which was inspired by his trips with Andreas-Salomé to Russia and written in a single night, was published in its final form in 1906 and prompted numerous adulatory letters from admirers. Fame was foreign to Rilke, and he felt uncomfortable with the adoration. The restless energy and constant traveling that ensued came, in part, as an attempt to imitate Andreas-Salomé's way of life and to feed their shared need for experiences to fuel their art.

The year 1911 was significant for both Rilke and Andreas-Salomé. Tired of spending so much time apart, Westhoff finally filed for divorce. Rilke supported ending the relationship and even encouraged his wife to undergo psychoanalysis with his friend Dr. Viktor Emil von Gebsattel. It was also at this time that Andreas-Salomé attended the Third International Psychoanalytic Congress in Weimar, Germany, where a meeting with Sigmund Freud would change the course of her life. The previous year, she had published an essay about erotic love, titled "The Erotic," and Freud—whose theories about repressed sexual drive informed many of his core psychoanalytic tenets—found Andreas-Salomé's work fascinating. He was well aware of Andreas-Salomé's status as an intellectual celebrity and flattered by her genuine interest to study with him. A group photograph of the congress shows Andreas-Salomé, wrapped in a long fur, seated in front of Freud and his associate Carl Jung.

When Andreas-Salomé returned home, she knew she would devote the rest of her life to pursuing Freudian psychology. Her deep interest in the burgeoning field, she explained, was motivated by the years she spent "sharing the extraordinary and rare spiritual destiny of another person, and growing among a people who were naturally oriented toward the inner life."[9] That other person she referred to is assumed to have been Rilke, as her relationship with him was the most enduring and profound of her life. Andreas-Salomé was anxious to share her newfound passion with Rilke and urged him to join her at a meeting with Freud.

Thus, one late-summer day in 1913, Sigmund Freud had a visit with Andreas-Salomé and her famous poet friend in Munich, where Freud was attending the Fourth International Psychoanalytic Congress. Rilke was so magnetized by Freud's ideas that he considered going into analysis himself. Andreas-Salomé encouraged the idea at first, but later, fearing that the pursuit would negatively affect Rilke's creativity, she dissuaded him.

As it was in any circle that she joined, Andreas-Salomé became ensconced in the center of Freud's intellectual activity. She would share meals with him and his family, and they would stay up well into the night discussing ideas. Andreas-Salomé regularly attended Freud's Wednesday lectures, and if she missed a class, the eminent psychologist would often struggle to deliver his speech. "I stared spellbound at the space that had been left for you," he once told her.[10] She indeed became one of the first female psychoanalysts of her era. Freud's special admiration for Andreas-Salomé only grew deeper with time, and in later years he kept a framed picture of her on his desk. It seems doubtful that he ever valued a woman's intellect as much as Andreas-Salomé's. While his own work tended to focus on the neurotic or unhealthy mind, her theories emphasized the mind's healthy pathways that strive toward wholeness. In fact, some suggest that Andreas-Salomé's ideas prompted Freud's colleague, the renowned psychologist Alfred Adler, to write about the integration of both "masculine" and "feminine" aspects of ourselves in becoming a fully realized human being.

Letters from Rilke's later years indicate that he read and absorbed Andreas-Salomé's psychoanalytical essays. He believed that artistic and sexual experiences were different expressions of the same yearning—a view that shares much in common with Andreas-Salomé's theories. Most notably, his ideas about the role of the feminine are essentially Andreas-Salomé's proclamations. In the future, he wrote, girls and women would no longer be viewed in relation to men but would instead be considered "something in itself, something that makes one think, not of any complement and limit, but only of life and existence: the feminine human being."[11] Andreas-Salomé borrowed from Rilke as well: She often used his poems as tools for treating her patients during analysis.

From 1912—the year Rilke wrote the first poem of his masterful *Duino Elegies*—until 1922, when he completed the tenth and final of his elegies, he continued to write and visit Andreas-Salomé. She had become his distant spine, a driving force that gave him the strength and confidence to finish this major feat. After reading the *Duino Elegies,* Andreas-Salomé offered Rilke praise. "How you have enriched me," she wrote to him.[12] His late-career poetry represented the culmination of a fulfilled potential. This was what Rilke had hungered for all his life.

"[A]ll that I am / Stirs me because of you," Rilke wrote to Andreas-Salomé in 1926.[13] When he penned that letter, he was in the late stages of leukemia; he would pass two weeks after it was sent, at the age of fifty-one. Rilke had told Andreas-Salomé the pain he was experiencing was unbearable, but to him, even the process of death was another phenomenon to be experienced and examined. Up until his final hour, he refused painkillers and hospitals, and kept a watchful eye as he greeted his death. "Come, you last thing, which I acknowledge," he wrote.[14] That was his final notation on the paper found by his bed.

Andreas-Salomé would eulogize Rilke by writing a book about his work. In it, she described mourning as not simply "a state of emotional preoccupation. . . [but] more precisely, an incessant discourse with the departed one, in order to draw him nearer."[15] Although she remained evasive about her marriage and considered her relationship with Nietzsche to have been an experience, she addressed Rilke as "a discourse, a conversation that seemed ever alive," as her biographer Julia Vickers wrote.[16]

Throughout her sixties and well into her seventies, Andreas-Salomé continued to practice psychoanalysis and often saw Freud's referrals as patients. She and Freud's daughter Anna would collaborate on a number of psychological theories, as well. At the age of seventy, she published an exceptional essay on psychoanalysis that Freud called "the finest thing of yours I've read, an involuntary proof of your superiority over all of us."[17] In 1935, while suffering from breast cancer, Andreas-Salomé had a mastectomy. She died of an infection a year and a half later, just one week before her seventy-sixth birthday.

> "We were not two halves seeking the other: We were a whole which confronted that inconceivable wholeness with a shiver of recognition."
>
> Lou Andreas-Salomé

Andreas-Salomé was, in many ways, the first embodiment of a modern woman. She cherished her own mind and lived on her own terms—behavior that was unheard of for a female of her generation. It would have been far easier for Andreas-Salomé to have immersed herself in Nietzsche's work and become his disciple, but she was committed to exploring and forming her own philosophy. Likewise, she could have simply remained the object of obsession and a muse to some of the most accomplished men of her time, but instead she steadfastly carved out her own intellectual and creative independence. And through it all, none of her relationships were as enduring and indispensable as the one Andreas-Salomé shared with Rilke. They guided each other through one of the most fruitful artistic exchanges in twentieth-century literature. Despite distance, age difference, and emotional turmoil, they managed to cultivate a lifelong connection built on love, partnership, and the exchange of ideas.

Carl Jung & Toni Wolff

The Soul Seekers

Carl Gustav Jung was one of the greatest thinkers of his era and the founder of analytical psychology. His ideas influenced not only the field of psychology, but also many others, including literature and anthropology. His theories on the collective unconscious, his formulations on personality types, and his thoughts about the interplay of constructs such as introversion and extroversion have become fixtures of popular discourse. And every year, laypeople flock to the C. G. Jung Institute's locations around the world for a variety of courses and seminars.

During the height of his career, Jung was considered a living icon, and questing souls made pilgrimages from far and wide to see the "sage of Zurich." Albert Einstein, James Joyce, and Nobel laureates Hermann Hesse and Wolfgang Pauli were but a few of the luminaries who either sought his advice, underwent analysis with him, or immersed themselves in his world of ideas. But what many do not know is that this brilliant healer and doctor was once filled with such anguish over being caught between the love of two women that he wanted to drown himself in a lake by his home.

In 1911, Jung was thirty-six and happily married to his wife, Emma—the second richest heiress in Switzerland and the mother of his four healthy children. He had a flourishing private practice and was an internationally known and respected research psychiatrist. He was the president of the International Psychoanalytic Association and heir apparent to Sigmund Freud. However, by 1913, he was facing a personal crisis of monumental magnitude. The independent thinker that he was, he could no longer accept Freud's theory that sexual energy was at the root of all mental dysfunction and had to break away from his mentor—a bold and difficult move at the time. Jung stopped teaching at the University of Zurich, which

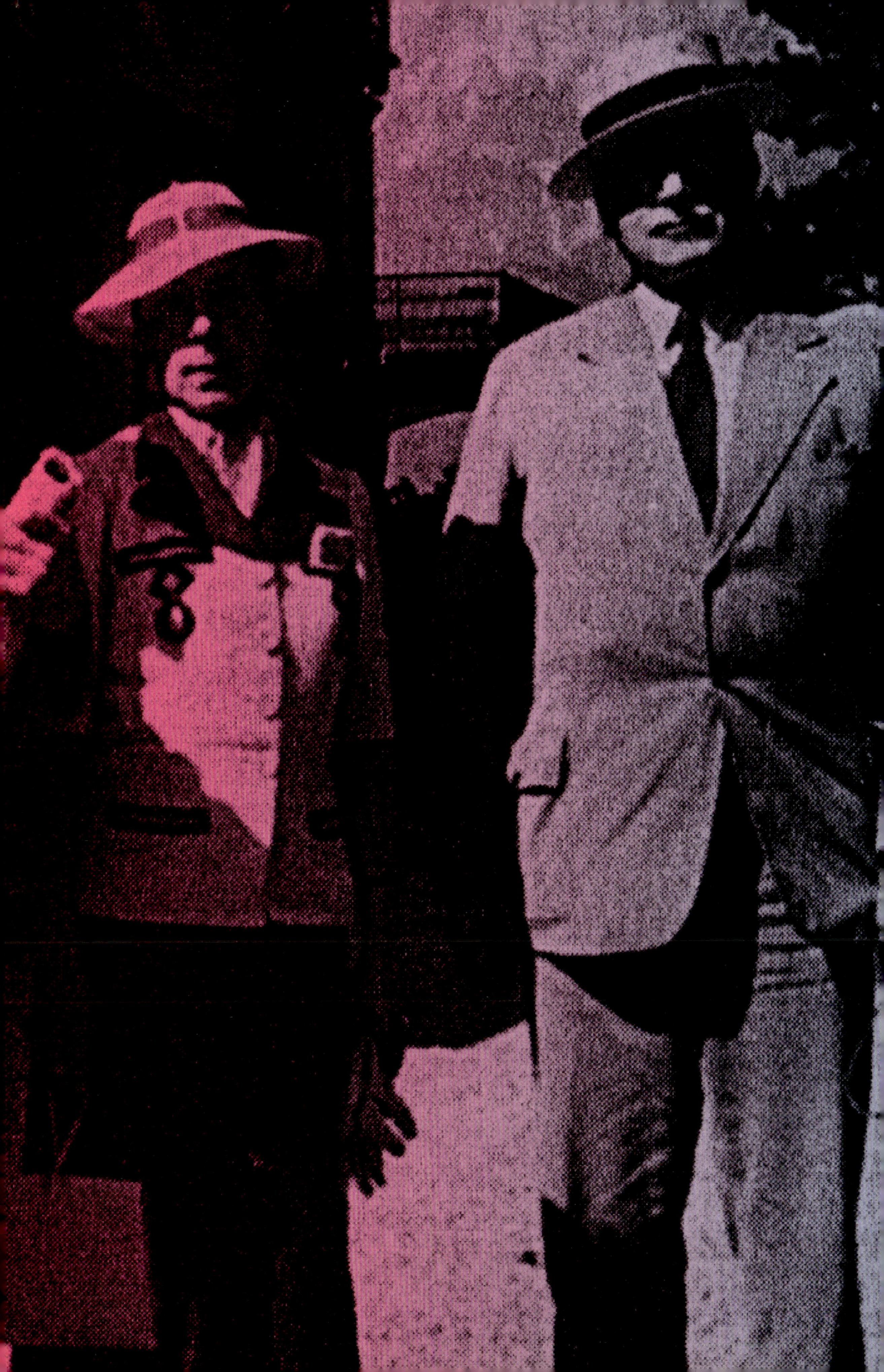

further isolated him from professional circles, and decided to devote his time to studying the unconscious.

His primary collaborator in this work, Toni Wolff, was the most influential woman in Jung's creative life. She would figure as the third member of a complicated love triangle in the Jung household. Few may have heard the story, for Wolff's name and contributions have been either overlooked or buried to minimize the unconventional connection she shared with him.

"We must make our mistakes," Jung once said. "We must live out our own vision of life. And there will be error. If you avoid error, you do not live."[1] This is how the story of Jung and Wolff's love—and the genius behind analytic psychology—begins: with a man who lived according to a particular inner vision, without regard for being right or wrong.

In 1910, the twenty-two-year-old Wolff was sent to Jung's office at her mother's request. Wolff's beloved father and mentor had died several months earlier, and the young woman was inconsolable. As a way of coaxing her to talk in their first session, Jung compared her grief to several episodes from Greek mythology. Wolff summarily chastised him for glossing over some details of the stories, and Jung listened as she retold each myth with detailed accuracy. At that moment, it dawned on him that this petite, beautifully coifed young woman grasped, perhaps even better than him, the very subjects that he had been exploring for the past year. He had a suspicion that the symbols embedded in mythological stories paralleled those found in dreams, and that both stemmed from the inner reaches of the unconscious. Such symbols, he believed, would provide the key to deciphering the messages of the unconscious.

Jung spent the subsequent sessions concentrating on his and Wolff's shared intellectual interests. From the start, they brought out the best in each other's thinking. Not afraid to challenge Jung's ideas, Wolff fueled his creativity and imagination, and she brought a much-needed feminine perspective to his research, ensuring that the duo's early theories in psychology were not only groundbreaking but also timeless. The intensity of their collaboration over the following decades would prove that "neither could have conceived alone what they were able to create together," as their biographer Nan Savage Healy wrote.[2]

Emma Jung would spend the rest of her years coping with the love triangle that her husband forced on their lives. It was an awkward situation for all three, to say the least. Wolff would never enjoy a fully committed and public relationship with Jung, and Emma was dismayed that she would have to share her partner with another woman. Jung, meanwhile, felt torn. "I had to obey an inner law which was imposed on me and left me no freedom of choice," he later wrote.[3]

The two women shared some traits. Both came from aristocratic Swiss families that denied them a university education. Stifled, with no apparent opportunity to advance their

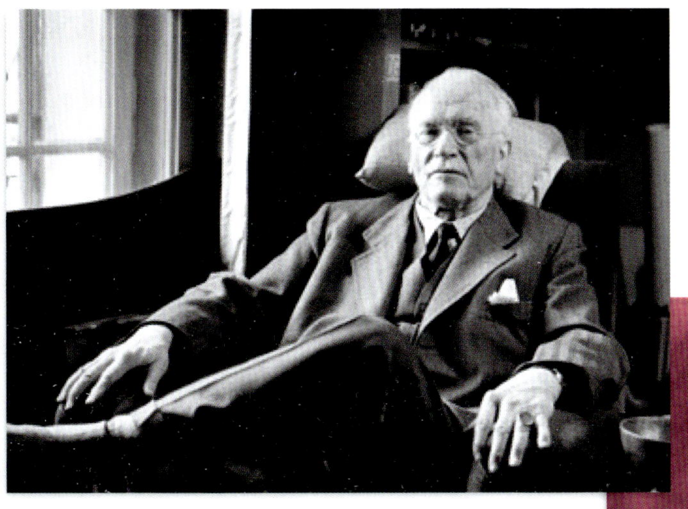

From top: Swiss psychiatrist Carl Gustav Jung, 1960; Antonia Anna "Toni" Wolff, early 1920s.

"Where love rules, there is no will to power, and where power predominates, love is lacking. The one is the shadow of the other."

Carl Jung

intellectual aspirations, their attraction and connection to Jung served as an outlet for their creative gifts. Emma certainly believed she could be more than just a wife and mother to Jung's children; she wanted to be a partner in his professional life, too. When Jung described the long hours he spent at the Burghölzli psychiatric hospital writing daily case reports about patients, Emma practiced her handwriting in preparation for the secretarial duties she intended to perform for him. But Jung preferred Emma to remain a homemaker and only enlisted her help in situations where her poise and social standing could benefit him professionally.

Unlike Emma, who was deferential to Jung's colleagues and content to perform secretarial tasks, Wolff behaved as his intellectual equal from the start. Dressed in well-cut, elegant dresses, Wolff would visit Jung's home office several times a week with books and manuscripts in hand to continue their joint exploration of mythic stories. She would spend hours studying and doing research at the university library—another privilege that Emma had no time or liberty to experience. No doubt, Emma resented her husband's growing intellectual dependence on Wolff, especially as family demands restricted her own time with her husband.

Jung relied heavily on Wolff's ideas in formulating his book *Psychology of the Unconscious,* which was published in 1912. In the meantime, their mutual fascination with one another was slowly changing the nature of their relationship. At midlife, Jung was at a crossroads, and he struggled with the strength of his feelings for Wolff. He stopped seeing her, hoping the attraction would subside. He was not only concerned for his own family life, but also aware that a relationship with Wolff would prevent the young woman from finding an appropriate husband. Soon, though, Jung had a nightmare that he almost lost Wolff and subsequently reestablished contact with her by letter. At that point, he noted, he knew their relationship was "inevitable."[4]

Later, Jung would provide two explanations for his intense attraction to Wolff. Both theories warrant further discussion, as they are the cornerstones of Jungian philosophy and useful in analyzing the dynamics of the couples showcased in other chapters of this book.

Jung believed that at midlife, one reevaluates priorities. Having achieved outward success during the first half of life, someone in his or her latter years has a higher obligation to become a fully individuated person—one who is aware of the many opposing elements in

> "Seldom, or perhaps never, does a marriage develop into an individual relationship smoothly and without crises; there is no coming to consciousness without pain."
>
> Carl Jung

his or her psyche, and who has the wisdom and fortitude to integrate them fully into his or her broadening personality.

Additionally, in Jung's view, highly creative people manifest two disparate personalities. The first is the traditional persona, which he called the "regular self."[5] The second, on the other hand, is largely spiritual and nonrational, and contains the individual's creative seed. Jung claimed that his second, more artistic and illogical personality connected with Wolff, while his first personality—his conventional persona—was drawn to Emma. Thus, in this triangular relationship, each woman only encountered one half of his true self.

The other equally compelling theory originated from Jung's research with Wolff, published in the book *Psychological Types.* In this groundbreaking work, Jung noted that the interplay of the feminine and masculine energies within each couple serves as the primary source of attraction between the pair. He maintained that each man has an unconscious feminine side within his psyche, which Jung called the anima, that the man carries with him through life. This anima is a constellation of a man's experiences of femininity from childhood on. And Jung theorized that a man becomes attracted to a woman if she displays traits that correspond with his anima. In women, the animus plays a similar role in defining the masculine side of a woman's personality.

Applying this theory, Jung claimed that he was attracted to Wolff because her essential being was the feminine reflection of his unconventional self. Wolff's attraction to him also makes sense in this light, for her primary experience of masculinity in her early life was through her adoring father, who encouraged her curiosity and valued her intellect. In many ways, Jung embodied the same prized masculine values for Wolff.

In her own highly original essays, Wolff corroborated some of the same perspectives, specifically in relation to women. In "A Few Thoughts on the Process of Individuation in Women," she identified two principal feminine archetypes: "the mother" and "the lover." The Virgin Mary is the most common symbol for the mother, as she is not only maternal but also a virgin and dissociated from sexuality. On the other hand, the lover is personified by the more sensual, ancient image of a woman who is connected to the body and the earth. Wolff noted that in Western culture, women seem to overidentify with the pure, virginal archetype and suppress their dark, hedonistic energy. In Jung's life, Emma—the shy, retiring mother of five who dressed in peasant-like attire—exuded the energy of a nurturer and mother. And the mysterious Wolff, with her piercing eyes and stylish dress, was more aligned with the carnal, provocative woman.

It was against the backdrop of these seemingly unconscious and intense forces that Jung and Wolff sought to live out their highly unconventional relationship. It is believed that Emma had contemplated divorce, but she knew that if she left Jung, he would fall apart. Her primary commitment was to her husband and his well-being, and so she slowly adjusted to a routine of compromise and repression.

It was two short weeks after Emma gave birth to her fifth and last child when Jung and Wolff left for a vacation in Ravenna, Italy, where they shared their first sexual encounter. One can only imagine the amount of pain and guilt associated with this decision, but Wolff became a permanent fixture in the Jung household thereafter. She attended most of the family's receptions and smaller gatherings, and each Sunday she was the only outsider at luncheons that had previously been private family affairs. The children even called her *Tante* Toni (Aunt Toni), earnestly at first. But as the kids caught wind of the true nature of their father's extramarital relationship, they became increasingly sarcastic and mean spirited. They resented that after meals, Jung would go off alone with Wolff, either to walk by the lake or to retreat to his study. Because Wolff shared a house with her mother, Jung was also able to spend every Wednesday afternoon with Wolff and her family without sparking undue gossip.

Soon, the three eldest Jung children heard whispers about their father flaunting his dueling relationships in public. Jung would walk into the Psychological Club with Wolff on one arm and Emma on the other, and the two women would sit in armchairs on either side of him to avoid inequity in status. When Jung went to England for his seminars, he took both Emma and Wolff with him. At first, everyone assumed Wolff was granted such favor because of her significance as a collaborator, but other forces were at work.

It was, in effect, the enormous strain of handling these sensitive situations that prompted Jung to contemplate suicide. He spent an immense amount of emotional energy trying to ensure that he treated both women equally and with respect. Jung did not think of Wolff as a common mistress and felt it essential that her dignity be preserved. He explained to Emma that the only solution was to consider Wolff "another wife," as his colleague James Kirsch put it.[6] Much to Emma's dismay, the three privately agreed to these relationship parameters and acted with a high degree of discretion so as to not scandalize the conservative Zurich community.

While their quasi-polygamous relationship may have seemed radical for the time, it wasn't uncommon in certain bohemian communities in Europe. Known as the "left-handed marriage,"[7] this sort of non-legally binding but nevertheless romantically committed union had a precedent among medieval noblemen who would take women of lower status as their second "wives" in a sacred ceremony. Jung called this "a psychic relationship"[8] that fulfills the soul's deepest potential, bringing the "unconscious side"[9] of the psyche (represented by the left hand) together with the heart, which is located on the left side of the body. In many ways, his relationship with Wolff reflected this sentiment.

Perhaps it was in reaction to all the seismic changes in his life that Jung experienced a period of deep disorientation. From the years 1913 to 1918, his unconscious was assaulted with images so bizarre that he found it hard to speak to anyone but Wolff. He later wrote that the experience was so overwhelming, he felt the most difficult feat would be to come out of these attacks with a sane mind. During this time, Wolff stood by him, functioning as his "most integral partner,"[10] in the words of their biographer Healy, and his "necessary human bridge"[11] to the outside world.

Thomas Kirsch, the president of the International Association of Analytical Psychology and the son of Jung's analyst friend James Kirsch, also noted that "[Wolff] became [Jung's] soul mate for psychological matters."[12] He found in Wolff a woman who was not threatened by the powerful energies as work; rather, she used her razor-sharp intuition to discuss possible interpretations of his experiences that could aid his integration. For the first time in his life, Jung found that he could converse at the deepest level of the soul with another person, and in

“The meeting of two personalities is like the contact of two chemical substances: if there is any reaction, both are transformed.”

Carl Jung

turn, Wolff's wisdom and guidance grounded him during those turbulent years. This is when their collaboration reached the height of its intensity. Wolff listened to all of Jung's visions, dreams, and fantasies, serving as an unacknowledged analyst. "Either she did not love me and was indifferent to my fate, or she loved me—as she certainly did—and then it was nothing short of heroism," Jung wrote. "Such things stand forever, and I shall be grateful to her in all eternity."[13]

Jung painstakingly illustrated these visions and observations in a red, leather-bound book that remained in a vault in Switzerland until its publication in 2009. Dubbed "the most influential unpublished work in the history of psychology,"[14] the book was met with such excitement and anticipation when it was published that it was pre-ordered months in advance and hit the *New York Times* bestseller list in no time.

During those years of turmoil, Wolff played an essential role in helping Jung devise his core tenets of complex psychology, and she provided substantial input for his *Psychological Types* manuscript, which was published in 1921. Like Jung, Wolff believed that a potent creative force is released when a man and a woman work together, and the merging of the feminine and masculine elements would incite new revelations. She and Jung may have done just that when Wolff helped him discover, develop, and name the key principles in *Psychological Types.* At the same time, she became a scholar in her own right. In her landmark essay, "Structural Forms of the Feminine Psyche," Wolff created an original model of the female unconscious. Her groundbreaking theory balances out Jung's more masculine perspective and is still widely used today.

Wolff also assumed a more public role in the larger psychoanalytic community, and later became the chair of the prestigious lecture committee at the Psychology Club of Zurich. In 1917, she was the first woman to be elected to the organization's executive committee, and in 1928, she became the club's president, a position she held for twenty-one years. Throughout her tenure, Wolff drove the life of the Psychology Club by lecturing, selecting speakers, and managing the organization's administration. Walking into the entryway of the clubhouse today, one is greeted by a beautiful portrait of Wolff that captures her intelligent eyes and graceful beauty.

As more patients arrived in Zurich to undergo analysis with Jung, he asked Wolff to help him with his overburdened practice. He certified her to see patients, and she became a highly regarded analyst herself, second in renown only to Jung. It is interesting to note that early patients worked with both of them separately, as Jung felt it was beneficial for analysands to receive a balance of male and female perspectives. Although Jung gained more robust attention, the physician and psychotherapist Tina Keller-Jenny, who worked closely with both Jung and Wolff, believed that Wolff was a more talented practitioner than her prominent partner. When Keller-Jenny told Jung that she considered Wolff to be a superior analyst, Jung agreed, saying that it is "the privilege of a woman to go with the patient into the dark places."[15]

Wolff's connection to Jung gave her life meaning and purpose. When Jung built a retreat house near the town of Bollingen, Switzerland, the couple would stay there reading and writing together for two to three weeks at a time. Emma, who did not care for Bollingen, spent less time there. A round, two-story tower, the womb-like house had no modern amenities. Jung had designed his bedroom and the kitchen in one unified space, which he associated with Emma and aptly called the "maternal"[16] tower. He later created a private study in a separate tower. In this place of reflection and investigation, he surrounded himself with

> "Either she did not love me and was indifferent to my fate, or she loved me—as she certainly did—and then it was nothing short of heroism. Such things stand forever, and I shall be grateful to her in all eternity."
>
> Carl Jung

painted representations of the unconscious material that appeared in his visions. This second construction represented Wolff, and Jung called it the "spiritual"[17] tower. It is striking that Jung erected literal structures that reflected his inner relationships with the two women in his life; perhaps symbolically, the two towers were not physically connected, either. As much as Jung found Bollingen a place of refuge, he noted that he was bothered by the architectural isolation of the two buildings and at times felt as if he were "disappear[ing] between" them.[18]

Disappearance was an appropriate word to use at the time. Emma and Wolff had become more openly dismissive of one another, and Jung would conveniently excuse himself from these charged situations. The two women did attempt to resolve their differences by asking Jung's colleague Carl Alfred Meier to work with them in what Meier would later call "the first group therapy session in analytic psychology."[19] Both Wolff and Emma suffered from their restricted roles. After years of feeling burdened by endless compromises, Emma was ready to carve out an identity of her own. She began studying and became a practicing analyst in her own right. Wolff, who was by then in her thirties, wanted more from life. Seeing Jung only two days of the week felt limiting. As a couple, they had established a solid life together as prominent members of the growing analytical community, and she wanted their personal life to reflect that. Jung, however, had no intention of leaving Emma and marrying Wolff.

Abandoning the dream of marrying Jung was among the most difficult challenges that Wolff faced during her lifetime. Weary of her marriage campaign, Jung slowly started pulling away from her. They still kept their scheduled meeting times, but by the early 1930s, Jung's inner attachment to Wolff was fading. Many have wondered why she continued to stay with him. But it seems logical that, after investing twenty years in both their working and romantic relationships, she would have found it hard to let go. Wolff also had a significant commitment to their joint research and wanted to remain active in the psychoanalytic community. Jung and Wolff may have not taken the opportunity to form a family of their own, but analytical psychology had become their creation and figurative child.

Indeed, Wolff continued to do important work in the ensuing years. She became the senior editor on a series of Jung's papers that were later published as *The Collected Works of C. G. Jung.* After all, she had helped Jung create many of those ideas, and though she took no credit for them, it behooved her to prepare them for dissemination. She also wrote several pieces in which she methodically organized analytical theories into synopses to help new students understand them. When the C. G. Jung Institute of Zurich opened in 1948, Wolff taught a whole generation of analytical candidates, while continuing to lead the Psychology Club, which remained her primary intellectual stage for the rest of her life.

However, Wolff's influence on Jung was beginning to wane. When Jung became interested in studying alchemy, Wolff at first tried to dissuade him. She feared that the esoteric work would marginalize them in the psychological community. But Jung was unconvinced and conveniently replaced Wolff with a willing, young researcher by the name of Marie-Louise von Franz. What Wolff was not aware of at the time was that Jung maintained strong relationships with people only as long as they advanced his creative efforts, and by refusing him, she had effectively sidelined herself.

In 1944, Jung suffered a heart attack, and his subsequent illness struck the final death knell in the already precarious Wolff-Jung relationship. While he was in the hospital, Emma kept all visitors at bay—including Wolff. In fact, Emma was so devoted to her husband that she seldom left his side for three months, relying on her children and servants to bring anything she needed to the hospital. When Jung finally returned home, Emma screened all telephone calls and saw to it that Wolff would have as little time with him as possible. Jung, on the other hand, had come back from the hospital with a renewed love and appreciation for his wife.

By the late forties, a more generous accommodation had sprung up between Wolff and Emma that lasted for the remainder of Wolff's life. Both Emma and Jung were well aware that this woman was completely alone, and that she had dedicated her entire life and her work to Jung; perhaps they did not want to carelessly cast her aside. In her remaining years, Wolff would spend time with both Jung and Emma, whether at their house or in Bollingen. Emma would even take care of Wolff when she was ill.

It came as a great shock to Jung to hear that Wolff had passed away suddenly in her sleep in 1953. Just four days before her death, Wolff had enjoyed a long, relaxed lunch with the

> "We must make our mistakes. We must live out our own vision of life. And there will be error. If you avoid error, you do not live."
>
> Carl Jung

Jungs and nothing had seemed amiss. Jung was greatly criticized for not joining Emma at the memorial service, but some speculated that he feared breaking down in public. In honor of his departed collaborator, Jung carved a stone with Chinese characters and placed it under a ginkgo tree on his property. The words translated as "Toni Wolff. Lotus. Nun. Mysterious."[20] Those who were close to Jung reported that he was filled with grief and remorse, and that he was frequently compelled to talk about her. Carl Alfred Meier also paid homage to Wolff by launching an effort to publish a collection of her essays. In the foreword, Jung credited Wolff with playing an active role in the development of analytical psychology, and wrote that he owed her a debt of gratitude for their collaboration.

Emma died just two years after Wolff's passing. This time, Jung was seen sobbing for his late wife, calling her "a queen."[21] To memorialize her, Jung carved a stone as he had done for Wolff. It read, "She was the foundation of my house," and Jung placed it by the "maternal" tower in Bollingen.[22]

It was only when both Wolff and Emma were gone that Jung connected the two towers with a second-story addition that featured an expanse of windows. Perhaps with the passing of the two most important women in his life, he was finally ready to bring to a close the decades-long separation of the two female energies within his psyche. Jung continued to publish books until his death, less than six years after Emma's passing.

Salvador Dalí & Gala

The Surrealist Set

"At the age of six, I wanted to be a cook," he once said. "At seven I wanted to be Napoleon."[1] At age fifteen, he settled on being himself—Salvador Dalí—and soon became one of the most iconic artists of the twentieth century. His works gave expression to the irrational elements of the unconscious. Dalí's dreamscapes, hallucinations, and fetishes were meticulously painted for all to see. Yet few know about the artist's relationship with Gala, his wife, muse, manager, protector, and partner of more than fifty years. The couple's life was as shocking and surreal as Dalí's artwork. He painted Gala obsessively, in a hundred different guises. She was portrayed as his one and only—the Virgin Mary, Venus, and Helen of Troy. He signed his best canvases with her name entwined around his and credited his success to her. "It is thanks to Gala that Dalí is the only living genius of our time except for Picasso," he wrote in his witty book *50 Secrets of Magic Craftsmanship.*[2]

Gala was born Elena Ivanovna Diakonova in 1894 in Kazan, Russia. Although she suffered from fragile health throughout much of her childhood, she received a high-level education and later worked as a schoolteacher. At age seventeen, she was diagnosed with tuberculosis and sent to the famous Clavadel sanatorium in Switzerland for treatment. While convalescing there, she fell in love with a fellow patient, the young French poet Paul Éluard. Just before the outbreak of war in 1914, the two parted—Gala returned to Moscow and Éluard to Paris—but they maintained a feverish correspondence, and in 1916, Gala made her way to France to marry her poet.

As Éluard became increasingly well known as a leader of the burgeoning surrealist movement, Gala was drawn to its vibrant artistic scene. Surrealism, a movement that began in Paris in the 1920s, had its roots in the desire to unlock the power of the mind. André Breton,

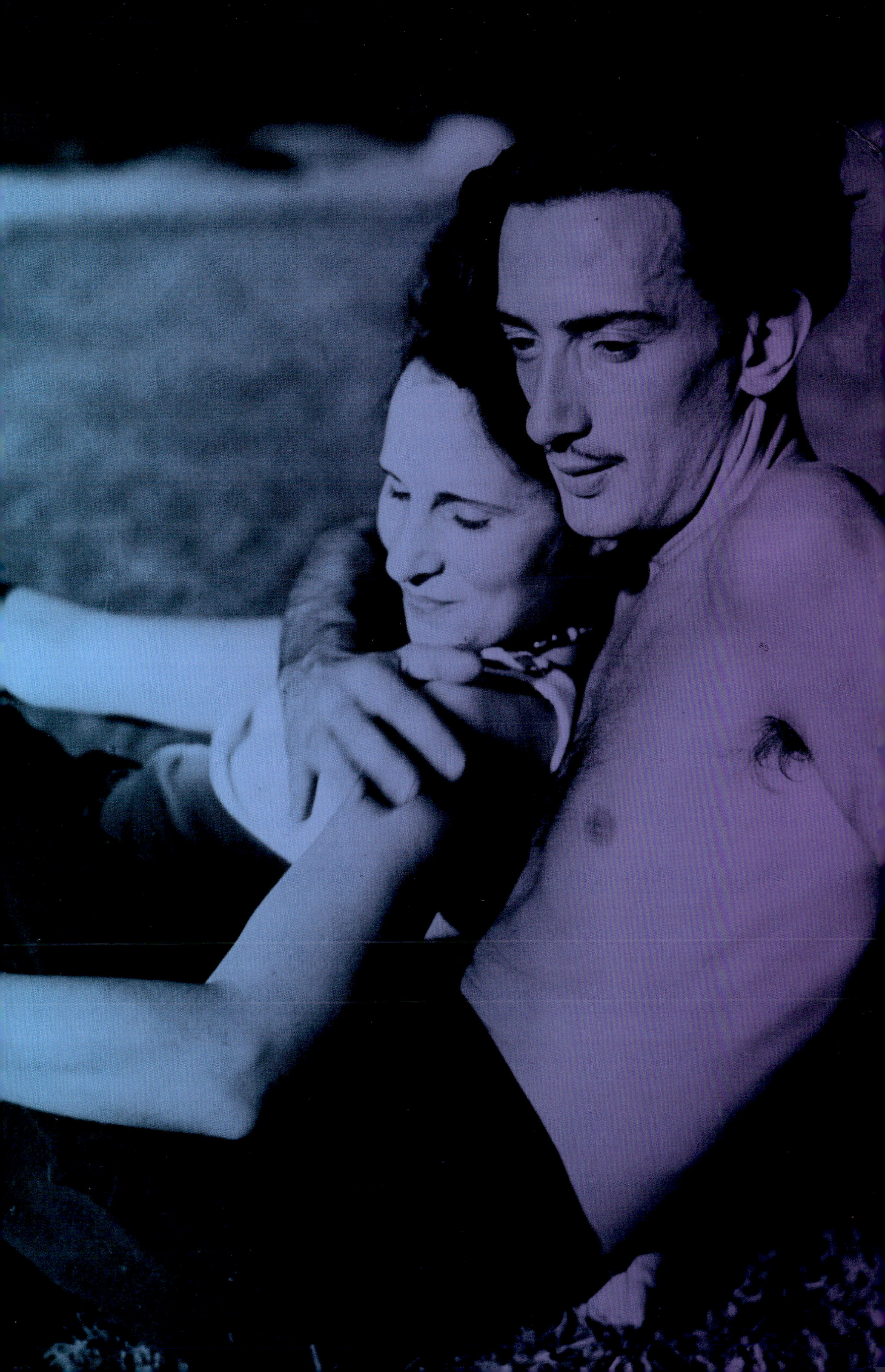

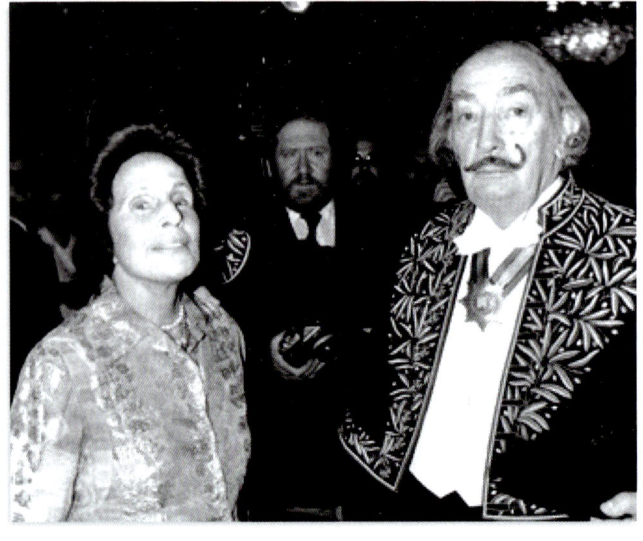

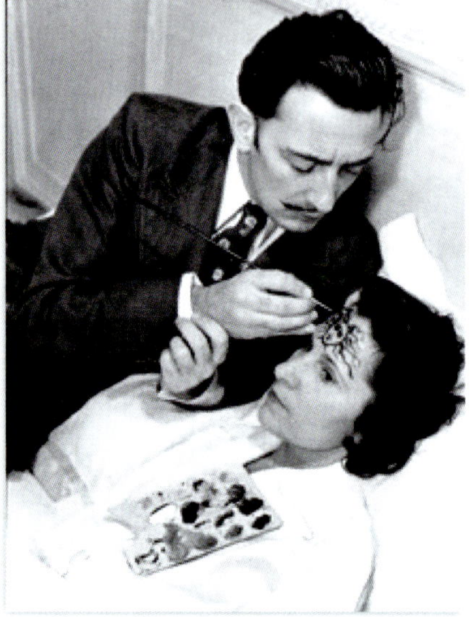

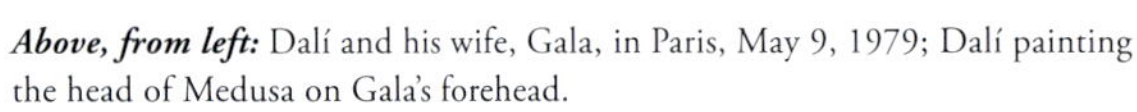

Above, from left: Dalí and his wife, Gala, in Paris, May 9, 1979; Dalí painting the head of Medusa on Gala's forehead.
Below, clockwise from top: Gala and Dalí in Port Lligat, August 1957; Dalí drawing Gala while in the U.S., 1940; Dalí dressing Gala in a costume for his event called Night in a Surrealist Forest, for which guests had to dress up as nightmares. The event was held in the Bali Room of Hotel Del Monte, Monterey, California, 1941.
Page 41: Dalí with his painting *The Madonna of Port Lligat,* for which Gala was his model.

> "I dedicate this novel to Gala, who was constantly by my side while I was writing it, who was the good fairy of my equilibrium, who banished the salamanders of my doubts and strengthened the lions of certainties."
>
> Salvador Dalí

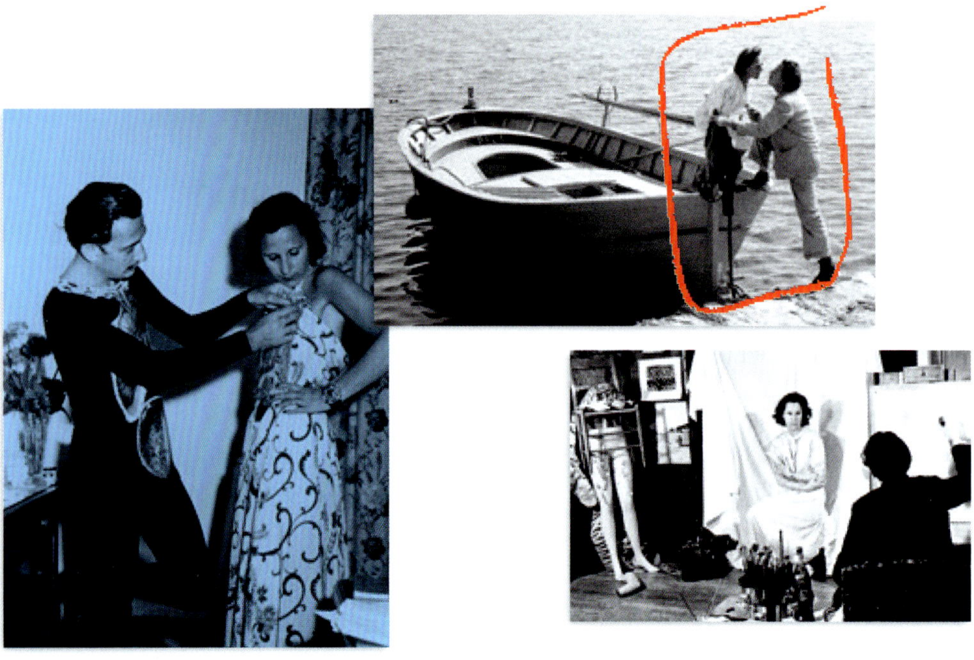

the movement's founder, argued that total recovery of our imaginative powers was the key to liberating the masses from the straitjacket of ordered society. This goal, he said, could be attained by tapping into our unconscious minds. Sigmund Freud's theories were particularly influential to the surrealists, as they validated the importance of exploring the unconscious and analyzing dreams to uncover symbolic meanings and understand the nature of repressed needs and desires. Surrealists believed that flouting convention and bypassing rationality were the gateways to a different realm of consciousness.

Fueled by surrealist fervor and prodigious sexual appetites, Éluard and Gala were eager to break taboos, and they opted for an open marriage. Tristan Tzara, a fellow poet and leader of the Dada movement, once noted that "Éluard liked group sex. He was keen for his friends to make love to Gala—while he watched or joined in."[3] One of the couple's dalliances was with the handsome German surrealist painter Max Ernst. It wasn't long before Ernst began sleeping in Éluard and Gala's marital bed on a nightly basis.

Salvador Dalí, on the other hand, had lived a life of what the author Tim McGirk described as "permanent erotic deprivation, relieved only by masturbation."[4] Self-pleasure became his only means to orgasm throughout his entire life—even when he was married to Gala—and Dalí became, perhaps, the only notable painter in the history of art to make masturbation a major theme of his work.

Born in 1904, in Figueres, Catalonia, Spain, the eccentric young Dalí learned early on that his tantrums would compel his mother and father to give him anything he wanted. An older son, also named Salvador, had died before Dalí was born, and so the doting parents took particular care with their second child. In his school years, he was timid and awkward, yet he displayed a penchant for exhibitionism, throwing himself down flights of stairs to become popular with the other boys. At university in Madrid, the gifted artist insulted the intelligence of the examiners, professing his superiority to them, and was summarily expelled. It was during this time that he immersed himself in the writings of Freud. The psychoanalyst's essays on sexuality and sexual perversions and his book *The Interpretation of Dreams* were of monumental significance to Dalí, who would have lifelong preoccupations with autoeroticism, sodomy, and coprophilia. Through his readings of Freud's work, he grasped that the messages the unconscious transmits to the conscious mind are veiled in symbols; he would later incorporate such symbols into his paintings. If Michelangelo charted the body's anatomy, Dalí would be the artist to plot the anatomy of the psyche.

It was the summer of 1929 when Gala and Dalí first met. That spring, Dalí and his friend, the filmmaker Luis Buñuel, had traveled to Paris to present their surrealist film *Un Chien Andalou*. The Spaniards' sixteen-minute-long tour de force electrified the audience, which included a who's who of the artistic community: Pablo Picasso, Le Corbusier, Jean Cocteau, Hans Arp, Joan Miró, Fernand Léger, Constantin Brancusi, and Breton. While in Paris, Dalí met with Éluard and invited him to spend the summer in Cadaqués, the picturesque beach town near Figueres where Dalí lived. And so, that summer, Éluard and Gala and their eleven-year-old daughter, Cécile, set off for Cadaqués. Gala was sitting on the sand, her naked back glistening in the sun, when Dalí set eyes on the androgynous beauty, who was ten years older than him. He was immediately lovestruck.

Gala, however, was initially revolted by Dalí. She did not know what to make of the madman. In the days that followed, Dalí unsuccessfully tried to gain her favor by waxing his armpits, wearing rags with one breast showing, and covering his body with goat's dung. Gala disliked his scatological humor and his obnoxious, erratic behavior; every time he tried to speak to her, he would break out in hysterical laughter. But over the course of their stay, she became intrigued by the artist's subtle brilliance. Slowly, she began to intuit that a tormented man lay behind the bizarre antics. She understood that Dalí was anguished by the disturbing images he was painting on the canvas, and that his unnerving laughter was a sign of sheer, uncontrollable terror. Gala had an uncanny gift for recognizing the struggles of an artist, and she soon began to help Dalí harness and direct his creative ideas. The two took long walks on the beach, leaving Éluard with Cécile at the nearby hotel. Somehow, Gala's presence transformed Dalí. His laughing fits and hysteria ceased, and his sole focus turned to staying near the imperious Russian muse. One September day, while they walked atop the rocky beaches, they made love, presumably for the first and perhaps the last time. For the next five decades, Dalí was able to provide immense wealth and fame to Gala, but he was incapable of sexual intimacy. Gala, who was sexually promiscuous, soon became a wife that was loved—even adored—beyond the distance of touch or desire.

When summer ended, Gala decided to remain with Dalí. She did return to Paris a few weeks later, but only to promote Dalí and his work in advance of his first solo exhibition at the Galerie Goemans. Gala was more convinced of his genius than Dalí was, and she threw herself headlong into championing his work. She tried to convince André Breton that Dalí was the physical incarnation of the surrealist spirit, and she sought out rich, young art collectors who would become his patrons. In the ensuing years, Gala would act as Dalí's agent, aggressively fighting for his rights with gallery owners and setting his art's sale prices. She would also become the translator for his visual language. When art dealers and collectors failed to appreciate one of his new paintings, it was she, armed with an evangelical belief in his artistry, who would persuade them to think otherwise.

When Dalí finally arrived in Paris with his many paintings for the exhibition (including his early masterpiece *The Great Masturbator*), Gala took him under her wing. He stayed in the home she had shared with Éluard and their daughter. But two days before the exhibition was set to open, the smitten couple dashed off to Barcelona for their "honeymoon."[5] Since Dalí had no money, it's likely that the weak-willed Éluard agreed to pay for the trip.

When Dalí went back to Figueres to announce his love for Gala, his father, the stern and conservative notary, was beside himself. How could his son be involved with a married mother, ten years his senior? He accused Gala of being a drug addict who had manipulated his son to become a drug trafficker. How else could they explain the money they had just earned? Dalí had, in fact, sold out his Paris exhibition and was now flush with cash. But soon the funds ran out.

Gala and Dalí were to spend the next few months living in a secluded, one-room stone hut, with no running water or electricity, in the Spanish wilderness near Port Lligat. Such a move represented a significant downgrade for Gala, who was accustomed to luxury back in Paris. Managing Dalí's fears was a colossal undertaking for her: He was racked with visions of being menaced by giant grasshoppers, and his sexual paranoia and fear of death had returned

> "To be able to live with your very wife as though she were a mistress into whose arms you were escaping from the soft, but too habitual conjugal bed!"
>
> Salvador Dalí

with a vengeance. Gala was his only sense of comfort; in his autobiography *The Secret Life of Salvador Dalí,* the artist said he knew that Gala "was destined to be my Gradiva, the one who moves forward, my victory, my wife."[6] The name Gradiva comes from the title of a novel by Wilhelm Jensen. In it, a man becomes obsessed with the image of a girl in an artwork and begins to encounter her in his dreams and, eventually, in real life; he names her Gradiva, and she brings him psychological healing. Indeed, Dalí's sanity was built around Gala, and he would come to rely on her for most things, from the menial to the more complicated. She would buy him train tickets, pick out his clothes, pin money to his jacket so he wouldn't lose it, prepare his canvases, and mix his paints. While Dalí painted, Gala sat beside him, reading aloud books on philosophy and mythology. Some speculate that Gala had become the mother that he had lost at age sixteen, but the obsessive nature of their relationship cannot be explained so easily.

Gala soon realized that living so far away from Paris, the center of the art world, made no sense, so the couple returned to live with Éluard and Cécile until Dalí's career was rightfully launched. At the time, many artists were repelled by Dalí's fixation on excrement, but Gala showed no signs of dismay. It wasn't that she liked or enjoyed Dalí's proclivities, but she showed a tolerance that intrinsically alleviated his existential shame about his sexual perversions. This, in turn, helped him sublimate his angst into his creative work. In many ways, Gala's role was to provide the optimal environment in which Dalí could make art. She would critique his work and guide him through new artistic thresholds. She became the gatekeeper to the elusive genius—his bridge to the outside world.

Though Gala and Dalí shared a deep bond, Gala would look elsewhere for sexual gratification. She pursued an active sex life well into her eighties, attracting the most handsome young men, many of whom resembled Dalí, for her pleasures. To some of these lovers, she gave money, signed Dalí drawings, or in the case of collectors and dealers, negotiated contracts for acquiring Dalí's work. Dalí, like Éluard, was said to know about Gala's affairs and even take delight in them. While he hated physical contact himself, he was creatively stimulated by Gala's liberation.

By 1931, Dalí had built a reputation for himself in Europe. At a solo exhibition that same year, he presented one of the most iconic works of the entire surrealist movement, *The Persistence of Memory.* But the foreign shores of America were beckoning him and Gala, who were bewitched by the compelling stories of the United States in the pages of *Town & Country* and *The New Yorker.* Picasso generously provided the funds for the couple's transatlantic crossing so they could attend an individual exhibition of Dalí's work in New York in the fall of 1934. Gala, who had become Dalí's rightful wife in a civil ceremony earlier that year, spent most of her time on the boat humoring her petrified husband. Dalí was scared of drowning and constantly wore a life preserver, even while lounging on the deck.

The nervous Spaniard stepped off the SS *Champlain* in New York carrying an eight-foot baguette under his arm and at least a dozen paintings tied to his person; he had heard New York was a rough place and was scared of being robbed. Flashbulbs went off as reporters rushed to report the arrival of the mustachioed artist and his muse. In interviews, Dalí explained to the American public that he painted his obsessions; his art was his therapy to remain sane. The story and its packaging tantalized the public. Thus, the myth of Dalí began to take shape. Gala knew that, if there was big money to be made, it would be in the United States. American museums and galleries were more attracted to surrealism than the mainstream

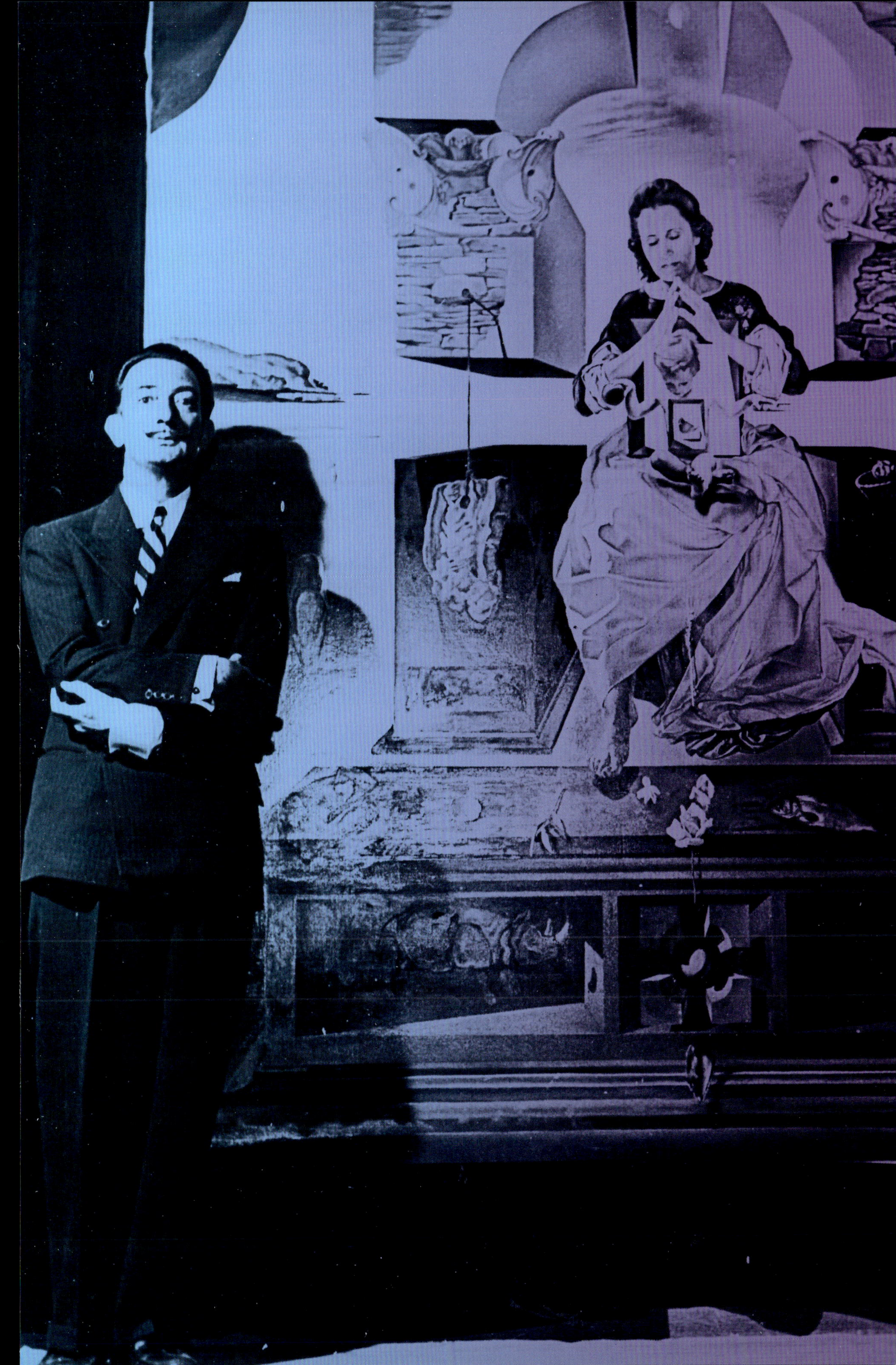

European art world was. In addition, American collectors seemed to have more cash on hand than their European counterparts. At least ten Dalí paintings were sold at the Julien Levy Gallery in 1934, including *The Persistence of Memory,* which was subsequently gifted to the Museum of Modern Art.

> "I must now complete for you the description of the setting of our ménage à trois by telling you how and to what degree painting loves my Gala."
>
> Salvador Dalí

On Gala and Dalí's last night in New York, the arts patron Caresse Crosby and Julien Levy's wife, Joella, threw a dream-themed farewell party that would go down in history. Dalí helped the hostesses produce fittingly surreal decor that included a bathtub full of water half-suspended over the stairway to the gallery. Respectable society women turned up to the event wearing birdcages around their heads or snakes wrapped around their necks. A man came in the guise of a pincushion. Funnily, compared to the guests' outlandish costumes, the Dalís looked quite normal, with Gala wearing a dress that showed off her shapely legs and a doll sprouting from the top of her head.

The couple earned more publicity and money in the U.S. during those few weeks than they had in an entire year in Paris. Dalí became well aware that he had to sell himself more than his paintings. Over the next couple of decades, the artist's spectacular self-promotional schemes would earn him and Gala worldwide celebrity status.

When Dalí appeared at the International Surrealist Exposition in London to give a lecture in June of 1936, he wore a diving suit with a car radiator strapped to the top of the helmet. Around his waist was a belt with a dagger, in his hand was a billiard cue, and he was escorted by two dogs. In true surrealist fashion, he mystified the audience by speaking in French through a loudspeaker, while upside-down slides flashed on the screen. When he got uncomfortably warm and, by some accounts, began to suffocate, his helmet had to be pried off his head. On another occasion, Dalí was invited to the Sorbonne, in Paris, to speak about the relationship between DNA and the spiral stalks in vegetables. He pulled up to the event in a Cadillac completely filled with cauliflower. He had the last laugh anyhow. His paintings were soaring in value.

During a visit to New York in 1936, Dalí made headlines once again, but this time for landing in jail. The luxury department store Bonwit Teller had commissioned Dalí to design surrealist-themed window displays at its Fifth Avenue emporium. The result was so macabre that the manager ended up switching out some of the bizarre props to make the scene more palatable. This did not please Dalí, as he was not consulted beforehand. Feeling that he had every right to preserve the integrity of his work, he dashed into the window to disarrange the set. As he was milling about, Dalí knocked over the bathtub full of water that sat prominently in the middle of the display, it crashed through the window, and he fell through right behind it. Luckily, Dalí emerged unscathed on the sidewalk, but while the crowd was delighted by the performance, the police were not. He was taken to the police station on East Fifty-First Street. The incident spawned a vast amount of press coverage, which only helped sales during his exhibition at the Julien Levy Gallery two days later. Man Ray's photograph of Dalí appeared on the front covers of the *New York Times* and *Life* magazine, which reported that Dalí was now one of the richest young painters in the world.

In Paris, Breton and the other surrealists were outraged by Dalí's flamboyant behavior and success, and dubbed him "Avida Dollars."[7] Dalí happily waxed his mustache into two crescents, twirled his cane, and watched Gala secure more lucrative commissions. Even Dalí's father was convinced of Gala's management skills. While showing his son's press clippings to another painter, he said, "Without Gala, Salvador would have ended up under a bridge in Paris."[8]

By the late thirties, currents of anarchism, communism, and fascism were sweeping through Europe. Spain exploded into civil war, and Federico García Lorca, Dalí's close friend, was assassinated by a right-wing military agency. Dalí, however, did not speak out against the fascist government. Fed up with Dalí's antics and what he viewed as Dalí's pro-fascist inclinations, Breton finally excommunicated him from the surrealist group. With the outbreak of World War II, the Dalís packed up and moved to New York, setting up house at the St. Regis hotel. They remained in the United States for the next eight years.

Hollywood was a lure that Dalí could not resist, and he soon began to spend time there, too. He painted portraits of film moguls, actresses, and actors, often charging up to $25,000 for a sitting. Alfred Hitchcock consulted with Dalí before shooting the dream sequence in his 1945 film *Spellbound.* Harpo Marx became a friend. At this time, though Dalí continued to enjoy massive commercial success, the quality of his work was beginning to suffer. In order to maintain his extravagant lifestyle, he took up commissions for magazines, appeared in televised advertisements, and mass-produced lithographs. Gala, who feared poverty above all, began to bully him to churn out more work. Throughout the next few years, he would lend his name to practically any product if the price was right.

There are many accounts of Gala's temper and tyranny. She wanted those around Dalí to worship and mold their lives around the whims of the genius artist, just as she had.

Dalí seemed to adore her strength of purpose, her vindictiveness, and her mercurial moods. For one, she was egalitarian in her outbursts; she had no qualms about insulting receptionists and French cabinet ministers alike. She once stubbed out a cigarette on a dinner companion's hand, claiming, "He was boring me to death."[9] Dalí found these tantrums to be deliciously entertaining. It is no wonder that their close friend Carlos Lozano dubbed them "a double act."[10]

Dalí may have feared her bullying, but he displayed a slavish devotion to his wife. In his first autobiography, he spoke volumes of his Gala—and of her every orifice. But his descriptions are remarkably detached, with little written about Gala's qualities aside from how she stimulated his sexuality and artistry. One wonders: With so much self-sacrifice, what did Gala get in return? Her connection to the indisputable genius may have been a primary point of attraction, and the extravagant lifestyle a further bonus.

When postwar abstraction became a major artistic movement, Gala helped Dalí to shed his old techniques and move into more classical, religious depictions. His eternal muse became the focus of his iconography. He painted Gala as *The Madonna of Port Lligat,* put her on a pedestal as the Virgin Mary, and depicted her as the spiritual mother. The same austere stillness pervades other portraits of Gala—all drained of erotic references. Dalí had now decided that she was his "female twin."[11]

The Dalís were swift to realize that a by-product of being rich and famous was that they could procure young, beautiful people who would be all too willing to quench the older couple's sexual appetite. They typically held court at Paris's Le Meurice hotel or New York's St. Regis. In Paris, they would descend from the Presidential Suite, previously occupied by King Alfonso XIII during his exile from Spain, to host their infamous Princes' and Paupers' Tea parties. These events were populated with a glamorous array of models, celebrities, aristocrats, dwarfs, transsexuals, and even ocelots. In different rooms, orgies of every permutation would be taking place. Dalí knew instinctively who had come prepared to take off their clothes, and some would make love in front of him for no reason other than that he had dared to suggest it. In his second autobiography, *Diary of a Genius,* Dalí recounted how he planned every detail of these debaucheries, constantly intervening to tell the actors what to do and what to stop doing.

As time wore on, the couple relied on the services of a fixer to arrange the realizations of Dalí's bizarre fantasies and Gala's revolving door of young lovers. Gala was not so keen on Dalí's libidinal exhibitionism. At her husband's coaxing, the aging seductress would don one of her old Chanel suits and join him at the start of his teas, but eventually she would disappear with one of her lovers. The true dynamics behind their outlandish behavior isn't fully known. Some say that Dalí used the teas to incite Gala's jealousy in order to get back at her for her sexual appetite.

Although Gala would become jealous of anyone who tried to get close to Dalí, he let two women into his inner circle: Nanita Kalaschnikoff, an aristocratic Spanish beauty who was also married to a Russian, and Amanda Lear, an attractive, tall, blonde model and singer whom Dalí claimed was once a Vietnamese man. Although each of these women would come to spend a great deal of time with the artist, neither threatened Gala's important position in Dalí's life. In fact, whenever Gala was away, Dalí would play the pop song "Baby Come Back" repeatedly and cry real tears. "My life would be meaningless without her," he once said.[12]

By the 1970s, Gala had grown weary of Dalí's constant neediness and his circus of sycophants. In Port Lligat, admirers willing to act out his surrealistic fantasies would arrive in the afternoon and congregate by his phallus-shaped swimming pool. To give Gala some

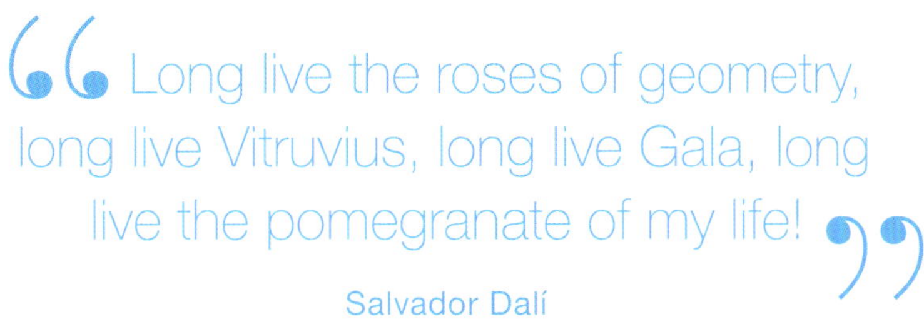

privacy, Dalí bought and refurbished a medieval castle for her in nearby Púbol. From 1971 to 1980, she would divide her time between the two residences, only allowing Dalí to visit the castle with her prior written consent. In 1971, when Dalí designed the special December issue of French *Vogue,* he dedicated it to Gala and told reporters how happy that arrangement made him, given his masochist proclivities.

There were two particular lovers who apparently gripped Gala's fascination. While in New York, the sixty-seven-year-old Gala caught sight of a darkly handsome young man by the name of William Rotlein who bore a remarkable resemblance to a young Dalí. She installed the new recruit in a room next to hers at the St. Regis, and they became lovers. Rotlein turned out to be a heroin addict who stole cash from Gala's purse. It seems that Gala inspired the same kind of total dependence in Rotlein as she had in Dalí. When Rotlein began to talk of marriage, Gala disappeared.

But the one lover whose charms kept Gala most captive was the man who played Jesus in the hit Broadway musical *Jesus Christ Superstar,* Jeff Fenholt. He had received a request to attend a Princes' and Paupers' Tea event held at the St. Regis. Dalí, at Gala's behest, asked him to remove his clothes to pose for his next masterpiece. Over the next seven years, Gala resorted to buying Fenholt a house on Long Island and gifting him several Dalí paintings to keep him coming back. "I feel like his grandmother and his lover," Gala confided to a friend.[13] Fenholt later sold the paintings at auction for peak prices, a sign that he may have been manipulating the infatuated woman for his own gains.

> "Every good painter who aspires to create authentic masterpieces must before anything else marry my wife. Thus you are advised: the painter's wife is called Gala."
>
> Salvador Dalí

From 1975 onward, Dalí's dance between lunacy and lucidity made it impossible for anyone but Gala to handle him. The two also had to deal with the sorry state of their business affairs. Fifteen years earlier, they had hired the art collector John Peter Moore as Dalí's right-hand man. He was popularly called Captain Moore, because he had served in the British army, but Dalí chose to call him "Psychological Warfare."[14] Indeed, he lived up to his nickname, as he manipulated the masses into buying thousands of Dalí reproductions bearing the artist's signature. He made a lot of easy money for the couple's foundation and became spectacularly wealthy himself. Moore soon began the deceitful practice of having Dalí sign blank sheets that could then be printed with any doodle and sold as Dalí lithographs. Spanish authorities later confiscated ten thousand allegedly fake prints signed by Salvador Dalí after the couple's death.

In 1968, Enrique Sabater replaced Psychological Warfare as the Dalís' private secretary, primarily because Sabater had agreed to receive only a 5 percent commission on art sales, whereas Moore had taken 10 percent. Sabater had been accused of theft, but Dalí did not care; he said he liked thieves. Besides, Sabater spoke Catalan and shared a similar background to Dalí. He also proved to be far shrewder than his predecessor. In just a few years, he became a multimillionaire. Some even speculated that his income was six times more than his employers'. The Dalís had suspicions that Sabater may have grown richer than them through shady dealings in his back office, but they had become too dependent on him to make any staffing changes. Sabater had to continue to act as the couple's secretary to justify his payroll, so the couple took pleasure in bossing him around like a slave. One of their preposterous commands was that he personally prepare fresh orange juice and wake them up at exactly four o'clock with two transvestites at hand.

A silver lining in the final years of Dalí's life was a retrospective held at the Centre Georges Pompidou in Paris in 1979, which attracted almost one million visitors before it moved on to the Tate Gallery in London. But the most touching event of that year came when Dalí was elected as a member of the French Académie des Beaux-Arts. For his induction, just two days before his seventy-fifth birthday, he had a special uniform made with a triangular Napoleonic hat. He carried an enormous Toledo sword with an image of Gala's eyes etched into the golden blade. Dalí gave the performance of his life. He gestured wildly, pounded his fists on the podium, and made a gripping speech that was a blend of his unconventional wit and delirious but affecting insights. Referencing his famed artwork *The Persistence of Memory,* with its melting timepieces spread about the canvas, Dalí shared, "When I work, time becomes empty and soft, and when the Divine Gala sits reading to me in the studio, I am in the blissful state of enlightenment."[15] The audience hung on his every word, and when his speech came to an end, as Lozano recalled in his memoir, "Dalí unsheathed his sword, and with the eyes of Gala glinting in the overhead lights, the fellows of the Académie Française rose in a standing ovation."[16]

Dalí's genius was as inexplicable as his life with Gala. Regardless of the longtime couple's endless bickering and more dramatic fights, regardless of their flaws and weaknesses—or, perhaps, because of them—the two found a love that went beyond the norms of a conventional marriage. When Gala died on June 10, 1982, following a severe flu, Dalí took refuge in her room, drew the curtains, and stopped eating. He would spend the remaining six-and-a-half years of his life as a recluse, slowly willing himself to die, until he finally passed due to heart failure in 1989, at the age of eighty-four. Dalí had wanted to be buried beside his Gradiva on the grounds of the castle. A tomb next to hers was prepared, supposedly with a hole between them, so the couple could hold hands in death. At the mayor's behest, however, he was buried under the museum in Figueres that bears his name. Before internment, the last of his secretaries took a mold of his face, as had been done with Napoleon—the man he wanted to be at age six, before he embraced being Dalí.

Serge Gainsbourg & Jane Birkin

The Lovers

When the French publishing house Larousse immortalized Serge Gainsbourg in the pages of its prestigious encyclopedia in 1991, the song its editors selected as the jewel of his oeuvre was the super-erotic "Je T'Aime. . . Moi Non Plus." It was his duet with the love of his life, the upper-class, doe-eyed English actress Jane Birkin, who was eighteen years his junior. Ironically, it started out as a song that Gainsbourg had written several years earlier for his then-lover, Brigitte Bardot; they had been having a torrid and public affair while Bardot was married to the German billionaire Gunter Sachs. At the last minute, Brigitte blocked the song's release for fear of embarrassing her husband. When the Birkin version of the song debuted, the lyrics—and the moaning and groaning soundtrack that accompanied it—caused outrage. No one in France had dared to express such explicit sensuality in song form. But for Gainsbourg, art had to be transgressive, confrontational, and barrier-breaking in order to have a lasting impact.

Rumors circulated that, for the song, Gainsbourg and Birkin had recorded one of their sexual encounters on a tape recorder underneath their bed. The all-too-witty Gainsbourg responded, "Thank goodness it wasn't, otherwise I hope it would have been a long-playing record."[1] Legend has it that as soon as Gainsbourg and Birkin finished the recording, the pair rushed back to their hotel—the famous L'Hôtel in Paris—descended down to its cellar restaurant, sat in a booth, and asked the staff to pop on their new song. The moment "Je T'Aime. . . Moi Non Plus" came on, everyone froze. Gainsbourg looked around and told Birkin, "I think we've got a hit."[2] The song was banned in Italy, Spain, and Sweden, and condemned by the Vatican. The BBC announced that it was "not considered suitable for

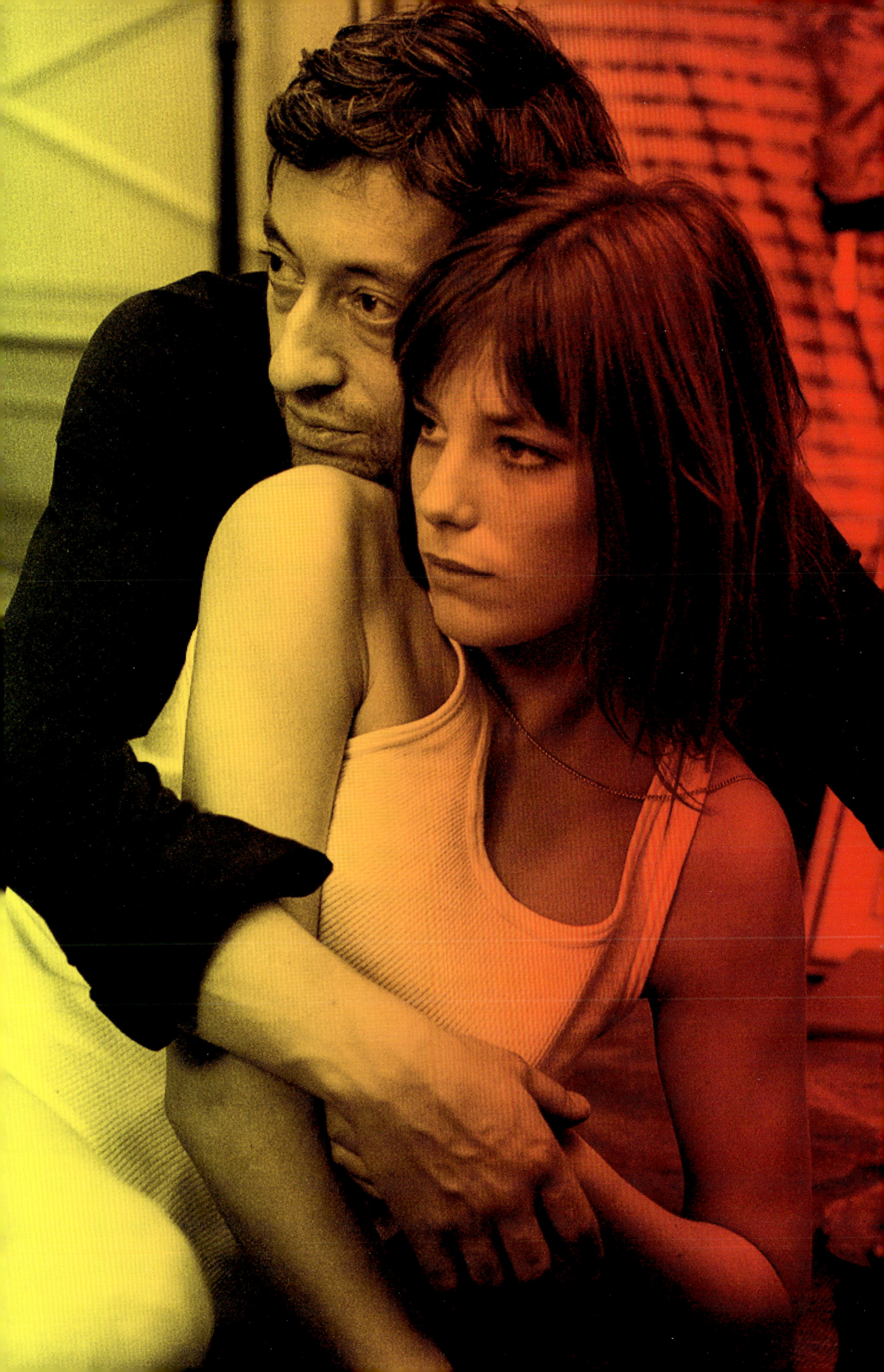

play,"[3] which only propelled it to become a number one hit in the U.K. More than six million singles were sold worldwide.

The notorious record launched Gainsbourg and Birkin to the status of Paris's archetypal 1970s couple. The news magazine *L'Express* first christened them the "scandalous couple,"[4] but soon they came to symbolize the artistically bent, sexually liberated duo who partied at nightclubs. Their lovestruck portrait adorned the September 1969 cover of *Rock & Folk* magazine. Within the year, pictures of the long-legged, miniskirted Birkin swinging a basket in one arm and clasping her provocative French beau with the other graced most French publications and tabloids.

Gainsbourg, who had spent the better of part of his career playing piano in nightclubs and bars, dousing his fans with disconcerting, cynical poetry about alcohol, women, and depressing jobs, finally had his megahit. He rewarded himself by going to the luxury jewelry house Cartier and buying a platinum Star of David. For a man who, as a teenager, was forced to wear the yellow Jewish symbol as a badge of shame and humiliation during the Nazi occupation of France, the platinum star was to show the world that he had proudly arrived.

Gainsbourg was born Lucien Ginsburg on April 2, 1928. His parents, Joseph and Olga, were Jewish immigrants who had fled the Ukraine following the Russian Revolution. Joseph was a talented pianist who worked in clubs and other venues in Paris and taught all three of his children to play piano from a young age. It was when Lucien was twelve years old that the German forces invaded Paris. Anti-Semitic graffiti and posters started to spread throughout the neighborhoods. Gainsbourg was insecure about his pronounced nose and protruding ears—features that resembled the anti-Semitic characterizations of the time—and the obligatory donning of the yellow star only deepened his sense of alienation. By 1941, an estimated 50 percent of the Jewish population in France was out of work. Joseph, who could no longer provide for his family, had to sneak away illegally to Limoges, in central France, where he was able to find a job with an orchestra. But the situation back in Paris worsened. Fearing for their lives, the rest of the family used false identification papers and traveled to Limoges to join Joseph. It was a harrowing time for them, but luckily, they were able to return to Paris unscathed after the war. The struggles of his adolescence would leave an indelible mark on Gainsbourg. His subversive lyrics, his iconoclasm, his driving need to control his environment, and his desire to be loved by the public were likely responses to the vulnerable feelings he had harbored during those years.

As a teenager, Lucien took up painting. He studied under Fernand Léger and André Lhote, and painted several canvases depicting androgynous, flat-chested women. Years later he would reflect, "All my paintings look[ed] like Jane. I painted her before I knew her."[5] In

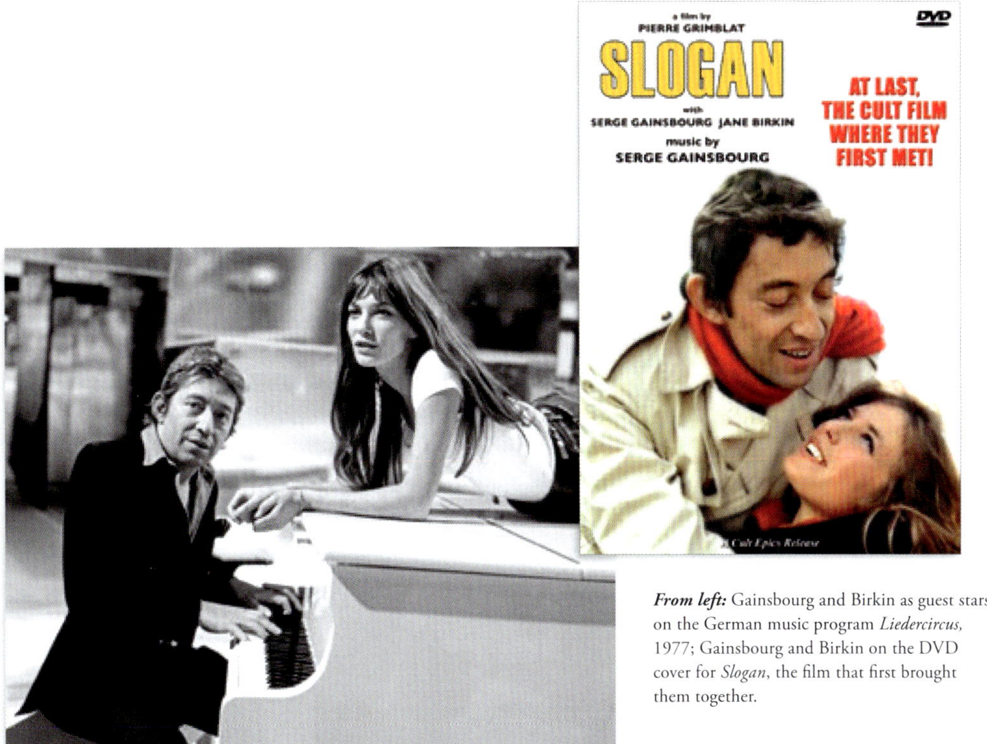

From left: Gainsbourg and Birkin as guest stars on the German music program *Liedercircus*, 1977; Gainsbourg and Birkin on the DVD cover for *Slogan*, the film that first brought them together.

his twenties, Gainsbourg fell in love with the fellow artist and model Elisabeth Levitsky, and they married in 1951. Within a mere six years, he had abandoned painting, changed his name to Serge—a reference to his Russian roots—begun playing piano at bars, and gotten divorced. Being sought after by women was a high priority for the self-conscious artist. One night, at a bar, he said to a fellow musician, "Even with my mug I'll make it. My goal is to make a lot of money and have the most beautiful women."[6] By the next decade, he would reach both goals. His first album took the prestigious Grand Prix du Disque award from the Académie Charles Cros in 1959, and the song he composed for the teenage performer France Gall won first place in the 1965 Eurovision Song Contest.

As Gainsbourg's star was rising, on the other side of the channel, in England, the aristocratic and striking Jane Birkin was being swept off her feet by the composer John Barry. Barry had cast the seventeen-year-old Birkin in his musical *The Passion Flower Hotel* and was smitten with her. Not even her concerned parents could stop her from marrying the older, divorced artist. Their marriage ended three short years later, in 1968, when Barry abandoned Birkin and their baby daughter, Kate, for another woman. By that time, Birkin had appeared in counterculture films such as *Kaleidoscope* and *Blow-Up* (where the exposure of her pubic hair caused a scandal in Britain), but offers for new roles had slowed. She was desperate to jump-start her career and accepted an offer to go to France to audition for the film *Slogan*.

Although Birkin was cast in the role, her first meeting with her costar, Gainsbourg, was disappointing. The famed beauty Marisa Berenson had been the front-runner to play the female lead in the movie, but director Pierre Grimblat was interested in giving the fresh-faced Birkin a chance. Clearly annoyed to be paired with an unknown, Gainsbourg asked Birkin, "How can you accept a part in France when you don't speak French?"[7] She found his dismissiveness worrisome. If they were to play the leading roles, she thought, there should be a modicum of chemistry. The despairing Birkin eventually asked, "Why don't you ask how I am?" To which Gainsbourg replied, *"Parce que ça m'est égal"* ("because I really couldn't care").[8] Birkin's only response was to break down and cry.

She asked that Grimblat arrange a dinner so the three of them could talk things over. They were to meet at Régine's, but Grimblat intentionally absented himself so the costars could spend some time alone. After that dinner, the two became inseparable.

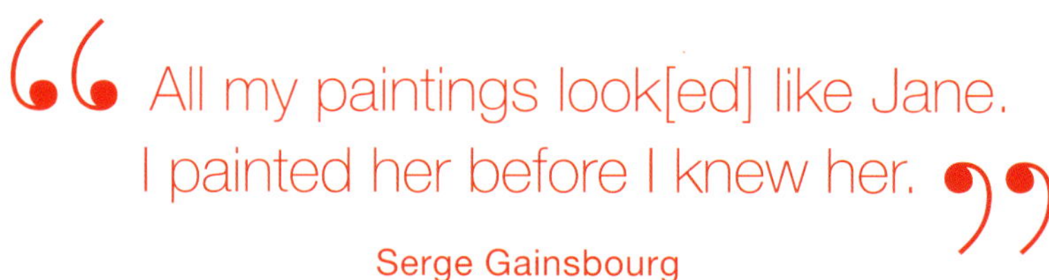

Gainsbourg, by now, was considered a great ladies' man, and even a misogynist. But to those who knew him well, he was a hopeless romantic. During their first evening together, Birkin and Gainsbourg stayed out until dawn. He took her to Madame Arthur, the cabaret where his father used to play the piano, and then to a Russian nightclub, where Gainsbourg gave the musicians one hundred francs each to serenade him and Birkin as they walked to their taxi.

They wouldn't leave one another's side until filming wrapped. But Birkin was wary of becoming a trophy wife to yet another famous partner. She told Gainsbourg that she intended to build her own career and was heading back to London. Gainsbourg sat up all night, overwhelmed with grief. Shortly thereafter, during a supper with Grimblat, another director, Jacques Deray, approached the trio at their table. On Grimblat's recommendation, Deray offered Birkin a leading role in his upcoming film, *La Piscine (The Swimming Pool),* starring the dashing Alain Delon. Her plans to return to London were postponed indefinitely.

Intensely jealous and fearful that Delon would make a move on his love interest, Gainsbourg got a flashy limousine and accompanied Jane and Kate to Saint-Tropez for filming. The aggressive musician wanted to make a big splash in front of the handsome actor. While in Saint-Tropez, Gainsbourg stayed with Kate at Hôtel Byblos while Birkin went to work every day. And when he left for Paris, Birkin returned to find that her beau had covered her bathroom mirror with lipstick hearts and the words *je t'aime, je t'aime, je t'aime.*

The year 1969 was auspicious for the couple. First, Gainsbourg's theme song for *Slogan* was released, with Birkin making her singing debut. *Slogan* also premiered in the summer of '69 to great critical acclaim. Birkin arrived at the screening wearing black underwear beneath a see-through minidress, and the scandalous couple took the coveted top spot in all the tabloids the next day. That same year, "Je T'Aime. . . Moi Non Plus" hit the airwaves, which created its own media blitz. When the album was released, Gainsbourg made sure that Birkin's name was listed before his in the song's credits. "He wanted me to be a star; that's what he did to people he loved," she later said. To cap off 1969, Gainsbourg photographed Birkin nude for the cover of *Lui* magazine. Birkin's singular look—a mix of British mod and French flair—would come to epitomize the "boho chic" aesthetic.

For the next couple of years, the pair traveled together and costarred in films. While Birkin was shooting a movie in Oxford, England, Gainsbourg began work on a concept album. Usually he would write his lyrics overnight, but on this album he wrote slowly, as he had time to spare while waiting for Birkin to return from the set. *Histoire de Melody Nelson* was a moody album that chronicled the love between a middle-aged Frenchman and an underage English girl. It doesn't take great imagination to see that Gainsbourg was mining his own experiences with Birkin as he produced this work. Birkin posed for the album's cover—topless, wearing a short red wig and bell-bottom pants, and holding a doll. In July of 1971, only four months after the album's release, Birkin and Gainsbourg would welcome another creation: a baby named Charlotte. Gainsbourg's only disappointment was that his father was not alive to see the birth of the new grandchild. Three months earlier, Joseph had suddenly died of a stomach hemorrhage. The grieving Gainsbourg found him a resting place in Montparnasse Cemetery, just twenty meters away from the grave of the poet Charles Baudelaire.

Before his sudden passing, Joseph had managed to find a home for his son's growing family on Rue de Verneuil in Saint-Germain, Paris. Gainsbourg's sense of aesthetics and decor was positively Dalí-esque. The house's interior was all black; Gainsbourg used to say that black neutralized the cacophony of colors and sounds spinning in his frenzied mind. What those close to him understood was that Gainsbourg had a great need for control. Each object in the home was meticulously arranged down to the smallest detail, and it would drive him mad if something was out of place. Many years later, Birkin would recall how the children weren't allowed to touch his piano or move anything in the house. "It was like living in a museum," she said.[9] When they went to restaurants, Gainsbourg would choose Birkin's outfit and hairstyle and order the food. If she was speaking and it was of no interest to him, he would nonchalantly look around or whistle as a sign that she needed to stop. Gainsbourg was not mean-spirited by any means. In fact, his generosity and love for Birkin knew no bounds, and she understood this deeply.

As their children grew, the couple adopted an unusual schedule to accommodate their nightlife: They woke up at three in the afternoon so that Birkin could pick up the girls from school and spend time with them. The two would have dinner with the kids, put them to bed, and then proceed to go out until dawn. It is interesting to note that both Gainsbourg and Birkin were still deeply committed to their work, despite their nonstop socializing. In fact, Birkin was working constantly, often on family-friendly, comedic films, and her popularity was steadily rising. Gainsbourg's career, however, had stalled. He admitted, "The problem is that the better things get, the stronger my desire to write 'unsingable' songs."[10] He wrote about Nazi imagery, madness, sex, farting, murder, and scatology. Gainsbourg was forthright in explaining how the reversal in his and Birkin's career dynamics affected him personally. "Relations between a man and a woman in the business can be very trying," he told the journalist Gilles Verlant. "Just when Jane reached the heights of stardom, I started to crack. It was very difficult, almost like I was 'Mr. Birkin.'"[11]

Yet Gainsbourg's devotion to Birkin never wavered. He accompanied her on film shoots and never wanted to spend more than a week apart from her. To remain by her side, he occasionally took lesser roles in her movies, such as *Sérieux comme le plaisir (Serious as Pleasure)* and *Trop jolies pour être honnêtes (Too Pretty to Be Honest)*. But one day in the spring of 1973, while Birkin was away on a shoot, Gainsbourg suffered his first heart attack. As Sylvie Simmons wrote in her biography of Gainsbourg, when he was a young nightclub pianist, a gypsy had read his palm. She "predicted that he would travel the world (done), lead a tormented love life (done), and come close to death at forty-five years old."[12] The fortune-teller appeared to be right on all three counts. While recovering from his heart attack, Gainsbourg began to miss the spotlight and called for a press conference from his hospital bed.

Around that time, Gainsbourg was writing the songs for Birkin's first solo album, *Di Doo Dah.* The ensuing years were filled with all kinds of joint projects. Gainsbourg wrote another album for Birkin called *Lolita Go Home,* which was released in 1975 and provocatively used one of the nude photos he took of her for *Lui* magazine as the cover art. Most surprising of all was their participation in a number of commercials for laundry detergent, soap, and razor blades. Gainsbourg had claimed it was an exercise in subversion by showing off Birkin instead of the product itself.

As the seventies drew to a close, Gainsbourg's career experienced a big, unexpected upswing. He made a reggae album in French, which went triple platinum, becoming the bestselling record of his career. The most controversial track was "Aux Armes et Caetera," in which Gainsbourg talk-sings the opening lines of the French national anthem over a laid-back reggae beat. The backlash from the song made the scandal around "Je T'Aime. . . Moi Non Plus" look rather meager. A French editor went as far as suggesting that Gainsbourg be stripped of his citizenship, while others discussed his outsider status as a Jew and the son of immigrants.

Gainsbourg's tour for the album was met with bomb threats and picketing. The most dramatic gesture was made in Strasbourg, where a retired paratrooper had warned the mayor

> "Just when Jane reached the heights of stardom, I started to crack. It was very difficult, almost like I was 'Mr. Birkin.'"
>
> Serge Gainsbourg

that, should Gainsbourg sing the song at his concert, he and his fellow veterans would "intervene physically and morally with all the strength at our disposal."[13] Gainsbourg did not want his fans to be robbed of a nice evening of music, so he took to the microphone and sang the original version of "La Marseillaise." The paratroopers in the front row were in utter shock. They took off their berets, stood up, and listened respectfully to the anthem. But at the end of the song, Gainsbourg flashed the French gesture of contempt. By the time he returned to Paris, Gainsbourg had become a hero for standing up to the racist right-wingers. His knack for using his music as a source of provocation of the current culture made him even more popular. He appeared on many magazine covers, now without his partner by his side.

On the home front, however, a subtle kind of unease was brewing within Birkin. She had grown as a woman and as an artist, but she didn't feel that Gainsbourg was fully seeing her for who she was. Perhaps the downfall of their relationship stemmed from Gainsbourg's overreliance on the packaged image that he had helped to create for her; that ingenue stereotype had left Birkin little space to express her other dimensions. Gainsbourg also had a drinking problem and would at times barge into the house inebriated and cause a ruckus. To shield herself and the kids, Birkin would rush off to nearby hotels in the middle of the night.

But the deeper reason for her departure was that Birkin craved to be her own person. Dressing up according to Gainsbourg's taste and going out every night was no longer compelling. She later said that she was thinking, "I don't want to be a doll anymore."[14] Gainsbourg seemed to show little understanding of her emotional state. When Birkin told him she was depressed, he simply brushed it off. She had him, the family, her career—what else did she want in life? In a sarcastic move, he wrote her a song called "Dépressive" and had her sing it on her 1978 album, *Ex Fan des Sixties.* "He didn't understand that the outside me didn't correspond with the inside at all," Birkin later recalled. "Then someone came along who understood how unhappy I was."[15]

That someone was the talented young director Jacques Doillon. Soon, the tormented Birkin took the girls and went to live with Doillon. Gainsbourg was shattered to the core, and true to form, he wrote a song about the man who had taken Birkin away, "Vieille Canaille—You Rascal You." As a way of numbing his pain, he showed up to public events and interviews drunk and disruptive. He dubbed this badly behaving part of his personality Gainsbarre. One day, Gainsbarre arrived on the set of *Je vous aime* blind drunk and tried to pick up his costar Catherine Deneuve. The actress understood that Gainsbourg was reeling from the pain of his breakup and called Birkin, hoping she could broker some kind of reconciliation between the two. Birkin, who still harbored deep feelings for Gainsbourg, came to his house, and in a fit of pride, he asked her to leave. But Birkin would never stay too far away. She would drop by Gainsbourg's house regularly to bring him food and check in on him.

One day in 1982, when Birkin had come to bring Gainsbourg one of her casseroles, she told him she was pregnant with Doillon's child. This news must not have been easy for Gainsbourg to take, but throughout the pregnancy, he made a valiant effort to reorient his relationship with Birkin and make their separation work. The story of the pair is all the more touching and extraordinary because of the way they bonded after their separation. Can couples who were once passionately in love, whose work and personal lives are deeply intertwined, forge a different kind of love after a devastating separation? Gainsbourg and Birkin did.

Slowly, they began talking to each other every day. When Birkin's child with Doillon was newly born, she called Gainsbourg first. He, in turn, sent baby Lou a gift of clothes and Russian fur booties, along with a card bearing the words "Papa deux" (Dad number two). He later became Lou's godfather. The following year, Gainsbourg would once again join Birkin on a film set, this time with Doillon and Lou. He began writing Birkin's next album, *Baby Alone in Babylone*—a touching tribute to their relationship. The first song Birkin recorded for it was "Con C'est Con Ces Conséquences" ("It's Stupid These Consequences"). It was the first time she was in the recording studio with Gainsbourg following their split, and firsts are

“I’d rather live alone than live with a face that looks at me with the wrong eyes.”

Jane Birkin

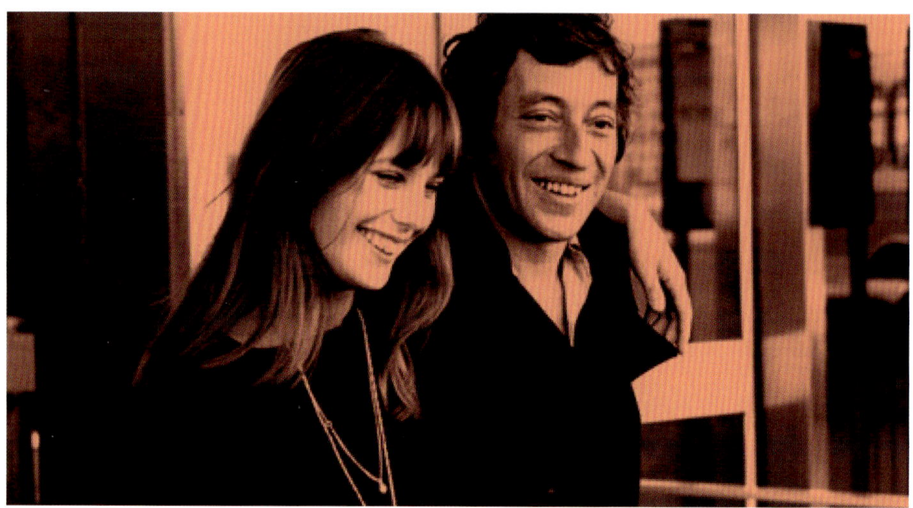

Birkin and Gainsbourg in 1969, one of the couple's most creatively productive years.

never easy. Tears rolled down her face as she sang his heartfelt lyrics, and Gainsbourg stood on the other side of the glass in the control room, crying along with her. "I realized that he was in fact asking me to sing words about his pain and the separation," Birkin later said. "I was singing his wounded side, his feminine side, the B-side of Gainsbarre."[16] The album went gold, and Birkin received the Grand Prix du Disque prize from the Académie Charles Cros—the same prestigious award that Gainsbourg had received early on in his career. Twenty-five years after his first musical triumph, a teary-eyed Gainsbourg accepted the award on Birkin's behalf, as she was off on a film shoot.

He wrote another spate of songs for Birkin two years later, for her album *Lost Song*. Birkin had confided in Gainsbourg that she was struggling to understand who she was becoming now that she was older and in a new stage of her life. They took to the piano and interpreted her feelings into moving lyrics. It is a marvel that Gainsbourg managed to produce such fine work for Birkin and other artists given his serious health problems. His alcoholism and prodigious cigarette smoking had caused delirium tremens, depression, vision loss, cirrhosis, cardiac flare-ups, and diabetes. Gainsbourg frequently had to stay in the hospital, and Birkin called nightly to check on him. One wonders what Doillon must have made of their relationship.

Gainsbourg, too, was in a serious relationship with the much younger Caroline Von Paulus—known as Bambou—and fathered a son, named Lucien, in 1986. But he had created a boundary between himself and his new family. Although he hated living alone, he installed them in another home in the thirteenth arrondissement. During his last month of life, he would sometimes sleep at Birkin's place. Back in his house on Rue Verneuil, Gainsbourg had kept Birkin's room exactly as she had left it, like a shrine in her honor. "In the end," Birkin said, "we became like an old married couple, sitting around and gossiping."[17]

The last album Gainsbourg wrote for Birkin, *Amours des Feintes,* was conceived while he was in the hospital recovering from yet another health scare. He urged her to record it as soon as possible, although Birkin was busy performing in a play in London. Perhaps he knew that he wasn't doing well. On the eve of his death, Gainsbourg went out to celebrate Bambou's birthday, but he had also bought a heart-shaped diamond from Cartier to be sent to Birkin. As usual, he went home alone after the festivities. The next day he was found dead in his bed from a heart attack. Birkin, Bambou, Kate, and Charlotte spent four days with him in the house, until his body was taken away.

> "In the end, we became like an old married couple, sitting around and gossiping."
>
> Jane Birkin

The announcement of the artist's death brought Paris to a standstill. Gainsbourg was so many things to the French public: a chain-smoking singer, a songwriter, a brilliant composer, a louche novelist, a photographer, an actor, an intellectual poet, a director, and a provocateur. French president François Mitterrand paid homage to the late artist by announcing, "Serge Gainsbourg elevated song to the level of art that will serve as an emblem of the sensibility of an entire generation."[18]

On March 7, 1991, Gainsbourg was buried near his parents, Joseph and Olga, in Montparnasse Cemetery—just a stone's throw away from the graves of the great philosophers Jean-Paul Sartre and Simone de Beauvoir. His death devastated Birkin and the girls. Less than a year later, Birkin and Doillon would split; Doillon claimed that he could not compete with Birkin's grief for Gainsbourg.

Birkin's iconic status only continued to skyrocket after Gainsbourg's death: The Hermès Birkin bag she designed would become one of the world's most sought-after accessories, she would have roles in upward of twenty films and release close to seventy albums, and she would become deeply involved with the nonprofit Amnesty International. In 2017, Birkin debuted a new album, called *Birkin/Gainsbourg: Le Symphonique,* that she created as a loving tribute to Gainsbourg; on it, she sings classical renditions of his songs accompanied by the Montreal Symphony Orchestra. Twenty-eight years after his passing, Gainsbourg's former partner and collaborator is still breathing life into the words that he lovingly wrote for her.

Jean-Paul Sartre & Simone de Beauvoir

The High Priest and Priestess of Philosophy

Aged twenty-three and poised to become the greatest philosopher of the twentieth century, Jean-Paul Sartre was ready to embark on a grand experiment with his fellow philosophy student and lover, Simone de Beauvoir. While studying at the Sorbonne in Paris, the diminutive and bespectacled Sartre had become smitten with the dark-haired beauty. They had fallen in love while preparing for their competitive final examination in philosophy, where Beauvoir came in second place to Sartre's first. However, the jury had debated whether to award the top prize to Beauvoir; the judges agreed that she was the better philosopher, but they gave it to Sartre nonetheless, because he was a man and it was his second time taking the exam. (He had failed it on his previous attempt.) The twenty-one-year-old Beauvoir thus became the youngest person in French history to pass the agrégation and graduate from the prestigious institution.

The pair had so much in common: an unabashed appetite for life, a fierce intellect, and a joint ambition to make a mark on history. Sartre could not have found a better match for himself. So, on a cool autumn day in 1929, he took the equally enamored Beauvoir to the majestic Luxembourg Gardens, looked into her flashing blue eyes, and made a proposition. He didn't ask Beauvoir to marry him, but instead offered a two-year lease on intimacy. He proposed that theirs would be an "essential"[1] relationship, where each party was free to engage openly in any number of contingent, secondary relationships. After two years, they would have an option to renew their commitment if the arrangement worked. Simone de Beauvoir and Jean-Paul Sartre would remain together for more than fifty years.

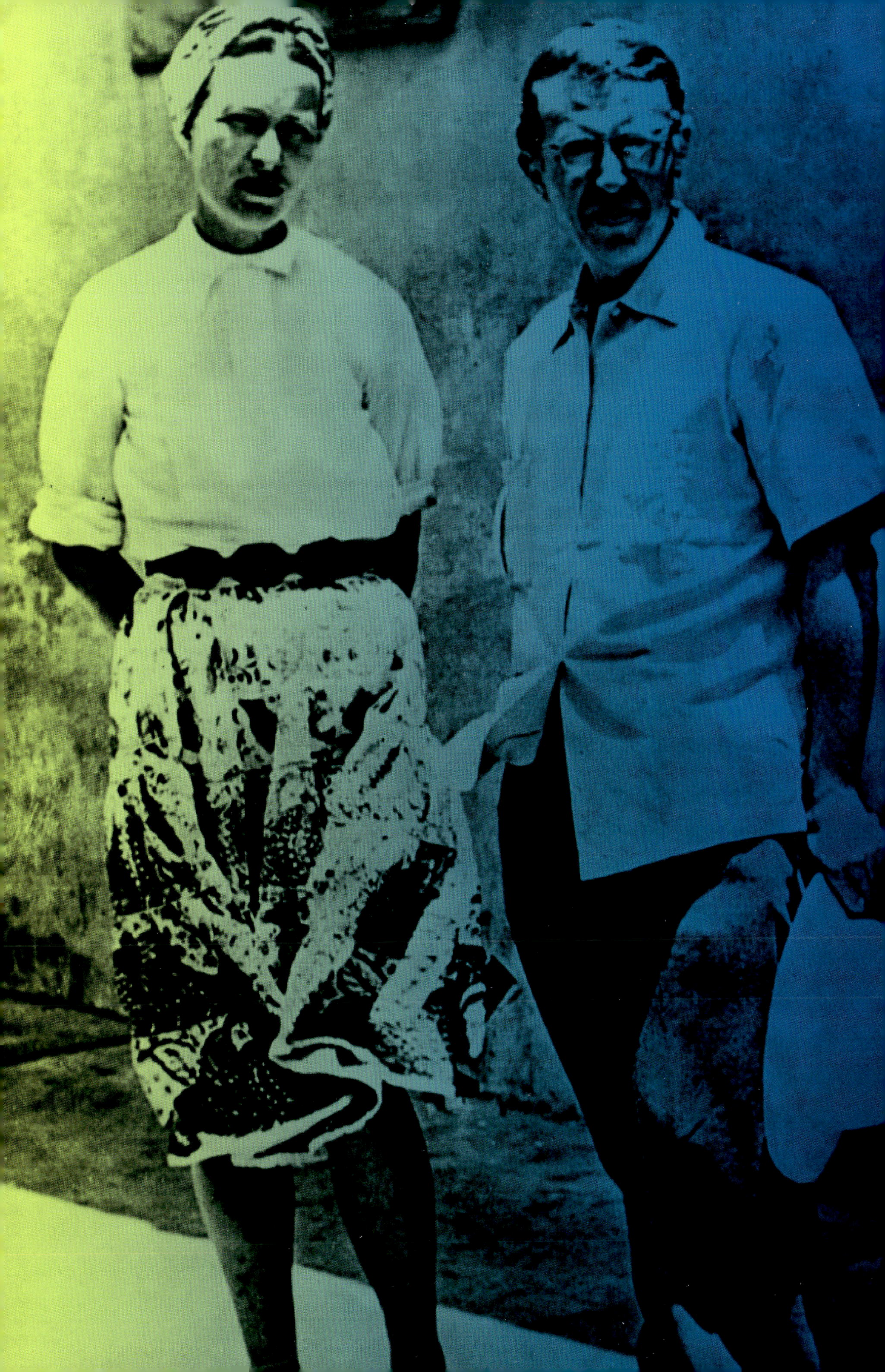

As Hazel Rowley wrote in her biography of the couple, "Sartre had made clear from the beginning that monogamy did not interest him. He liked women (far more than men, he always said), and he did not intend to stop having affairs at the age of twenty-three. Nor should Beauvoir, he said."[2] Why should they allow bourgeois conventions to determine their lives? Sartre, who would one day become the most widely recognized and influential proponent of the postwar philosophical movement called existentialism, vehemently believed in individual freedom and choice. Beauvoir found the proposition to be both frightening and exhilarating. She had never met anyone with such vitality and brilliance, who offered a boundless horizon of possibilities. Besides, she had harbored ambivalent feelings toward marriage herself. How could a declaration that is made at one point in time hold true for the ever-evolving self in the future? she would argue.

She had seen the pitfalls of a stale marriage in her own family; her father often came home late after nights of carousing with other women. Beauvoir certainly did not want to replicate the kind of dependence that marriage had created for her unhappy mother. Nor did she want to become a needy and possessive wife whom Sartre would grow to resent. To break from accepted norms would be a deeply significant act that would carry a social stigma. She was living in a world in which women were sheltered and protected. Beauvoir had thought herself wildly rebellious for setting foot in a café for the first time at age twenty. Women did not smoke or drink in public; they were expected to remain virgins until marriage. By remaining unmarried, she knew she would bring shame onto her parents. Her partnership with Sartre would be a radical departure from convention, but she was ready to make the leap.

In time, their coupledom became almost mythical in the way it reflected the tenets of existential philosophy; hence, their relationship was extensively documented not only by the press but also by Beauvoir herself. She would become one of the most famous memoirists of all time by penning a four-volume autobiography in which she defended and explained her uncommon relationship with Sartre. In her existentialist posturing, she took control of their public image by editing her version of their story. *Memoirs of a Dutiful Daughter* (1958), *The Prime of Life* (1960), *Force of Circumstance* (1963), and *All Said and Done* (1972) were wildly successful tomes that inspired legions of young people to explore open relationships in the vein of Beauvoir and Sartre's. But most would not be privy to the complexities of their relationship until their private correspondences were published posthumously.

What would be ingrained in the public's mind was the image of the two iconic intellectuals writing alongside one another, ensconced in the cafés strewn across Paris's Left Bank. Their favorite was Café de Flore on Boulevard Saint-Germain. They would write upstairs, at different tables, amid cigarette smoke and cups of tea. Sartre's handwriting was orderly and professional, while Beauvoir's was hardly legible. They became one another's sounding boards, literary critics, and supporters. Their partnership shaped both their philosophical writings and their fiction. They wrote in a remarkable range of genres: plays, novels, philosophical essays, travel narratives, autobiographies, memoirs, biographies, journalistic works. In 1945, the duo cofounded the journal *Les Temps modernes,* and Sartre assumed the role of editor. The publication and its writings exerted a significant influence on the intellectual life of France, Europe, and beyond.

Sartre's first novel, *Nausea,* was a landmark of French contemporary fiction that sealed his image as a maverick thinker. His plays were the most popular productions of Paris's theater season; his philosophical essays (especially *Being and Nothingness*), his biographical writings *(Saint Genet* and *The Family Idiot: Gustave Flaubert, 1821–1857)*, and his autobiographical masterpiece, *The Words,* were met with critical acclaim. In 1964, he won the Nobel Prize in

> "There is one thing that hasn't changed and cannot change: that is that no matter what happens and what I become, I will become it with you."
>
> Jean-Paul Sartre

Literature, but Sartre refused to accept the honor. As for Beauvoir, who was affectionately called the Beaver for her diligence and hard work, she is credited as the mother of the modern women's movement who galvanized a new generation of forward-thinking women with her groundbreaking feminist book, *The Second Sex* (1949).

As a part of their pact, Sartre and Beauvoir vowed to tell each other everything. They shared their daily struggles, their thoughts, and their ideas about their upcoming projects; they even provided each other with titillating reports of their affairs. Would the disclosures of their sexual experiences cause friction between the couple? For Sartre less so than for Beauvoir. From the start, Sartre declared that he disliked jealousy. It's better to control our passions before they control us, he would claim. To him, emotional reactions were impediments to living freely. Beauvoir would find her own way of dealing with her bouts of jealousy. She rationalized it as emotional weakness, a means of unnecessarily projecting one's need for safety onto another person. But her rationalizations only worked to some extent. At first, she was convinced that she loved Sartre more than he loved her, and would become anxious when he would embark on one of his new romances. Beauvoir learned to manage her feelings by

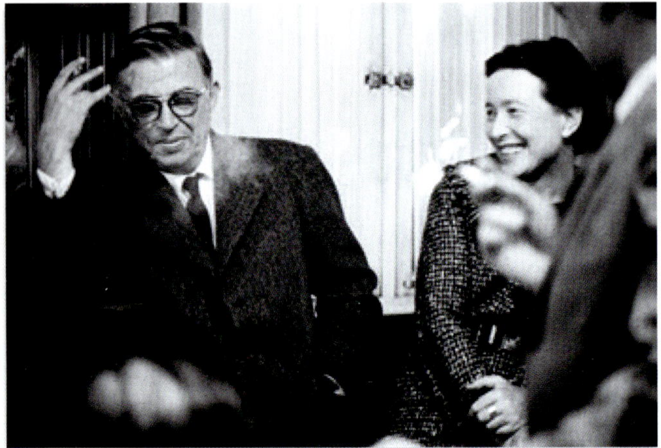

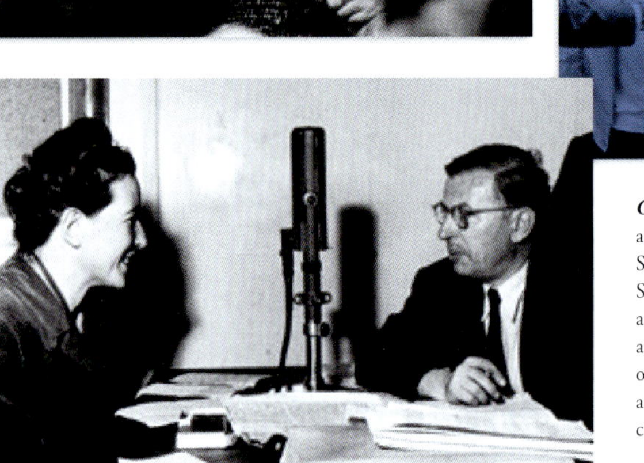

Clockwise from top left: Sartre and Beauvoir at the Théâtre de la Renaissance in Paris, where Sartre's play *Les Séquestrés d'Altona* was presented, September 1959; Journalists surrounding Sartre and Beauvoir on a Paris street after they were arrested for selling a newspaper advocating the overthrow of the French government; Beauvoir and Sartre in Saint-Germain-des-Prés, Paris, circa 1945.

cunningly keeping close with Sartre's "contingent"[3] women, even having affairs with them first and then introducing them to her partner. The writer and literary critic Lisa Appignanesi said it best: "[Beauvoir] accepted the freedom [Sartre] insisted on and became its custodian."[4]

Sartre and Beauvoir's preferred relationship style was to either mimic each other's dysfunctional relationships or to involve a third, shared love interest. They adopted a pattern whereby they would take a very young, confused woman under their wing, spend time with her, help her with her education and career, inevitably sleep with her, and later support her financially. As a young teacher, Beauvoir aroused an extraordinary number of schoolgirl crushes. She was an attractive woman, but what these aspirational girls desired most was her sense of freedom and her noteworthy achievements, which they hoped to emulate.

The first in the long line of student admirers was the ethereal seventeen-year-old Olga Kosakiewicz. After Beauvoir slept with her, Sartre tried unsuccessfully to seduce her for two years. When Olga went off with the handsome writer Jacques-Laurent Bost, Sartre was alarmed: The twenty-two-year-old Bost was not only having an affair with the inaccessible Olga but also with Beauvoir, who was thirty at the time. To distract himself, he turned his attention to Olga's younger sister, Wanda. Wanda had made it clear that she was physically repelled by him, which made Sartre even more determined in his pursuit. After two years of ardent letter writing and courtship, Wanda agreed to sleep with him. In time, Sartre and Wanda stopped having sex together, but he would financially support her for the rest of her life, cast her in several of his plays, buy her an apartment, and visit her twice a week.

Beauvoir was at first exasperated by Sartre's tumultuous relationship with Wanda, and by his fascination with Olga, and tried to make sense of her conflicted feelings. At Sartre's urging, Beauvoir would write a novel that drew on her experiences: Her book *L'Invitée* (which translates to *She Came to Stay*) features a character, based on a hybrid of Wanda and Olga, who overstays her welcome and is ultimately killed by the Beauvoir character. But, even at the height of his passion for Wanda, Sartre felt intimately connected to Beauvoir. She would read over his manuscripts and offer him feedback, and he, in turn, dedicated his 1938 book, the English title of which is *Nausea,* affectionately, "[t]o the Beaver."[5]

> "She was ready to deny the existence of space and time rather than admit that love might not be eternal."
>
> Simone de Beauvoir

When Beauvoir slept with another student, a pretty, sixteen-year-old Polish émigré named Bianca Bienenfeld, Sartre did too. He knocked on Beauvoir's door the following morning to tell her about his evening with Bienenfeld. He did the same with another former student of Beauvoir's, Nathalie Sorokine. She was a tall blonde with Slavic good looks who seemed to have gravitated toward the handsome Bost as well. The incestuous pattern of relationships would continue. When Beauvoir started an affair with the young, handsome Claude Lanzmann, Sartre proceeded to have one with Evelyne, Lanzmann's sister. She would become one of the women whom Sartre would later support.

By her own admission, Beauvoir and Sartre had more or less stopped having sex with each other by 1945, although they saw one another daily. In a letter she wrote to one of her lovers, Beauvoir explained her relationship with Sartre as one of deep friendship, rather than romantic in nature. "Love was not very successful," she stated. "Chiefly because [Sartre] does not care much for sexual life. He is a warm, lively man everywhere, but not in bed."[6] Given this assessment, one would venture to understand that Sartre's constant skirt chasing had more to do with his desire for conquest than with his sexual passions.

Sartre had been the pampered son of a widowed mother who devoted all her love and energy to her precocious child. But when he was eleven, his mother remarried. The resentful young boy took this as a mark of betrayal and abandonment. Sartre would spend the rest of his life attracting what he would call "drowning women"[7]—overly sensitive, vulnerable souls who would remain emotionally and financially dependent on him until he passed away. Certainly, for Sartre, those involvements could have been an unconscious way of ensuring that these women would never abandon him. It was of no consolation that he was physically unattractive.

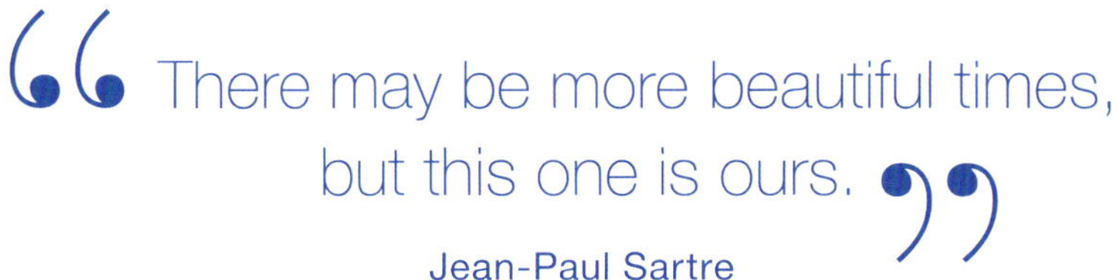

At around five feet tall, walleyed, and with blemished and pockmarked skin, he did not have a positive physical impact on the opposite sex. But what he lacked in handsomeness, he made up with the force of his personality. Sartre used his words and wit to great effect and became the kind of seducer he'd always hoped he would become. He would win over women by showering them with love letters and attention, only to withdraw into his work. The girlfriends would then complain about his lack of affection and become possessive and jealous. Sartre groaned about his demanding menagerie of women, but secretly he must have relished them needing him.

At the height of his success, he moved in with his mother—by then widowed again—and spent most of his money on supporting current and former mistresses. The harem of women he kept would live within ten minutes of him, but none—with the exception of Beauvoir—knew the truth about his life, as he made what he called his usual "medical rounds" to each girlfriend on scheduled dates and times. In this respect, Beauvoir set herself apart from the rest; Sartre admired and relied on her greatly.

Just as Beauvoir and Sartre's physical attraction to one another began waning, their notoriety as a couple reached new heights. In 1945, Beauvoir's novel *The Blood of Others,* and the first two novels of Sartre's Paths of Freedom trilogy, *The Age of Reason* and *The Reprieve,* all appeared at the same time in the bookstore windows. That same year, Beauvoir's play, *The Useless Mouths,* opened in Paris, and the first edition of their new journal, *Les Temps modernes,* debuted in kiosks throughout the city. Sartre and Beauvoir were so sought after that they couldn't walk leisurely in the streets without being besieged by photographers and autograph seekers.

When Beauvoir was struggling to find the next theme to write about, it was Sartre's probing question that set her on the path to further introspection: What does it mean to be a woman? Her thought-provoking response became her monumental opus, *The Second Sex,* which caused a storm of outrage and was banned by the Vatican. With great intellectual courage, Beauvoir explored the lost or missing narrative of women through biology, history, and mythology. Her book attacked society's overarching patriarchal bias, but also asserted that women are so conditioned by culture that they consent to this subservience.

Several chapters in *The Second Sex* discuss how freedom itself is full of insurmountable obstacles for women. But the question remains: Did Beauvoir, who dared to live as freely as Sartre, who seemed an equal to him in their intellectual pursuits, feel free herself? In one chapter, called "The Woman in Love," she described how a woman who loves a man mirrors his desires. "The supreme happiness of the woman in love," she noted, "is to be recognized by the loved man as a part of himself."[8] One only wonders if Beauvoir's constant accommodations to Sartre's countless affairs, as well as her own romantic trysts, were her way of acting like him. In her letters describing her sexual exploits, Beauvoir seemed ambivalent and condescending of her lovers, just as Sartre was in his letters. Was she secretly imitating him, or seducing him with voyeuristic pleasure to keep him interested?

Beauvoir also discussed how the independent woman is often doomed to feel divided when personal and professional goals pull her in different directions. She would have firsthand experience in this regard, as she had to give up one of the more significant relationships in her life in order to continue with her work and remain with Sartre. In 1947, she had met the writer Nelson Algren in Chicago while she was in the United States on a speaking tour. They fell in love, deeply and sexually, and tried for several years to maintain their transatlantic relationship. Algren wanted her to move to Chicago and marry him. She pleaded with him, "I could not live just for happiness and love, I could not give up my writing. . . in the only place where my writing and work may have a meaning."[9] After all, she wrote in French and had a predominantly French readership. Algren was also deeply hurt when Beauvoir repeatedly accommodated their travel plans to fit with Sartre's schedule. She tried to explain: "For nearly twenty years [Sartre] did everything for me; he helped me to live, to find myself, he sacrificed lots of things for my sake. . . I could not desert him. I could leave him for more or less important periods, but not pledge my whole life to anyone else."[10]

The relationship ended badly. Years later, Algren wrote a scathing review of Beauvoir's memoir, in which she had defended her open relationship with Sartre. "Anybody who can experience love contingently has a mind that has recently snapped. How can love be contingent? Contingent upon what?" he wrote.[11] Nevertheless, Beauvoir chose to wear the silver ring he had gifted her until her passing.

At the same time, Sartre was deeply enmeshed in a transatlantic relationship with the lively and charismatic Dolores Vanetti. They had met while Sartre was speaking in the States, too. Overtaken by strong emotions, he even pledged to marry her. But in the end, their relationship fell apart because of Beauvoir. Vanetti could not bring herself to accept another woman in Sartre's life. The women who were smart enough to understand the depth of the Sartre-Beauvoir relationship eventually backed away. Another example was Lena Zonina, who had been Sartre's official interpreter during his many visits to Russia. Sartre wrote her long, passionate letters over many years, referring to her as "Ma femme."[12] Beauvoir wrote that Sartre's hands were shaking when he read Zonina's farewell letter. "The more I read the Beaver's memoirs, the more I understand that I could never decide to change things," Zonina wrote. "You know that I feel friendship for the Beaver. I respect her, I admire the relationship you have. . . But you and the Beaver together have created a remarkable and dazzling thing which is so dangerous for those people who get close to you."[13]

The year 1963 proved to be incredibly productive for the couple. Beauvoir's book *Force of Circumstance* came out that year, and again she went to great lengths to describe the unique bond that she shared with Sartre. "There has been one undoubted success in my life: my relationship with Sartre," Beauvoir wrote. "In more than thirty years, we have only once gone to sleep at night disunited."[14] That year Sartre's autobiography, *The Words,* was received with great fanfare. Following its publication, the great existentialist won the Nobel Prize in Literature, which he refused to accept. He declined, he explained, because he detested awards on principle and felt that official accolades would add undue influence on the power of his pen. That, he said, would be unfair to the reader.

Now that he was nearing sixty, Sartre mulled over appointing a legal literary heir and executor. It made no sense to choose Beauvoir, as she was almost the same age. So, he turned to the youngest member of his existentialist circle (which he called "the family"[15]), Arlette Elkaïm. The Jewish Algerian philosophy student had originally reached out to Sartre in 1956, when she was nineteen. They struck up a friendship and may have had a fleeting fling, but he continued to see her regularly, and even bought her an artist's studio in Paris and a house in the South of France. Elkaïm, who had never held a job, became financially dependent on him. Sartre legally adopted her and later made her quite wealthy as the heir and manager of his estate. Needless to say, the rest of the women in his "family" were outraged.

By the time Elkaïm became Sartre's legal daughter, Beauvoir had found a protégé of her own. Sylvie Le Bon was a seventeen-year-old college student who had written Beauvoir an

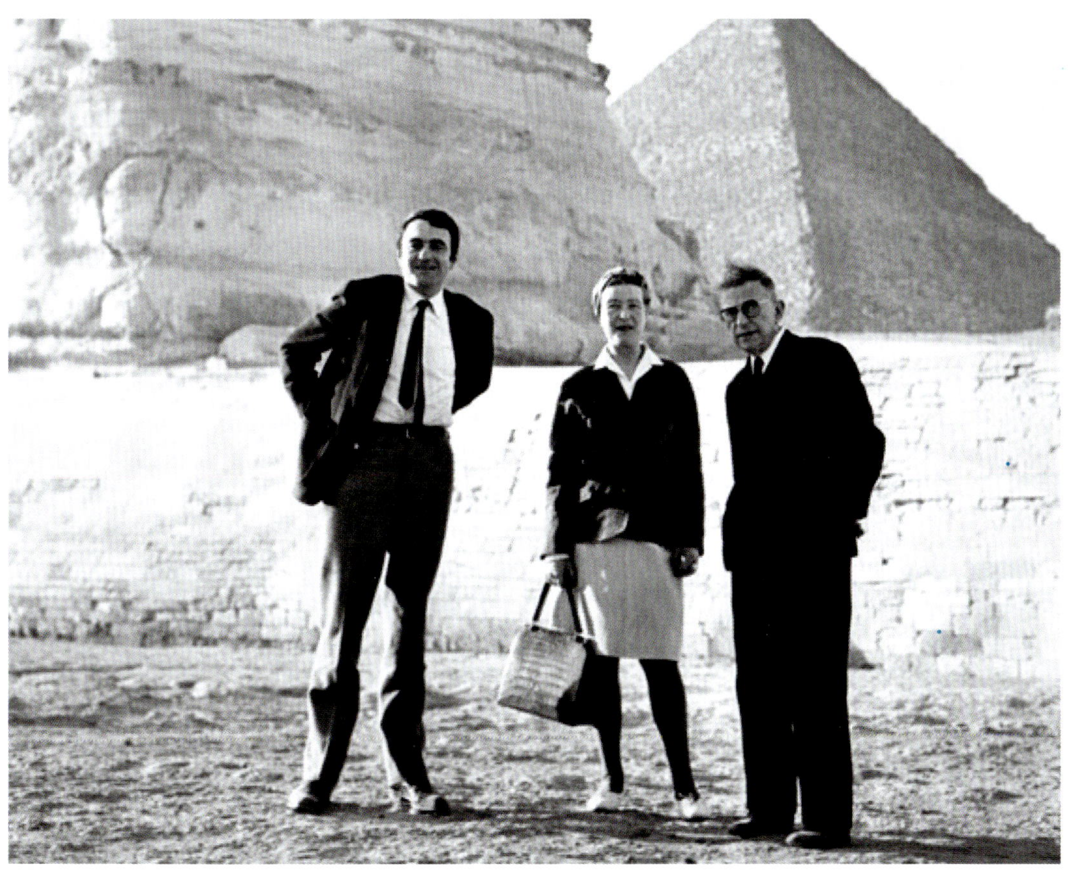

Beauvoir and Sartre with Claude Lanzmann (left), an editor at their journal, *Les Temps modernes,* standing in front of the Great Sphinx of Giza, Egypt.

admiring letter in 1960. Friends found Le Bon's resemblance to Beauvoir, and their shared interest in books and travel, remarkable. The two claimed that theirs was a deep-rooted friendship. Le Bon was reluctant to become her mentor's legally adopted daughter, wanting to avoid the comparison to Sartre and Elkaïm, but she also understood Beauvoir's real need for realizing a younger heir and executor, and finally acquiesced.

Sartre's steadily declining health plunged both him and Beauvoir into further introspection. As usual, Beauvoir processed her thoughts and emotions best through the act of writing. When her mother was sick and in the hospital in her final days, Beauvoir experienced a new sense of compassion for the woman she had so often rebelled against. Sartre encouraged her to put pen to paper and memorialize this great adventure between mother and daughter. *A Very Easy Death,* released in 1964, was the most tender book Beauvoir would author, filled with gripping and emotional passages. She then proceeded to write a clear-eyed and forceful book on aging *(The Coming of Age)* that spent several weeks on the bestseller list. During this time, Sartre tried his best to finish a project that he had started more than a decade earlier. His awe-inspiring book *The Family Idiot,* which he finally published in 1971, was a psychobiography of the novelist Gustave Flaubert. Sartre's brilliant analytical skills were on full display as he attempted to synthesize Flaubert's life through the prisms of psychoanalysis, social psychology, cultural context, and individual behavior. This ambitious book was deemed one of Sartre's most extraordinary works. The only book Beauvoir would write that Sartre did not read was *Adieux: A Farewell to Sartre,* which was a moving portrayal of her partner's physical decline that she published after his death.

> "For nearly twenty years [Sartre] did everything for me; he helped me to live, to find myself, he sacrificed lots of things for my sake. . . I could not desert him. I could leave him for more or less important periods, but not pledge my whole life to anyone else."
>
> Simone de Beauvoir

By the start of the seventies, Sartre had lost his eyesight after suffering a stroke, and now relied on Beauvoir to read him his books. It was only three years before his passing that Sartre would make one of his most public declarations of love and gratitude for his companion: In an interview to commemorate his seventieth birthday, he told the news magazine *Le Nouvel observateur* that his intellectual relationship with Beauvoir had been, above all others, the most significant bond in his life. He also credited his longstanding partner with filtering and refining his many ideas. It was not just because she was so intelligent, he said, but also because she understood him better than anyone else did. When the interviewer asked if he honestly critiqued her work, he responded, "Absolutely. As hard as possible. There is no point in not criticizing very severely when you have the good fortune to love the person you are criticizing."[16]

During Sartre's final days in the hospital, Beauvoir was with him constantly. There, at his bedside, Sartre took Beauvoir by the wrist and, with his eyes closed, muttered, "I love you very much, my dear Beaver."[17] The next day, unable to talk, he offered his lips to her. It was a rare gesture for him to make, and as Beauvoir reached in to kiss him, she knew that these would be their final moments together. When he passed away on April 15, 1980, she spent a few hours alone, lying next to her closest companion of fifty-one years.

Sartre's death made front-page news around the world. In France, the philosopher was a national icon; President Valéry Giscard d'Estaing even visited the hospital and spent an hour beside his coffin. Tributes and calls came streaming in. "Sartre inhabited his century like Voltaire and Hugo inhabited theirs," said the newspaper *Libération.* An estimated fifty to eighty thousand mourners packed the streets of Saint-Germain and Montparnasse to say their final goodbyes to the great philosopher as the hearse carrying Sartre's body went to Montparnasse Cemetery. Beauvoir never fully recovered from the overwhelming grief of losing her partner, and on April 14, 1986, she too slipped away, six years after him, almost to the hour. Her ashes were buried in a joint grave with Sartre's—their names linked for eternity.

"Women, you owe her everything!" So ran a headline that announced Beauvoir's death. Heads of state and notable thinkers, including Prime Minister Jacques Chirac and the American feminists Gloria Steinem and Betty Friedan, marked the passing of one of the world's most influential philosophers by issuing formal statements. "If any single human being can be credited with inspiring the current international woman's movement, it's Simone de Beauvoir," Steinem said.[18] Betty Friedan added that Beauvoir was an "authentic heroine in the history of womanhood."[19]

For many who grew up in the fifties and sixties, Sartre and Beauvoir each represented a new type of hero. Both sincerely believed that men and women could relate to one another on equal footing, that a new paradigm of relations could be forged between the genders that didn't involve marriage. In her book *The Second Sex,* Beauvoir advocated that once women found their own strength and forms of independence, both men and women would be liberated to have more authentic relationships. "We have pioneered our own relationship—its freedom, intimacy, and frankness," she once said of her partnership with Sartre.[20] She also conceded that their liaisons with third parties were not as successful as they had intended. Of course, it would be easy to condemn Sartre and Beauvoir's carrousel of partners as perverse and narcissistic; there were plenty of cases in which our hero and heroine straddled the worlds of saint and sinner. But one can't underestimate what the two built out of their fifty-one-year experiment in living. For five decades, their daily conversations gave rise to books, plays, and manifestos, along with a bond that, while occasionally irritated by other passions, never ruptured.

If you happen to walk along the cobblestone streets of Saint-Germain and Montparnasse, you will most likely come across many of the couple's old haunts: the cafés, jazz bars, and their apartments. On Rue Cels, you will find the Hôtel Mistral, an imposing yet modest hotel where Sartre and Beauvoir lived on and off during the war. A small plaque has been placed on its facade to commemorate the legendary couple. Underneath it is an excerpt from one of Sartre's letters to Beauvoir. It encapsulates their shared sense of adventure and commitment to become one another's witness as they made their journey through life. It reads: "There is one thing that hasn't changed and cannot change: that is that no matter what happens and what I become, I will become it with you."[21]

Bill Masters & Virginia Johnson

The Sex Gurus

"What have you got to tell me about sex?" Chancellor Shepley asked.[1]

The man sitting across from Washington University's chancellor was a stern-faced, bow tie-clad star academic and physician at the university's medical school. Dr. Bill Masters had published more than forty academic articles in his decade of tenure at the university. His innovations in obstetric and gynecological surgery and hormone research had secured his position as a topflight fertility expert, and people from across the globe came to his office for guidance and treatment. It was even purported that the glamorous and childless Princess Soraya, the wife of the last Shah of Iran, had visited the doctor to see if she could bear an heir to continue the dynasty.

Masters—not one to mince words or ease his way into a conversation—looked matter-of-factly at the chancellor and said, "Well, sir, I have to tell you, I am overwhelmingly aware that I don't know anything about sex. And I don't believe you do, either."[2] Chancellor Shepley broke out in anxious laughter.

It was true. Throughout history, so many people had written books, plays, and poems about the allure between men and women. Yet no one understood a thing about the underlying mechanics of sexual behavior and response. So much research had been conducted on human reproductive anatomy, but nothing was known about the physiology of sex. Religion, cultural mores, and politics had kept a tight rein on such discussions. Masters knew this firsthand. His years spent interviewing infertile couples had taught him that no one honestly disclosed the details of their sexual behavior—even to their trusted doctor. So, the logical next step for him was to study sex itself by direct observation. What mind-body connections take place before, during, and after intercourse? No one had any idea.

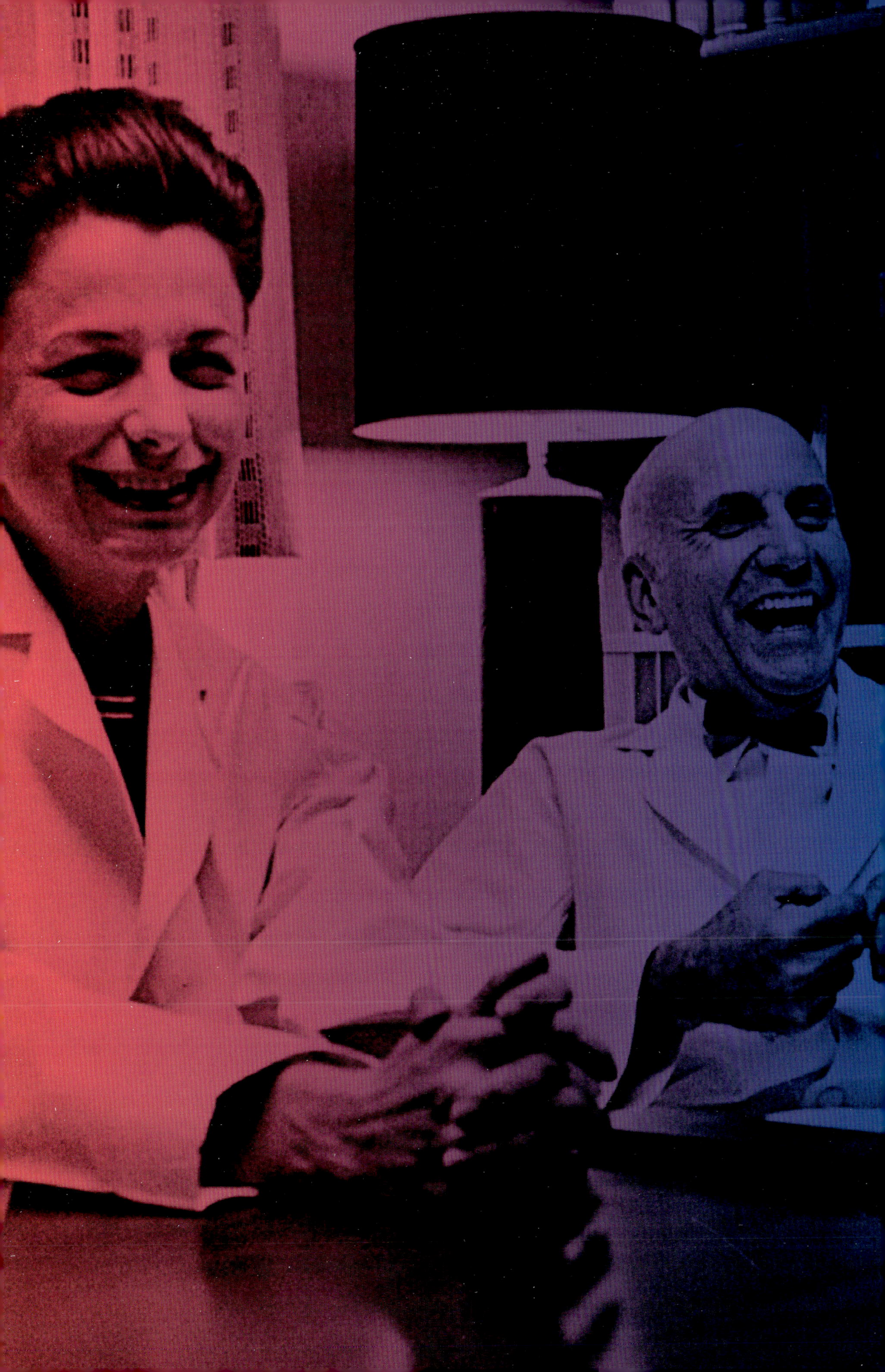

The exploration of sexuality, especially during the repressive 1950s, was risky and radical, but Masters desperately needed the university's backing to give his project a measure of credibility. In Ethan Shepley, he found an unlikely ally. The chancellor's encouragement of academic freedom and intellectual pursuits never wavered, and he granted the ambitious physician permission to go ahead with the first phase of his study.

But when Shepley heard the details of Masters's research strategy, he turned pale. Masters wanted to interview and observe the prostitutes of St. Louis and the surrounding areas through a peephole or two-way mirror in bordellos—with their consent, of course. Why prostitutes? Because they were, presumably, experts in their field. Masters even persuaded the St. Louis police chief, who was indebted to him for delivering his second child, and the local archbishop, whom he had won over by discussing how his research would bolster marital happiness, to quietly support his new project.

Masters interviewed 118 female and 27 male prostitutes, and from that sample he selected eight women and three men for observation of various sexual acts. "I was always interested in why the prostitute approached a targeted male the way she did," he said.[3] After each encounter and interview, he would diligently record all his findings.

Although Masters had gathered a great deal of information, he knew his research was essentially flawed. Prostitutes were not representative of the average American woman, and anatomically, many of them chronically suffered from irritated uteri and pelvic areas. He set his sights on finding educated women as subjects, but recruiting volunteers was a challenge. He could not simply ask female students and staffers on campus to have sex in his laboratory for observation. What he needed was a female research partner who would bring dignity, balance, and professionalism to the study. She would provide the much-needed woman's perspective on sexuality and also help recruit volunteers. Masters's wife, Libby, had no interest in aiding him, as she was busy raising their children. His only option was to find an assistant.

Aged thirty-one, the twice-divorced Virginia Johnson was in need of a job. She had recently decided to enroll as a sociology student at Washington University, but she would have to work in order to pay her tuition and support her children. It was Christmas break in 1956 when Johnson walked through the snow-covered campus to interview for a position in one of the most esteemed medical schools in the Midwest. She had no inkling that she and the man she was about to meet would spend forty-three years collaborating on research and would come to be known as the priest and priestess of human sexuality.

"I had heard of Masters and his work with infertility, and that's what I thought I was being hired for when I took the job," Johnson later recounted.[4] At the time, Masters's study on the physiology of sex was shrouded in secrecy, with very few people at the university aware of the details. Upon being hired, Johnson was given a desk in the maternity ward, where her first task was to compile subjects' personal histories. But she found it odd that some hospital employees would snicker as she passed by in the cafeteria. It was not until a young male colleague divulged the full extent of the research that Johnson discovered what was going on in Masters's soundproof lab. Much to Masters's surprise and delight, Johnson was unfazed by the revelation. That reaction invariably played a decisive role in Masters involving her further in the sex study.

Masters may have preferred a female physician as a partner, but in the 1950s, a woman with a medical degree was a rarity, and those few who did practice medicine would not have jeopardized their careers and reputations to do sex research. Besides, a female doctor of a higher stature would likely have provided her own input and imposed guidelines onto the study, which may have not worked well for the ambitious Bill Masters. While Johnson didn't have a bachelor's degree or the training and title of a medical resident, she possessed certain characteristics that made her an ideal research partner for him. She was smart, intuitive, hardworking, and had exemplary social skills. Johnson used those attributes to push Masters's controversial project forward.

Masters put in the time to train Johnson, tutoring her in anatomy and biology. Meanwhile, she showed an enthusiasm and commitment to the work that went beyond the call of most assistants. Johnson worked long hours and over weekends and holidays, and she studied and read other research on human sexuality. Since Masters was busy with his ob-gyn practice and the infertility clinic, Johnson shouldered most of the study's burdens. Within a year, she transitioned from a secretary to a savvy research assistant.

That the study was overseen by both a male and a female allowed volunteers to feel more comfortable with the sensitive nature of their participation. Johnson's gender and friendliness made her a prime recruiter of female university students, staffers, and faculty wives, who would perform prearranged sexual acts while hooked up to wires.

During the initial phase of their study, Masters and Johnson observed close to seven hundred men and women and an estimated ten thousand complete cycles of sexual response. That Johnson managed to sign up so many participants is a marvel. Forthright and witty in her approach, Johnson made a great feminist appeal to the young female candidates: She encouraged them to join the study to help break cultural barriers, to learn about themselves and their bodies, and to make an important contribution to science. Other participants—both male and female—joined in order to overcome their shyness toward the opposite sex, release sexual tension, or improve sexual performance.

With her warm and engaging demeanor, Johnson would dispel subjects' lingering anxiety in the laboratory by calmly explaining the procedures and the equipment. She would stick the wires and probes on the participants to record their heartbeats and brain waves and introduce them to their unknown, masked partners. It was not a natural setting in which to have sex by any means, but somehow Johnson was successful in reengaging them, making participants feel comfortable and even getting them to return again for further research. Her important contributions to Masters's work cannot be overstated.

Worried about what Sigmund Freud had called "transference" of feelings between therapist and patient, Johnson kept a friendly distance from the volunteers. But in the highly sexually charged lab environment, something seemed to be brewing between the two researchers. One night, Masters, who had always preached professionalism, approached Johnson after their evening discussions and proposed that they begin a sexual relationship.

The proposal was couched in his no-nonsense, scientific, detached reasoning, without a trace of romantic overture. Masters claimed that conducting their own experiment into male-female intimacy represented the natural next step in understanding their observations. He also made the case that sex with one another would abate the chances of them improperly transferring any built-up libidinal energy onto a volunteer. However, there may be a more troublesome side to the story. Dr. Robert C. Kolodny, who worked with the pair for two decades as their closest aide, believed that, had Johnson not accepted Masters's offer, she would have been quickly replaced. "No—I was not comfortable with it, particularly," Johnson insisted several decades later.[5] She had just begun to build a new life for herself as a single mother of two, but she feared her employment would be jeopardized if she were to refuse. In an era when there was little recourse for women who were sexually harassed in the workplace, Johnson rationalized the proposal as a part of her job description.

There was no pretense of emotional attachment. In fact, at the time, Johnson was seriously involved with an older man, a much-admired judge named Noah Weinstein. Their relationship would soon fall apart; Weinstein found Johnson too immersed in her research, and Masters was always a looming figure in their relationship. Masters, on the other hand, appeared to have the perfect family, but he seemed more married to his work than to his wife; the couple even slept in separate beds. While Masters was researching and studying sex, he seemed to have very little of it at home.

It was one late evening, after their volunteers had left the lab, that Masters and Johnson first consummated their relationship. The hospital staff may have harbored suspicions about the affair, but they looked the other way. After all, it was not uncommon for doctors to become involved with female staffers. Masters's wife, Libby, on the other hand, chose not to

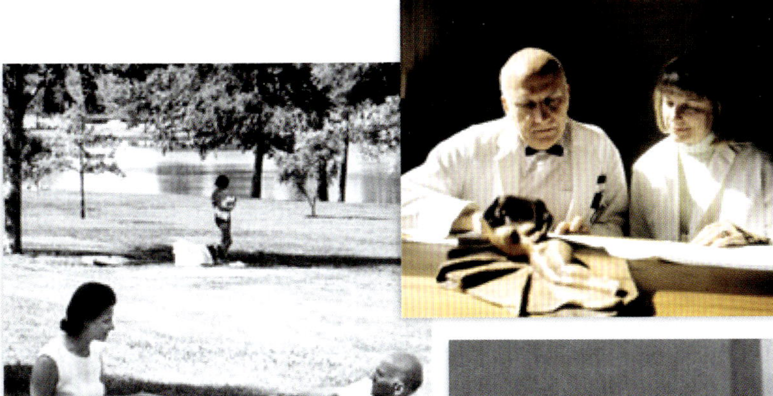

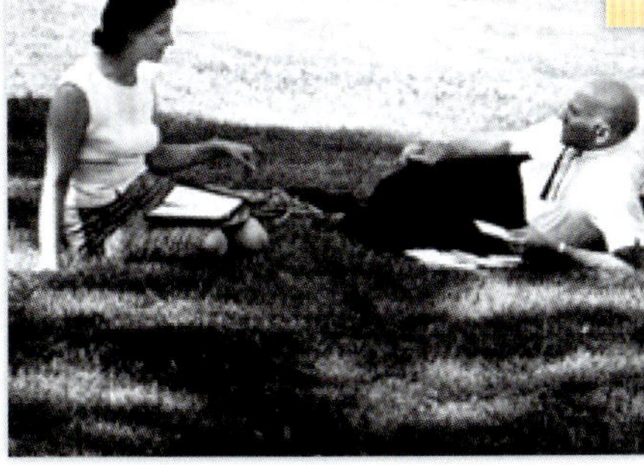

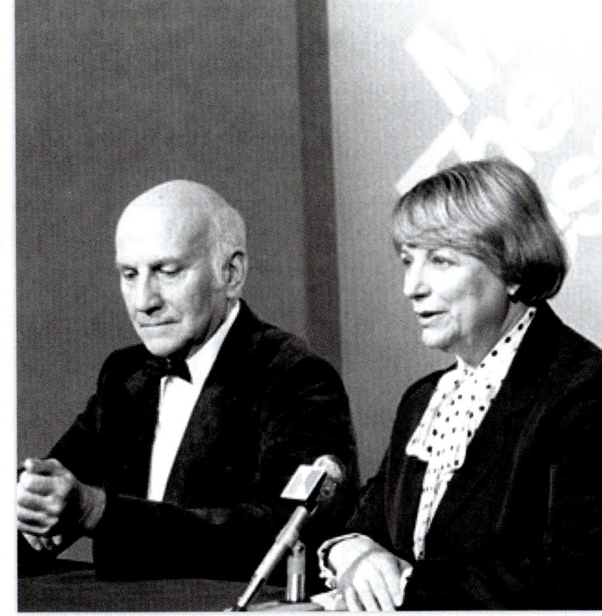

Clockwise from top left: Johnson and Masters relaxing on the lawn in Forest Park, New York, 1966; Masters and Johnson reading a document at their desk, which features a sculpture of a couple, in Saint Louis, July 1973; The couple presenting on homosexuality in Washington, D.C., April 22, 1979.

acknowledge it. Johnson was invited to many social events and fundraisers with the couple and was a regular presence in their house. Libby even took care of Johnson's children when Johnson was called away to work.

"The Human Female: Anatomy of Sexual Response" was the first published study in which Johnson shared a coveted byline with Masters. More publications followed, and soon Masters's research became a source of distress and controversy on campus. It started when Masters shared his sexually explicit research footage and findings at an ob-gyn conference at the university. The presentation was a scientific one, but the faculty was dumbfounded by the graphic images that flashed before their eyes. Over the ensuing months, the mounting pressure to stop Masters's project propelled the headstrong academic to leave the university altogether. In 1964, he decided to end his surgical practice at the hospital and to give up his tenured professorship to launch an independent, nonprofit research institution. Initially called the Reproductive Biology Research Foundation, the organization was renamed the Masters and Johnson Institute in 1978.

Masters was relentless in pursuing his goals. When prestigious publications refused to publish his sex research, he kept prodding them. He sought out smaller publications and pitched incessantly. When others questioned Johnson's training and credibility, Masters publicly credited her for many of their findings. No longer at the mercy of the university administration, he officially gave Johnson the title of research assistant and increased her salary. When she felt self-conscious and inadequate before presentations, Masters went to great lengths to tutor her and rehearse their answers. By 1964, Johnson had become a polished and well-informed communicator, and she directed her focus to pushing the study forward.

The complexity of Masters and Johnson's relationship is striking. Masters had inappropriately propositioned his assistant, but he also proved to be a dedicated mentor who ensured Johnson's professional growth and recognition. And although Johnson may have had misgivings about her sexual encounters with Masters at first, in time she began to enjoy their physical relationship. "We were really sexual athletes," she later boasted to friends.[6]

Their physical intimacy changed the dynamics of the duo's work. Masters began deferring to Johnson's opinions more often. She had become an indispensable part of the foundation's success and provided original insights, not only regarding female sexual response, but also about therapeutic solutions for sexual dysfunction. As Thomas Maier pointed out in his biography of the couple, "In many respects, [Johnson] was leading the way, fashioning a more thorough, integrated approach to dealing with human sexuality than [Masters] ever envisioned."[7]

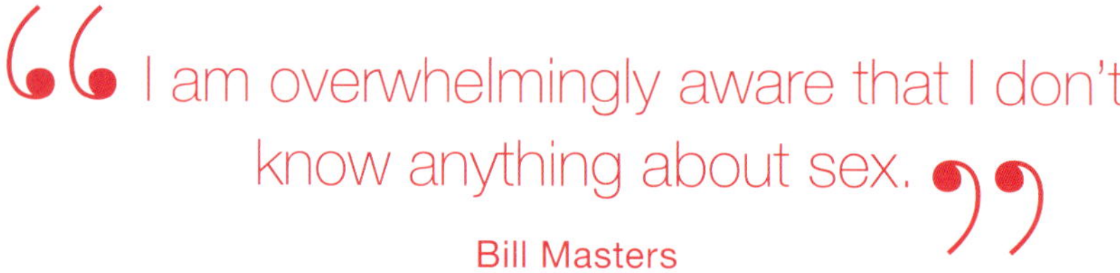

April 1966 brought a watershed moment for Masters and Johnson. These once-obscure researchers released their textbook, *Human Sexual Response,* and were immediately catapulted into the national conversation. Designed primarily for doctors and residents in need of basic training, the tome soared onto bestseller lists, selling more than three hundred thousand copies over the next four years. *Newsweek* called their work "the most daring and explicit experiments ever conducted in the scientific studies of sex."[8] The *New York Times* essentially described the duo as a scientific team that was educating a nation.

With the advent of the birth control pill and the rise of the feminist movement, many people were reassessing the parameters of their sexuality, and some of them consulted *Human Sexual Response* as they did so. The clinical evidence compiled in the book challenged the narrow, misogynistic views of women's sexuality. Freud, in his limited experience, had suggested that the male sex drive was stronger than and superior to that of the female. Medical literature, in turn, often portrayed women as frigid beings whose desire for sex only stemmed from their biological need to procreate. But Masters and Johnson showed otherwise. Their studies emphasized the physiological similarities between men and women and illuminated how both genders experience four sequential phases of sexual response: excitement, plateau, orgasm, and resolution. The authors devoted 141 pages of text to female sexual response—triple the amount of space spent on the male reaction—and revealed that women have the potential to experience multiple orgasms. Their landmark findings transformed both women's and men's views of themselves and inspired many to seek greater sexual fulfillment in their lives. Such insights shaped and fueled America's sexual revolution over the next two decades.

Having documented the physical mysteries of sex, Masters and Johnson turned their attention to helping people overcome sexual dysfunctions. In an innovative dual-therapy approach, Johnson and Masters separately interviewed both members of a couple. The process enabled them to identify both similarities and cross-gender variations in the subjects' answers, which ultimately brought about unique insights. "At least 70 percent of the therapy was her idea," Masters later said.[9] Johnson's years of interviewing and comforting volunteers during their initial research paid off greatly in the therapeutic setting. She instinctively came up with the pioneering "sensate focus" technique—a series of physical exercises aimed at restoring intimacy between couples. Their therapy program, which typically lasted two weeks, yielded an 80 percent success rate—a remarkable feat compared to the abysmal results of other forms of treatment.

With the publication of their second book, *Human Sexual Inadequacy,* Masters and Johnson were heralded as sex gurus. Based on their work at the clinic, the book described different forms of sexual dysfunction and specific therapies that could be used to target them. Johnson's distinctly female perspective improved women's understanding of their own sexuality. In 1970, *Time* magazine celebrated Masters and Johnson by featuring them on its cover. The notoriety brought them fame, wealth, and celebrity clients.

The following year, the American public heard that Masters and Johnson had decided to marry. The media treated their union as a happy ending to their work relationship, but the truth was that Masters had impulsively sprang into action upon discovering that Johnson was seriously considering marrying another man. He feared losing her—or, rather, her professional partnership—and was ready to leave his wife and family for her. Although Libby must have had her suspicions about their relationship, Masters's sudden departure left her devastated. In the end, it seemed that Johnson was as apprehensive as Masters about jeopardizing the future of their world-famous partnership. Lucrative book deals and speaking engagements were at stake, and she had worked so hard to earn her spot by his side. So, she ultimately accepted the proposal.

Although love and attachment were hardly considerations in their union, Masters and Johnson published a book in 1974, called *The Pleasure Bond,* that expounded on the virtues of sex within the framework of love and commitment. Somewhat ironically, people noted that Masters and Johnson's own passion for each other diminished after they had decided to marry.

They published two more books in the ensuing years. *Homosexuality in Perspective* (1979) was especially controversial; in it, the authors touted their success using conversion therapy to "cure" homosexuals. Activists and social scientists sharply criticized their study, while the religious right seized on the findings to validate the view that homosexuality was a lifestyle choice. Eventually, conversion therapy was discredited and condemned by most major medical groups, and it was revealed that Johnson had been apprehensive about the book from the start. She had tried to discourage Masters from pursuing the project, but he could not be swayed. She had even considered distancing herself from it. After the fiasco, Johnson decided to exert more influence on their work at the institute.

Perhaps it was due to his age, or because he was displaying early signs of Parkinson's disease, but around this time Masters seemed less engaged in his work. His hands would often tremble, and during presentations he would lose his train of thought. He had become even more withdrawn, preferring to stay home and watch football or read his favorite detective novels. For the lively and engaging Johnson, this lifestyle felt oppressive and boring. Yet during Masters's years of decline, she still cared for her husband.

By 1990, the institute's caseload had diminished significantly. Johnson ruminated on how she could leave Masters and retire from the clinic. But it was not an easy decision; she had spent most of her adult life with him. Bud Wilkinson, a close friend of Johnson's, was very astute in analyzing her dilemma. "You can love someone without being in love with them," he explained. "You maybe love what he represents. You love the collaboration and the partnership in the work. You love the recognition. But do you love the person? That comes down to another issue."[10]

What Johnson could not have expected was that Masters would be the one to end their twenty-one-year marriage. On Christmas Eve of 1992, he announced that he had found the true love of his life: Geraldine Baker Oliver—a woman he had adored and tried to propose to fifty-four years before. He had run into her in the eighties and had kept in touch with her over the years. By 1992, Geraldine's husband had passed away and Masters recognized an opportunity. At age seventy-seven, this was his last chance at love.

Although their marriage fell apart, Masters and Johnson continued to work together. Within a year of their divorce, they came out with yet another book, *Heterosexuality.* The two may have suffered miserably while married, but they were exceptional partners at work. Indeed, the personality traits and characteristics that make for an effective business partnership do not always translate well to personal relationships. What the two researchers shared above all was an unwavering commitment to their work; however, there was not enough intimacy or emotional attachment in their decades-long relationship to make their marriage successful. While Masters and Johnson offered insights about sex and the interaction between men and women throughout their illustrious careers, more than thirty years of research could not account for the strange chemistry and deep-seated connection two people share in a relationship.

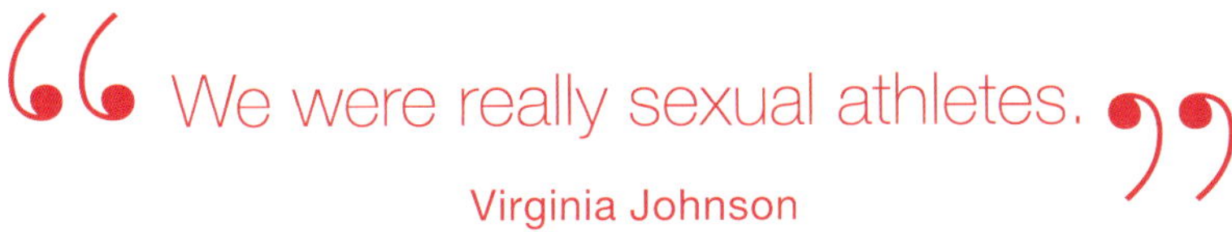

The year 1994 signified the end of an era for Masters and Johnson: Masters decided to retire, their work together came to an end, and the institute was shuttered. Less than a decade later, in February 2001, Masters died of complications from Parkinson's disease. Johnson passed away of natural causes in July 2013.

Recently, millions of Americans became reacquainted with the pair's remarkable story through the critically acclaimed Showtime television series *Masters of Sex.* Bill Masters and Virginia Johnson will always be remembered as pioneers and revolutionaries who changed our understanding of the physical mysteries of sex.

Ruth Bader & Martin Ginsburg

The Changemakers

With the marshal's "Oyez, oyez, oyez" resonating in the background, Justice Ruth Bader Ginburg takes her seat at the highest court in the United States. She is known for her fiery opinions in the courtroom, and she has the accoutrements to match. When a jabot, or decorative collar, with scalloped glass beads glitters against her somber black robe, it signals her fierce dissent; a woven one in yellow with gold detailing conveys that she will be reading the majority opinion.

It was about forty years ago that Ruth, or RBG as she's come to be known, stood in the very same court, arguing a series of gender-equality cases before nine stone-faced male justices. RBG is quick to clarify that she was upholding "the constitutional principle of the equal citizenship stature of both men and women,"[1] rather than arguing for women's rights. This brilliant attorney would ultimately win five out of six of these cases before the Supreme Court, catalyzing seismic changes in the way men and women were treated and viewed in society.

Ruth had imagined a world in which men transformed themselves alongside women, and in which women worked in coalition with men to get rid of outdated and restrictive gender roles. "In my life, what I find most satisfying is that I was a part of a movement that made life better, not just for women," she declared. "I think gender discrimination is bad for everyone, it's bad for men, it's bad for children. Having the opportunity to be part of that change is tremendously satisfying. Think of how the Constitution begins. 'We the people of the United States in order to form a more perfect union.' But we're still striving for that more perfect union. And one of the perfections is for the 'we the people' to include an ever enlarged group."[2]

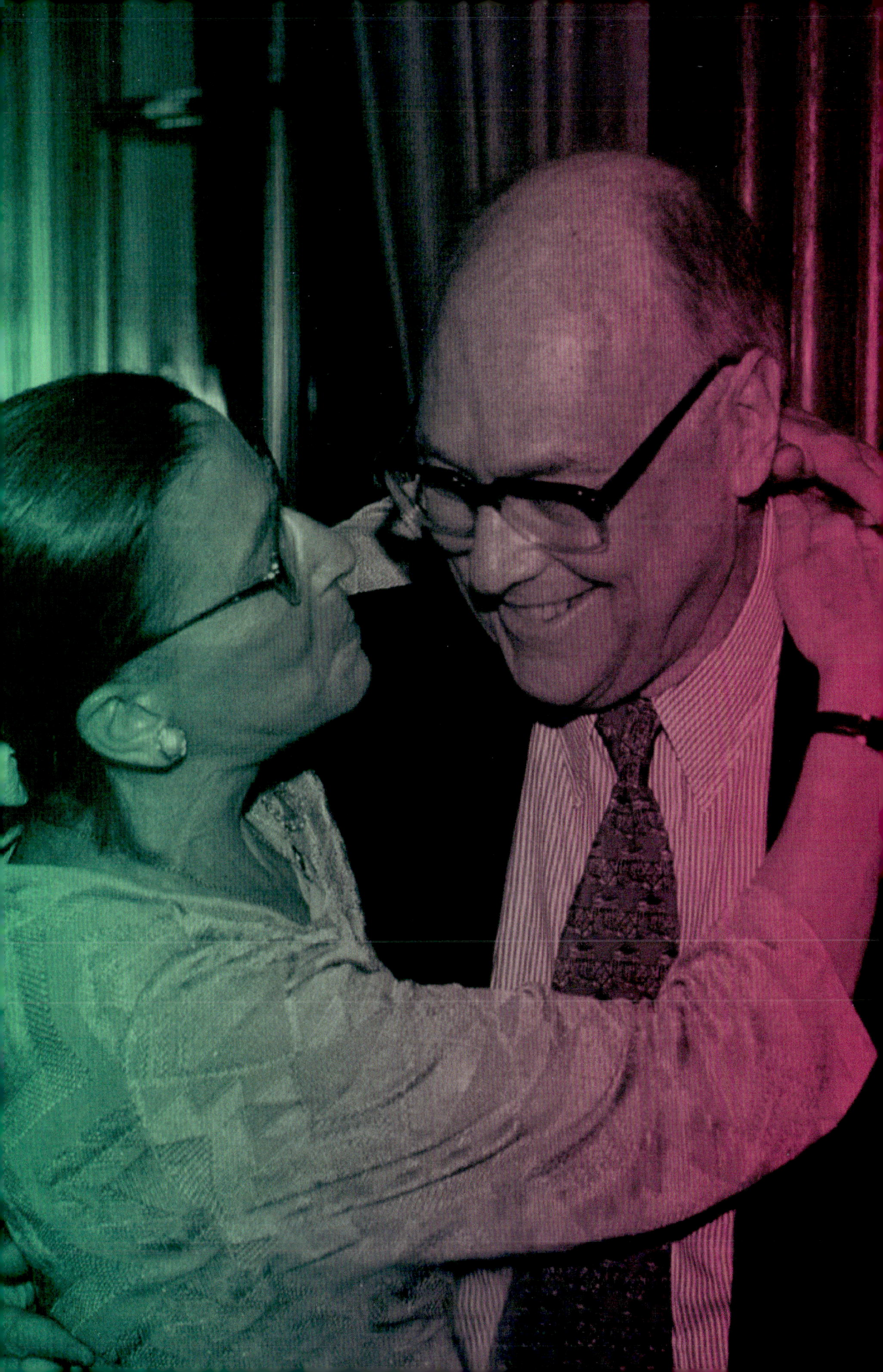

The world she hoped for was one in which men and women joined in a new kind of partnership, where each was freed of stereotypes, with mutual participation in the workplace and at home. In reality, though, she was already living this kind of union with Martin Ginsburg, her husband of fifty-six years. "I have been supportive of my wife since the beginning of time, and she has been supportive of me," Marty once said. "It's not sacrifice; it's family."[3]

The Ginsburg marriage was an extraordinary love affair that lasted until Marty's death from metastatic cancer in 2010. Grounded in mutual respect and equality, the couple's relationship survived their respective bouts of cancer and the inevitable challenges of raising a family while pursuing fulfilling career and life goals. Such a marriage was especially unique for the generation that came of age during the repressive 1950s.

Ruth Bader Ginsburg has earned a place in the limelight as one of the most powerful women in the United States, but this story is as much about Marty as it is about Ruth. RBG has spoken often of her husband's support in both her personal life and her career. "Marty coached me through the birth of our son, he was the first reader and critic of articles, speeches, and briefs I drafted, and he was at my side constantly, in and out of the hospital,

> "If you have a caring life partner, you help the other person when that person needs it. I had a life partner who thought my work was as important as his, and I think that made all the difference for me."
>
> Ruth Bader Ginsburg

during two long bouts with cancer," she wrote in her 2018 autobiography. "And I betray no secret in reporting that, without him, I would not have gained a seat on the U.S. Supreme Court."[4] Likewise, Marty felt that supporting his wife's growth was a significant part of his life's mission. Before his passing, he once remarked to a friend, "I think that the most important thing I have done is to enable Ruth to do what she has done."[5]

The couple met on a blind date at Cornell University. She was seventeen; he was a year older and, according to her, the only person she'd ever dated who seemed to care about her intellect. Marty would tell people that he had liked Ruth before she became interested in him, so to woo her, he showed her how much he respected her. The pair had much in common, although they had different temperaments. Marty was outgoing and enjoyed wisecracking, while Ruth was quiet and contained her emotions. From the start, he intended for them to marry and work together. "The idea was to be in the same discipline so there would be something you could talk about, bounce ideas off of, know what each other was doing," he later said.[6] At the time, Harvard Business School did not accept women, so they settled on law, and both were accepted to Harvard Law School.

In June 1954, they married in Marty's family home, just days after Ruth's graduation from Cornell. Moments before the ceremony, Marty's mother, Evelyn, placed a set of wax earplugs into Ruth's hands and said, "Dear, I'm going to tell you the secret of a happy marriage: It helps sometimes to be a little deaf."[7] Ruth has said that she followed this advice diligently, both at home through fifty-six years of a marital partnership and in the courtroom. "When a thoughtless or unkind word is spoken, best tune out. Reacting in anger or annoyance will not advance one's ability to persuade," she noted in 2016.[8]

Since Marty was a year older, he had already enrolled in Harvard while Ruth was finishing her last year at Cornell. He was soon called for active duty in the army, which sent the couple to Fort Sill, Oklahoma, for two years. Free from career pressures and family obligations, the two learned to live with each other and build a life together. During this time, Ruth qualified to be a claims adjuster for the Social Security Administration. When she offhandedly mentioned that she was three months pregnant, Ruth's employer told her she could not go through training, and her pay was summarily decreased, despite her workload remaining the same. Though men and women had vastly different experiences in the workplace at the time, "Fortunately, in my marriage, I didn't get second-class treatment," RBG later said.[9]

After two years in Oklahoma, Ruth earned readmission to Harvard. She had some concerns about entering law school. At the time, women accounted for less than 3 percent of the legal profession in the United States, and only one woman had ever served on a federal appellate court.

It was rare for a woman to study law at Harvard, and she wondered how she could manage the rigorous program while taking care of her young daughter. This time, her father-in-law, Morris, gave her the needed push to begin. "Ruth, if you don't want to go to law school, you have the best reason in the world, and no one will think the less of you," Morris told her. "But if you really want to become a lawyer, you will stop feeling sorry for yourself and you will find a way to do it."[10] RBG has often credited her daughter, Jane, with her success in law school. Ruth went to class each day and studied until four o'clock p.m., but for the rest of the afternoon she and Marty would take Jane to the park. This bonding time not only nourished her but gave her a renewed will to return to her studies. "Each part of my life provided respite from the other, and gave me a sense of proportion that classmates trained only on law studies lacked," she later said.[11]

However, during Ruth's second year of law school, the couple faced one of their biggest challenges. Marty was diagnosed with a rare type of testicular cancer, and the prognosis was grim. He underwent radical surgery and daily radiation for six weeks. Making sure that Marty stayed on track with his studies, RBG attended her husband's classes as well as her own, copying notes for him. Too sick to type, Marty would lie on the couch and dictate his third-year paper to Ruth; often it was around two o'clock a.m. when she would begin her own work. Ruth's dedication and Marty's perseverance paid off: He recovered, graduated on time, and found a job as a tax attorney at a firm in New York. In order to be close to her husband, Ruth transferred to Columbia University and earned her degree there.

After graduation, Ruth was given a recommendation to clerk for Supreme Court Justice Felix Frankfurter, but he refused to hire a woman. Finally, she landed a job clerking for Edmund Palmieri, a federal judge for the Southern District of New York. Two years later, Ruth was presented with an interesting opportunity. Law professor Hans Smit asked if she would coauthor a book about civil procedure in Sweden. Learning Swedish and traveling to another country to study its legal system was a tall order, but Ruth found the proposition intriguing. She had always lived with either her parents or her spouse and was curious to experience life on her own for a short while. Marty stepped up by taking care of Jane and promised to visit Ruth in Sweden, where she would spend six weeks conducting research.

What RBG learned in Sweden would change her life. In the postwar era, Swedish women were entering the workforce in much larger numbers than American women were. At the time, the Swedish government was interested in making structural changes in organizations and enacting laws to help deconstruct the dichotomy between male and female roles. Swedish advocates believed that once men and women were freed from the straitjacket of the breadwinner-homemaker dynamic, they would have greater latitude in living fuller lives. They argued that the imprisonment of men in the masculine role was as deep of a problem as the confinement of women to a feminine ideal of beauty and housekeeping. This was indeed a radical idea for the era, but it primed Ruth to view the women's liberation movement within the framework of equal liberation for men. And it was with this unique insight that RBG later devised careful, incremental plans for litigating gender discrimination cases before the U.S. Supreme Court.

Upon her return to the U.S., Ruth worked as a law professor at Rutgers University in New Jersey, and began volunteering with the local chapter of the American Civil Liberties Union (ACLU). The organization was overwhelmed with complaints from women reporting discriminatory practices in their workplaces, and RBG took those cases. Among the women she represented were one who had been fired shortly after becoming pregnant and girls who

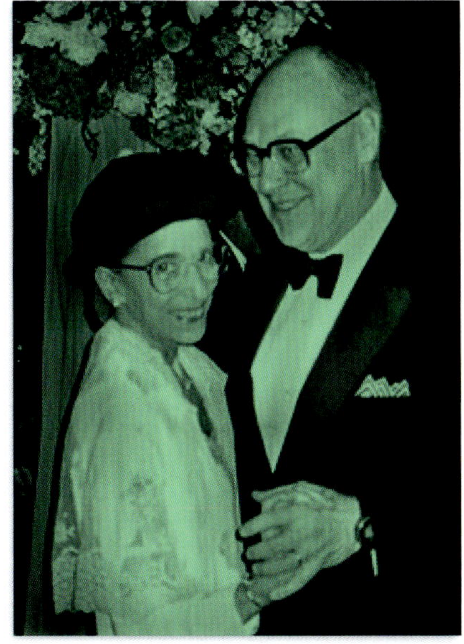

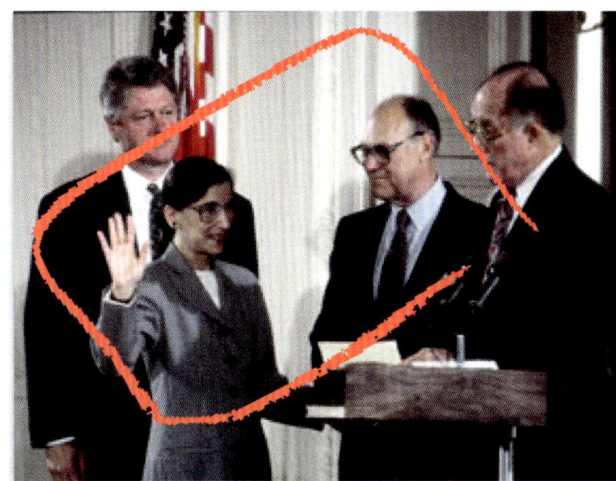

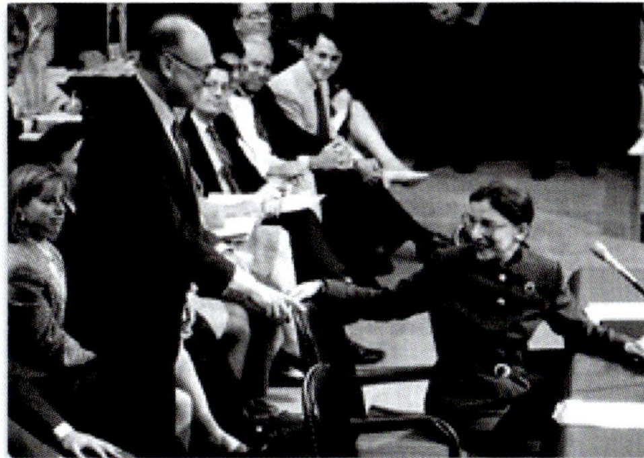

Clockwise from top left: Ruth Bader and Marty Ginsburg, Washington, D.C., June 8, 1998; Supreme Court Chief Justice William Rehnquist (right) swearing in new justice RBG as President Bill Clinton and Marty Ginsburg look on; Marty and Ruth Bader Ginsburg at her confirmation hearing, August 3, 1993.

had been barred from attending a prestigious engineering camp for low-income students. She continued this important work even after she gave birth to James, her second child, in 1965. By the time James was seven years old, Ruth had become the first female tenured professor at Columbia Law School, where she helped to change outdated policies. At the time, women who worked at the university lacked maternity coverage and received lower pension benefits and pay than their male counterparts. RBG filed a class action lawsuit on behalf of the female teachers and administrators and won.

It was around the time when Ruth cofounded the ACLU's Women's Rights Project, in 1972, that Marty agreed to scale back his work to support his busy wife. He, too, had an incredibly impressive professional life as a top-flight attorney earning a significant income. By the late seventies, Marty was ready to transition out of his law practice and accepted a teaching position at Columbia Law School. But in 1980, when President Jimmy Carter appointed RBG to the United States Court of Appeals for the District of Columbia Circuit, Marty moved with her and started teaching at the Georgetown University Law Center. When reporters asked why he moved teaching posts, he facetiously responded that his wife had been given "a good job"[12] in the area. Marty's confidence in his own self-worth elevated their relationship to a place where Ruth could grow into the person she aspired to be.

The Ginsburg relationship was a model of reciprocity. This did not necessarily mean splitting tasks and decisions down the middle, but rather taking on responsibility in areas where the other was lacking. For example, as Marty said, "I learned very early in our marriage that Ruth was a fairly terrible cook, and, for lack of interest, unlikely to improve."[13] So he became a fantastic cook and prepared most of the family's meals; the couple often discussed the law over his dinners. The Supreme Court Historical Society even published Marty's greatest recipes in a cookbook called *Chef Supreme.* In turn, Ruth went over the children's homework every day.

The two were partners not only in marriage but also in law. Marty was the one who turned Ruth's attention to the tax case that would lead to her national notoriety. Ruth knew that she needed to try a case that would catalyze the courts to examine gender equality with a broader lens, but the right one had not presented itself. One night, while Ruth was working in the bedroom, Marty called out to her from the dining room. He showed her an article about a traveling salesman by the name of Moritz, who was single and lived with his eighty-nine-year-old mother in Denver. Moritz had hired a caretaker to aid his ailing mom while he was on the road, but he was not allowed to deduct that expense on his tax return; the IRS only granted such deductions to women, widowers, or the husbands of incapacitated women. The government had never previously considered that a man could assume a sole-caregiver role; its policies senselessly denied benefits based on one's gender. The Ginsburgs recognized that this could be a keystone case for gender equality. When Ruth won *Moritz v. Commissioner of Internal Revenue* in the lower courts, the solicitor general appealed the decision to the Supreme Court. If the Supreme Court upheld the decision—which it ultimately did—other federal laws that applied to one gender and not the other would be called into question. Of course, that was Ruth and Marty's intention from the outset. For the next ten years, RBG set about litigating scores of cases that would systematically chip away at policies that enabled gender discrimination.

It was January 17, 1973, when Ruth stood before the justices of the Supreme Court for the first time. The federal law she was challenging in *Frontiero v. Richardson* drew on the stereotype that between a husband and wife, the man should be the independent one. Marty was seated behind her as RBG argued on behalf of Sharron Frontiero, a lieutenant in the U.S. Air Force who was seeking a dependent's allowance for her husband and was denied. The federal law held that wives, but not husbands, of military service members could be classified as dependents. Ruth brilliantly argued that the differing criteria for male and female spousal dependency violated the due process clause in the Constitution's Fifth Amendment.

The justices ruled in favor of Frontiero; however, they fell short of establishing a broader rule that would make most gender-based classifications unconstitutional. Although it was a win for her client, RBG had hoped for a more sweeping judgment. Nevertheless, she learned a valuable lesson from trying her first case before the Supreme Court. "Generally, change in our society is incremental," she said. "Real change, enduring change, happens one step at a time."[14]

> "I think that the most important thing I have done is to enable Ruth to do what she has done."
>
> Martin Ginsburg

Just two years later, Ruth stood before the Supreme Court again, this time to advocate on behalf of Stephen Wiesenfeld, a widower who had tried to claim Social Security benefits following the death of his wife—the primary earner in his family—and had been denied. The law only allowed women to obtain such benefits. Paraphrasing the words of a female district court judge, Ginsburg argued that such "a gender line. . . helps to keep women not on a pedestal, but in a cage."[15] Her client won by unanimous decision. The ruling would mark an important turning point in the feminist movement's appeal for gender equality in both the professional and domestic spheres. Now, under the rule of law, equal protection among genders would apply to the distribution of benefits. More broadly, the judgment signified that women's earnings were of equal importance to men's.

In 1993, when President Bill Clinton nominated RBG to serve on the U.S. Supreme Court, the *New York Times* reported on the unusually active role that Marty had played in her appointment. Clinton administration officials disclosed that it had been Marty's persuasive back-channel lobbying that got Ruth's name added to the list of potential candidates. Of course, he was thrilled and proud when his wife became just the second woman in U.S. history to be appointed as a Supreme Court Justice. RBG embarked on this new chapter in her life with great enthusiasm and some trepidation. Could she deal effectively with the magnitude of the work? Once again, Marty proved to be her biggest supporter. When reflecting on her husband's role in her growth, RBG shared, "The principal advice that I have gotten from Marty throughout my life is that he always made me feel like I was better than I thought myself. I started out by being very unsure. Could I do this brief? Could I make this oral argument? To now where I am."[16]

While the nation may have viewed Justice Ginsburg as a serious, reserved woman, there was a playful side to her that Marty used to bring out. Her former law clerk David Toscano saw it up close when he walked into the chambers and saw Ruth jokingly chasing her husband around the desk with scissors. At parties, when she was likely to hang back and avoid socializing, Marty would join her and graciously guide her through the room. He lovingly took care of her through her two bouts of cancer—one in 1999 and another in 2009. He would drag her out of the office so she could take a break and ensured that she ate a good meal and got some rest. Marty, too, faced cancer once again. Before his last trip to the hospital, he left a letter for his wife on a yellow pad by their bed. It read:

> *6/7/10*
>
> *My dearest Ruth—*
>
> *You are the only person I have loved in my life, setting aside, a bit, parents and kids, and their kids. And I have admired and loved you almost since the day we first met at Cornell some 56 years ago.*
>
> *What a treat it has been to watch you progress to the very top of the legal world.*
>
> *I will be in JH Medical Center until Friday, June 25, I believe, and between then and now, I shall think hard on my remaining health and life, and whether on balance the time has come for me to tough it out or to take leave of life because the loss of quality now simply overwhelms.*
>
> *I hope you will support where I come out, but I understand you may not. I will not love you a jot less.*
>
> *Marty* [17]

On June 27, 2010, less than a week after their fifty-sixth wedding anniversary, Marty passed away. It happened during one of the Supreme Court's busiest times of the year, when all of its big decisions were released. Ruth was scheduled to announce an opinion on a key case the very next day. Both of her kids encouraged her to go, as it would have been what Marty wanted her to do.

So, the grieving justice went to court that day with a black ribbon in her hair. Chief Justice John Roberts read a tribute to Marty, and Justice Antonin Scalia—one of Ruth's closest friends on the bench—wept. Days later, Ruth placed the folded American flag from

> “The principal advice that I have gotten from Marty throughout my life is that he always made me feel like I was better than I thought myself.”
>
> Ruth Bader Ginsburg

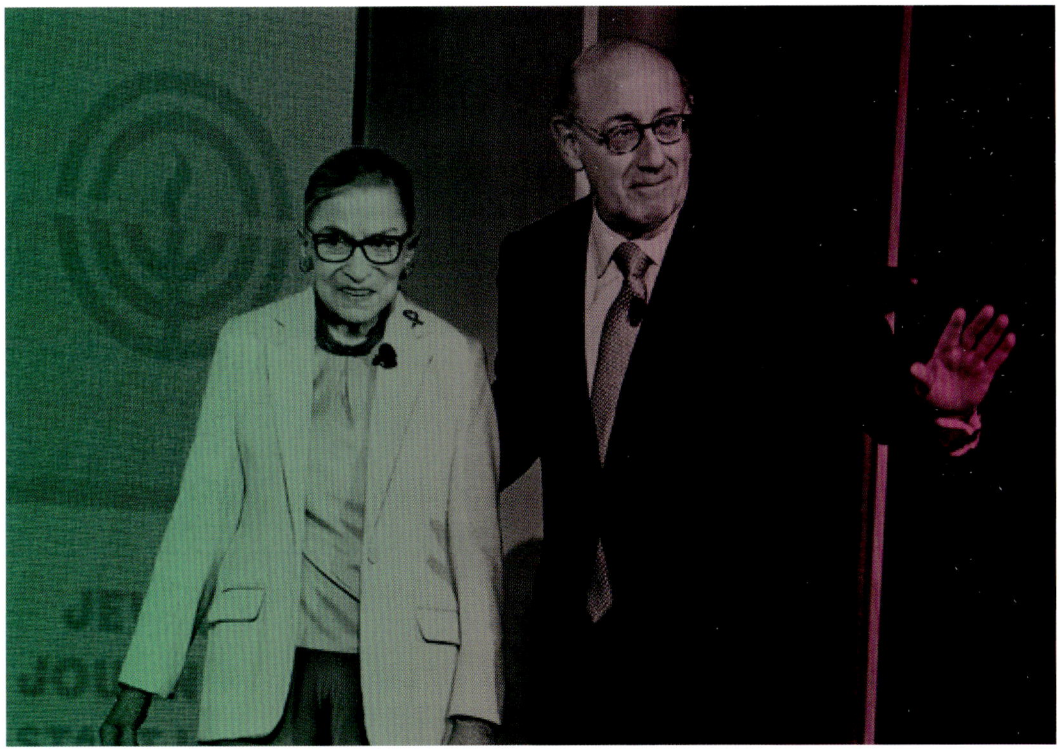

Ruth Bader Ginsburg arrives onstage at the General Assembly of the Jewish Federations of North America at the Washington Hilton in Washington, D.C., for a wide-ranging interview with attorney Kenneth Feinberg, November 14, 2016.

Marty's burial on the windowsill of her chambers. Many had thought that the seventy-seven-year-old widow would step aside and make room for a younger successor, especially during President Barack Obama's last term. But her refusal to shuffle off the stage is another way that RBG is expanding the public's awareness of what it is to be a fierce older woman of power.

Nowadays, Ruth is excited about what the future holds for women and for couples. She has always argued that the oversimplification of gender roles restricts our ability to fully explore our true potential, both as individuals and as partners in dynamic relationships. As she said in a 2017 interview, “Women's enhanced opportunities hasten the time when women and men will become true partners in shaping society's course.”[18] Of course, RBG and Marty were the trailblazing couple who embodied the equal relationship she has envisioned for the world.

Queen Elizabeth II & Prince Philip

The Royal Suite

It was June of 1953 when approximately one million people flooded London to celebrate the historic coronation ceremony at Westminster Abbey that formally launched the reign of the young Queen Elizabeth II. Elizabeth was mindful that the world would be tuning in to see the pomp and pageantry of this momentous occasion. She also knew that she had to exude a particular combination of poise and self-assuredness befitting a queen. So, leading up to the big day, she practiced her speech, rehearsed the processional, and reviewed the details of the event with a critical eye. She even sat at her desk and practiced wearing St. Edward's Crown, first used at the 1661 coronation of Charles II, to get accustomed to its weight. The bejeweled crown is so heavy that Elizabeth once joked that it could have broken her neck. Perhaps its weight appropriately symbolized the demands that would be made upon her for the rest of her life.

The city buzzed with excitement on that drizzling coronation day. On their way to the church, the queen and her husband, the dashing Prince Philip, Duke of Edinburgh, sat in the great Gold State Coach and went past hundreds of thousands of onlookers and well-wishers. Seated in the carriage, Philip joined his wife in waving at the crowds, but inside the abbey he did not participate in the crowning. Elizabeth proceeded down the aisle alone, she took the coronation oath alone, and she alone was crowned. Once the queen sat on her throne with her scepter, it was the Archbishop of Canterbury who first paid homage to her, then the prince. And when he did, he approached the throne bareheaded in his long red robe, knelt before his wife, and placed his hands between hers and recited his oath of allegiance. Philip gazed down at her hands. Elizabeth had worn the coronation ring on one hand and her

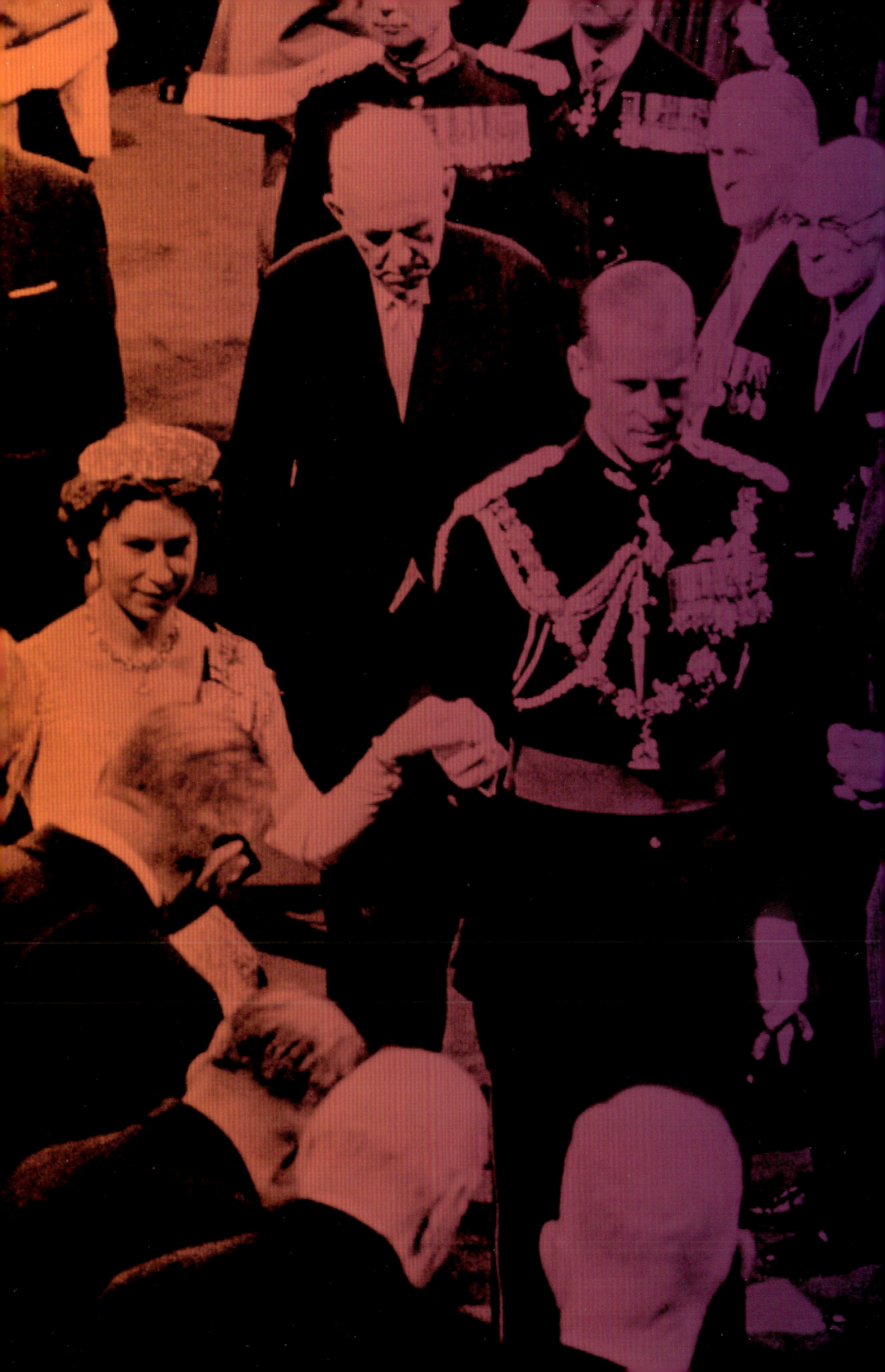

diamond engagement ring on the other. Two rings, representing two sets of responsibilities. The call of duty would always come first, but how would the queen, who was besotted with her husband, balance her roles of wife and working mother with being a public figure and the symbol of a nation? And how would the ambitious and energetic Philip set aside his personal aspirations to support his wife?

Their relationship is as unique as their station in life. Elizabeth and Philip possess something that even the most iconic celebrities do not: As mere mortals, they embody the image of a mythical, fairy-tale couple. Being on display and the target of constant scrutiny have created challenges, yet the two have managed to sustain a close bond throughout their more than seventy-year union.

> "Tolerance is the one essential ingredient of any happy marriage."
>
> Prince Philip

Upon reflection, some people can pinpoint a particular event in childhood that changed the course of their lives. In Elizabeth's case, it was a summer day in 1939, when she met Prince Philip of Greece at the age of thirteen. Elizabeth had accompanied her parents on a visit to the Royal Naval College in Dartmouth, where the eighteen-year-old Philip was training. It comes as no surprise that the young Elizabeth became smitten with this distant cousin of hers. A blue-eyed and blond-haired charmer, Philip cut a handsome figure in his naval uniform. However, few could have predicted that the two would keep in touch and ultimately marry eight years later. As the queen's cousin Margaret Rhodes once noted, from the day of their first meeting, Elizabeth "never looked at anyone else."[1] Elizabeth's life had always been planned out for her, but in one respect the dutiful daughter went against the wishes of her family, who would have preferred a titled English aristocrat for a son-in-law. Unlike more appropriate suitors, Philip could boast no land holdings or fortune; he was neither an Etonian, nor a Guards officer, nor a huntsman. But he did have charisma, intelligence, an exuberant personality, and a royal bloodline.

Philip's parents were indeed of royal descent. His mother, Princess Alice, was the great granddaughter of Queen Victoria, making Elizabeth and Philip third cousins. His father, Prince Andrew, was the younger brother to the king of Greece. Being the fifth child and only son, Philip grew up in a household of doting women. But by all standards, his childhood was marred by upheaval and trauma. By 1922, when he was only one year old, the future of the Greek monarchy was in peril: Philip's grandfather had been assassinated in 1913, his uncle forced to abdicate the throne, and his father arrested and nearly condemned to death. It was only through backchannel maneuverings that Andrew and his family were able to secretly flee the country and spend the rest of their years in exile. With this reversal of fortune, the family relied on the beneficence of well-heeled relatives and friends to make ends meet in France, where they first settled. When Philip was eight years old, he was sent to Cheam, one of England's oldest preparatory schools. Shortly thereafter, his mother, Princess Alice, suffered a nervous breakdown, and even consultations with the famed psychoanalyst Sigmund Freud did not alleviate her symptoms. She was ultimately committed to a sanatorium for several years. Philip's mother virtually disappeared from his life for the rest of his childhood, and exacerbating this sudden change, all four of his sisters got married within nine months of one another. By age ten, the prince no longer had a home to return to, as his sisters were gone and his father had moved into a small flat in Monte Carlo with his mistress. The precarious circumstances made Philip into a resilient, self-reliant young man, who in adolescence turned to his maternal uncle Lord Louis Mountbatten for support and a sense of family.

As tumultuous and unconventional as Philip's family life was, Elizabeth's was structured and safe. She enjoyed a privileged and stable upbringing and remained more or less out of the limelight, as it was her uncle King Edward VIII who was in line to inherit the throne. But only months into his reign, Edward instigated a crisis by proposing to the twice-divorced American Wallis Simpson. Their impeding marriage was controversial for several reasons. Prime Minister Stanley Baldwin believed Simpson's marital status made her unsuitable, both socially and politically, as the king's consort. The Church of England, which disapproved of divorce, asserted that King Edward could not fulfill his role as the head of the church if he married a divorcée while her former spouses were still alive. Edward became one of the shortest-reigning monarchs in British history when he abdicated, to marry Simpson, only eleven months after ascending the throne. His brother Albert, Elizabeth's father, succeeded him as king. Albert was known as King George VI.

So, at just ten years of age, on the cusp of the Second World War, Elizabeth was stirred onto a different track—one that would train her to become the United Kingdom's future monarch. It was unheard of for girls to go to university in those days, especially for women of her class and generation. However, Elizabeth was extensively tutored in legislative processes and constitutional law. In fact, future prime ministers would later be impressed by the depth of her knowledge.

In the meantime, Philip, at just twenty-one, had not only become one of the youngest first lieutenants in the Royal Navy but also a hero of the Battle of Cape Matapan during World War II. By the end of the war, Philip had decided to pursue a career in the navy. Within a few years, though, he would begin to wonder how his impending marriage to Elizabeth would affect his ambitions. No doubt, this action-oriented, hands-on, young prince would have to reorient himself toward a different kind of life, where he would give up a great deal of autonomy. By marrying the future monarch, he would become a public figure, live in his wife's ancestral residences, and assume the docile role of the queen's consort. Early on in his marriage, however, he revealed his intentions and feelings for Elizabeth in a letter to his mother-in-law. "[M]y ambition," he wrote, "is to weld the two of us into a new combined existence that will not only be able to withstand the shocks directed at us but will also have a positive existence for the good."[2]

Following their 1947 wedding, the first order for the young couple was to set up their newly formed household at Clarence House, the nineteenth-century residence adjacent to Saint James's Palace. The move to Clarence House was of particular significance to Philip, as it was the first family home he'd had since the age of ten. From the start, Elizabeth was sensitive to her husband's need to assert himself. She described him as "terribly independent" and wanted him to be the "boss in his own home."[3] So, she let Philip take the lead in redesigning Clarence House. By all accounts, the first four years of their marriage seemed to have been fulfilling, as Philip was able to combine his royal duties with his naval ones. But around the time their first child, Prince Charles, was born, Elizabeth's father, King George VI, suffered a severe blood clot in his leg. With the king's failing health, Elizabeth and Philip had to step in to represent the sovereign on various state visits and engagements. It soon became clear that they would be needed full-time. Philip therefore had no choice but to take an open-ended leave from the navy, effectively ending his military career at the age of thirty.

This transition proved to be a challenge for the active and independent prince; he was not only obligated to give up a promising career in the navy but also had to invent his new position with no role models to follow. Under Queen Victoria's reign in the nineteenth century, the prince consort served as the queen's adviser and private secretary. But after Victoria's death, the monarchy became an official institution, and those privileges were stripped from the consort's role. Thus, Philip became the first consort who was constitutionally excluded from the very substance of his wife's official life. For Philip, there was the added pressure of going against the traditional gender roles of the early 1950s, where the husband was considered to be the dominant figure and the head of the household.

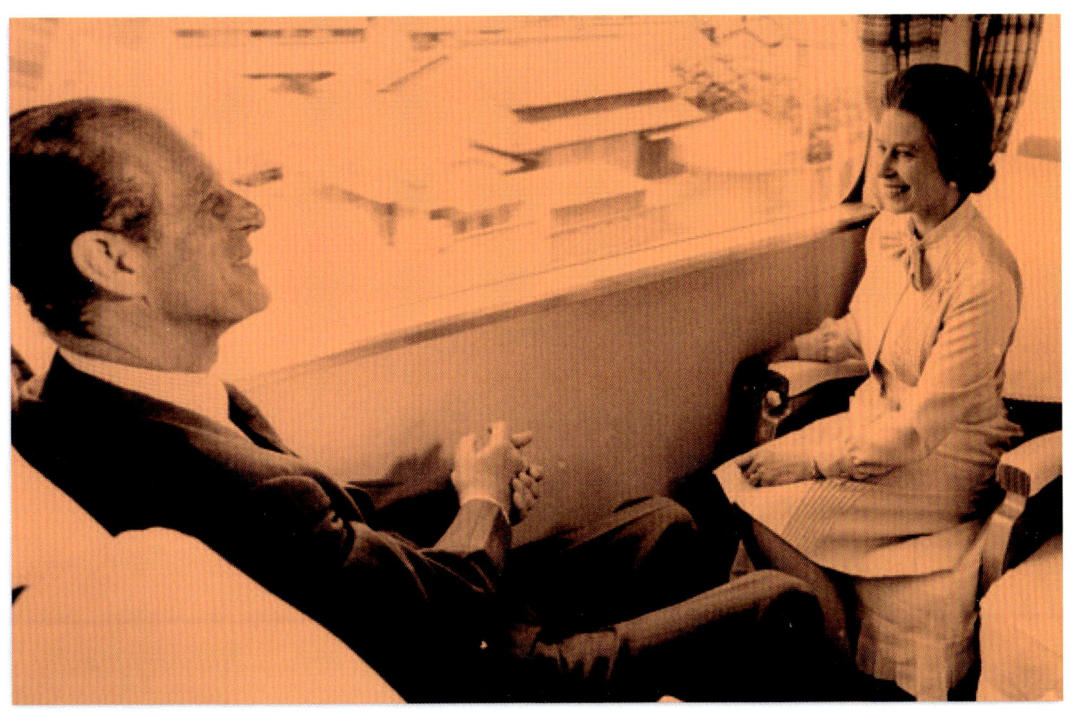

> “[My] ambition is to weld the two of us into a new combined existence that will not only be able to withstand the shocks directed at us but will also have a positive existence for the good.”
>
> Prince Philip

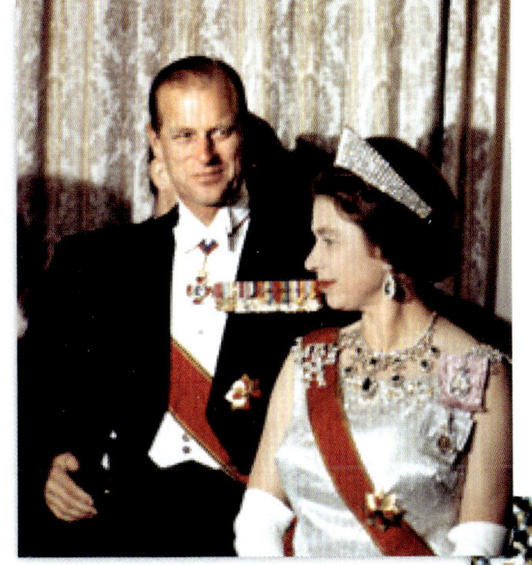

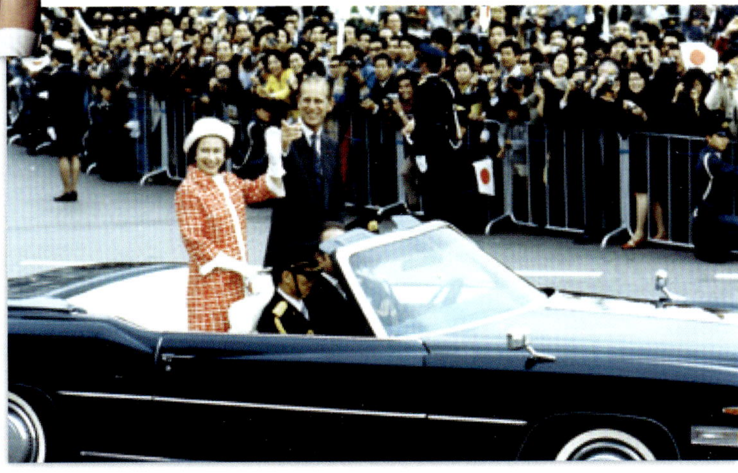

Clockwise from top: Prince Philip and Queen Elizabeth II talk on the Shinkansen bullet train on their way to Tokyo from Nagoya, Japan, May 12, 1975; During a parade in Tokyo, Queen Elizabeth II and Prince Philip wave from a car, May 9, 1975; The royal couple at a celebratory banquet in honor of German President Gustav Heinemann in London, October 1972.

Their first official tour as representatives of the ailing king gave them a taste of the life that would await them once Elizabeth ascended the throne. Their days were, in the words of biographer Gyles Brandreth, "a relentless, endlessly repetitive roller-coaster ride of royal duties and good works."[4] The breadth and pace of their first trip to Canada was exhaustive, with more than seventy stops and visits. It was at these public appearances that their respective roles would take shape. Elizabeth was noted to exude a restrained, serious presence, and Philip, who had to walk a few respectful steps behind her, grinned and shared lighthearted banter with others.

In 1952, while Elizabeth and Philip were visiting Kenya, their private secretary broke the grim news that the fifty-six-year-old king had died from a blood clot in his heart. When the distraught couple returned to London, the protocol of receiving the new queen took precedence over the grief her family was experiencing. For instance, the king's mother, Queen Mary, who had just lost her son the day before, could not hug her granddaughter but curtsied to her new queen. At age twenty-five, Elizabeth now assumed a hereditary position consecrated by God—a post that bore the challenge and responsibility of representing not only her country but also a range of Commonwealth nations of varying faiths and cultures.

The grief-stricken Elizabeth set about her business of writing letters and telegrams and receiving heads of state within days of her ascension. Winston Churchill, the nearly eighty-year-old prime minister, was both surprised and impressed by this twenty-five-year-old's sense of duty and work ethic. Throughout the ensuing decades, Elizabeth's schedule would begin with meetings with her private secretaries and deputies—with whom she would discuss domestic and foreign travel, ecclesiastical and military appointments, and the credentials of newly appointed ambassadors—followed by meetings with members of the clergy, military officers, and distinguished guests.

But what made Elizabeth's position even more unique was that she had to balance her sovereign duties with the demands of her growing family. Charles now had a younger sister, named Anne, and both would ask for her in the evenings. So, in order to participate in her children's nightly bedtime routine, Elizabeth changed her scheduled meetings with the prime minister from 5:30 p.m. to 6:30.

Elizabeth was indeed an anomaly, both in her generation and among the British upper class, for being a working mother and having a husband in a subordinate position. Philip, meanwhile, found his new role to be stifling. As the queen's consort, he wanted to proactively introduce changes in the court. But the institution had its own momentum, and Philip was expected to fit in with its traditions. "There were plenty of people telling me what not to do," he explained to Brandreth. "I had to try to support the queen as best I could without getting in the way."[5] He knew that the palace courtiers thought of him as an outsider, and at times he would mockingly refer to himself as the "refugee husband."[6]

There were other slights and snubs that increasingly weighed on the prince. When Elizabeth became queen, Philip wanted them to continue living in Clarence House; he even submitted a proposal recommending that they remain in their home yet conduct the business of the monarchy at Buckingham Palace. But the queen's private secretary and Churchill both opposed the idea. Tradition dictated that the monarch's family would reside in Buckingham Palace, so that was the way it had to be done. The final insult came in 1952, during discussions about the family's name. Philip wanted his children to bear the surname Mountbatten. Once again, Elizabeth's private secretary and Churchill felt strongly that the queen should honor the affiliations of her grandfather and father by keeping the Windsor name. Philip was simply incensed, and would complain to his friends, "I am the only man in the country not allowed to give his name to his own children. I'm nothing but a bloody amoeba."[7]

> "[Philip] has, quite simply, been my strength and stay all these years, and I, and his whole family, and this and many other countries, owe him a debt greater than he would ever claim, or we shall ever know."
>
> Queen Elizabeth II

By the time their third child, Andrew, was born in 1960, Elizabeth wanted the new prime minister, Harold Macmillan, to revisit this sensitive issue. Elizabeth had "absolutely set her heart"[8] on making a change for Philip's sake. The prime minister understood her predicament and duly noted in his diary, "The Queen only wishes (properly enough) to do something to please her husband—with whom she is desperately in love."[9] After a series of discussions among government ministers, an arrangement emerged. The official decision was that "the royal family would continue to be called 'The House and Family of Windsor,' but the Queen's 'de-royalised' descendants—starting with any grandchildren who lacked the designation of 'royal highness'—would adopt the surname 'Mountbatten-Windsor.'"[10] One could only imagine that Prince Philip was all the more pleased when his daughter, Princess Anne, disregarded this policy and signed her marriage register as "Mountbatten-Windsor" thirteen years later.

Elizabeth and Philip are sharply contrasting characters, but they have shown, in good measure, a tolerance and understanding necessary for a successful partnership. Their overriding bond has evoked a shared sense of purpose that has sustained them through their seven-decade marriage. A close look at footage from their public appearances shows that they resemble a royal Fred Astaire and Ginger Rogers with their expert choreography. Philip knows when to step back or lean in to keep things flowing during the hours of conversation Elizabeth is expected to partake in. In public, he walks one step behind her; however, in private, they seem to behave like most couples. In fact, it has been noted that "Prince Philip may be the only man that treats the queen simply as an ordinary human being and not some kind of public figure."[11] Elizabeth, in turn, finds their relationship one of the rare few in which she can allow herself to relax and completely be herself. According to family and friends, over the years she has become bolder with him, and he gentler with her.

Elizabeth has acknowledged Philip's dedication as her consort by officially making him a prince of the United Kingdom—a more elevated title than the royal duke designation he had held since their wedding day. Over the past decades, Philip has also immersed himself in establishing and supporting a variety of charitable organizations. As chancellor of both Cambridge and Edinburgh universities, he encouraged innovation, especially in technology. The prince has authored or coauthored close to forty books—many of them anthologies of speeches or essays on religion, philosophy, science, and conservation. He has additionally spoken at length about scientific applications to agriculture, medicine, and the military, and founded the Commonwealth Study Conferences, an educational and leadership-development event. Yet all of these activities fold into his primary role of supporting the queen.

Eventually, Philip was able to inject new ideas into the court that would increase accessibility to the royal family. At a time when there were grumblings about the royals being cloistered, too formal, and out of touch, he instituted and cohosted with the queen regular, informal Buckingham Palace luncheons and conversations for "meritocrats" from the worlds of business, the arts, sports, science, and religion. These monthly gatherings have enabled the queen to connect more with the outside world and new ideas. He has also supported diversifying her staff and throwing royal garden parties for a wider spectrum of people. Given his deep interest in technology, it comes as no surprise that Philip was also the first member of the royal family to use television as an effective communication tool for the monarchy. He hosted his own television program, a documentary about his Commonwealth tour featuring film footage he had shot. The prince also urged Elizabeth to broadcast her traditional Christmas message, which he helped to draft, on television in 1957. Millions of people tuned in, which successfully broadened the monarchy's reach. An equally important goal was to make the queen more relatable as a person. Philip set about showing Elizabeth hard at work in a variety of settings, to get across to the public "the 'relentlessness' of her job, and to open the curtain on her private life as a wife and mother in places never before seen by the public."[12]

At an age when most of her generation had settled into comfortable retirement, the queen's unique position required her to keep an active pace and to expand her perspective to stay current with the changing culture. Billions have watched her evolve from a beautiful ingenue, to a businesslike working mother, to a wise and occasionally hip grandmother. On March 6, 1997, she launched the first royal website, containing approximately one hundred fifty pages of information about the monarchy. The queen also opened her own YouTube channel in December 2007; it got one million hits in the first week. Elizabeth continues to enjoy a high public-approval rating, which reached about 80 percent in 2017, and a national poll conducted by ICM Research for *The Sunday Telegraph* newspaper in 2012 found that 35 percent of those surveyed considered Elizabeth II Britain's "greatest ever monarch."[13]

Throughout their seventy-one years of marriage, the queen's relationship with Philip has deepened, and both have turned to one another for support and constancy. On their fiftieth wedding anniversary, shortly after Princess Diana's passing, Philip paid tribute to his wife by sharing, "Tolerance is the one essential ingredient of any happy marriage."[14] In a speech, the queen also made it known that "[Philip] has, quite simply, been my strength and stay all these years, and I, and his whole family, and this and many other countries, owe him a debt greater than he would ever claim, or we shall ever know."[15]

With the deaths of Elizabeth's mother and sister in 2002, Philip became more than ever her emotional touchstone. When it was time to celebrate the queen's sixth decade of reign, Philip was seated on a gilded throne next to her. For the auspicious occasion, she rededicated herself to the country in front of both houses of Parliament and thanked Philip for being her "constant strength and guide."[16]

Now at ninety-three years of age, Elizabeth is the oldest and longest-reigning current monarch, and Philip, at ninety-eight, is the longest-living consort. Elizabeth has steered the monarchy into the twenty-first century, and yet she has also been a source of stability, serenity, and continuity to the United Kingdom and the world. In her sixty-seven years of reign, she has shown up for the various demands of her life—exactly what Philip and Elizabeth have done for one another while melding their relationship and duties into a successful partnership.

Charles & Ray Eames

The Design Duo

It was written in his plain handwriting on a Cranbrook Academy of Art notepad, and it read:

> *Dear Miss Kaiser*
>
> *I am 34 (almost) years old, single (again) and broke. . . I love you very much and would like to marry you very very soon. I cannot promise to support us very well—but if given the chance will shure [sic] in hell try.*[1]

At the bottom of the note is a sketch of a hand with an arrow pointing to the ring finger. He had asked, "What is the size of this finger?"[2]

Within a month of this proposal, Ray Kaiser and Charles Eames married. Over the next four decades, the collaboration between Ray, a painter who rarely painted, and Charles, an architecture-school dropout, would shape the face of twentieth-century design.

Charles and Ray met in 1940 at the Cranbrook Academy of Art in Michigan. Each had come to the school by very different routes. Ray was a talented young painter who had studied with the avant-garde German émigré Hans Hofmann. Fully committed to modernism as an aesthetic, she had recently enrolled in classes at the academy. Charles—who was married, dashing, and somewhat of a maverick—was the school's newly installed head of the industrial design department. His training was in architecture, although he never fully earned his degree. Rumors abounded that he had infuriated his teachers with his "unfailing devotion to the practices of Frank Lloyd Wright"[3] and was asked to leave after two years of study.

The two met when Ray was called in to help prepare drawings and models for Charles's submission, with the designer Eero Saarinen, to the Museum of Modern Art's furniture-design

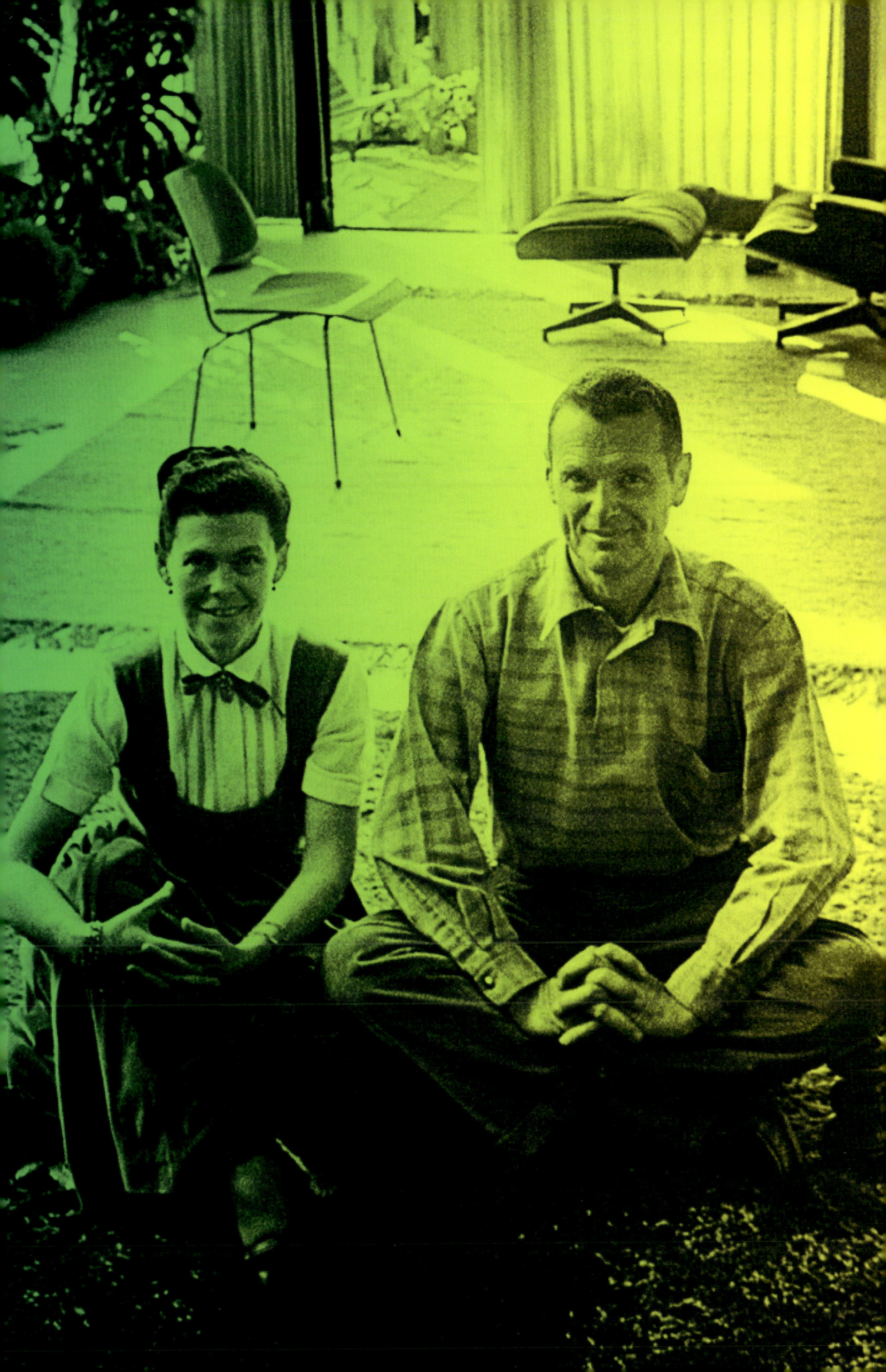

competition. There was an indelible attraction from the moment they met. By May 1941, the smitten Charles had divorced his first wife, Catherine Woermann, and written his proposal letter to Ray. After a road trip honeymoon to Los Angeles, they eventually built a home in Pacific Palisades—now known as the Eames House—where they hung tumbleweed collected during their car journey.

This architectural masterpiece remains marvelously preserved, and in many ways mirrors the couple's energetic personalities and their drive to seek what Charles called "the uncommon beauty in common things."[4] And the tumbleweed that had marked the beginning of their journey together still whimsically spins from the ceiling in the couple's living room.

The creativity of these two American designers knew no bounds. Over the course of four decades, the husband-and-wife team had an incontestable influence on multiple industries, including modern architecture and industrial and furniture design. The Eameses are best known for their revolutionary 1946 molded-plywood chairs, their 1950 fiberglass chair, and their 1956 lounge chair and ottoman set, which are among the bestselling chair lines to date. These midcentury classics have found their way into homes, stadiums, restaurants, and airports around the world.

But the Eameses were much more than just furniture designers. They were communicators, educators, and collectors of design concepts. Indeed, their desire to express their passion for certain ideas and objects led them into make their "idea" films, multimedia presentations, and exhibition designs. All of those creative outlets—as well as their architecture—brought them international acclaim, and their many short films (more than eighty) won them awards at film festivals in the United States, Europe, and Australia. They even received an Emmy Award for their work on the film *The Fabulous Fifties.*

In the period of great optimism and determination to build a better future following World War II, Los Angeles became a mecca for innovative artists and designers. The Eameses fit right in with this creative community and played a pivotal role in shaping California modernism. From the very start, Charles and Ray Eames thought of themselves as designers and aimed to use new materials and industrial processes to produce quality everyday goods at prices affordable to most people. Once they arrived in Los Angeles, the young couple settled into a Richard Neutra-designed apartment in the Westwood neighborhood. There they established their first workshop in the unit's spare bedroom and built a homemade machine—nicknamed Kazam!—into which they fed a variety of woods and glues that Charles snuck home from his job as a set architect at MGM Studios.

While experimenting with sculpturally molding plywood with Kazam!, Ray kept in touch with Hans Hofmann and the painter Lee Krasner, and abreast of the New York art scene. The beautiful covers she designed at the time for *Arts & Architecture* magazine show the influence of Hofmann, Alexander Calder, and Joan Miró in her biomorphic compositions. In many ways, Ray

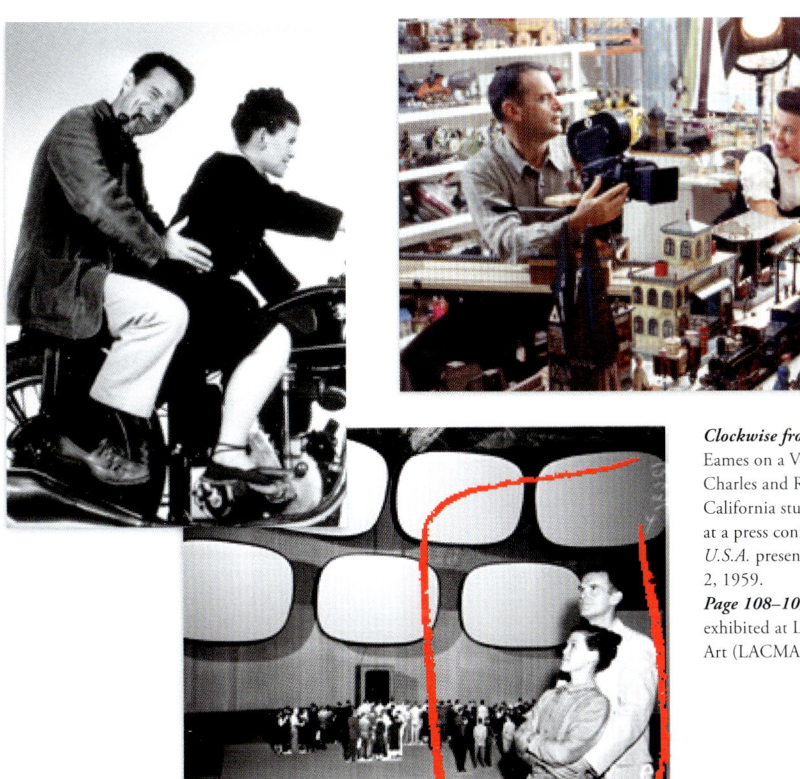

Clockwise from top left: Charles and Ray Eames on a Velocette Motorcycle, 1948; Charles and Ray filming toy trains in their California studio, May 5, 1958; The designers at a press conference for their *Glimpses of the U.S.A.* presentation in Moscow, September 2, 1959.
Page 108–109: Photo mural of the Eameses exhibited at Los Angeles County Museum of Art (LACMA).

translated these abstract forms into the Eames DCM (Dining Chair Metal) designs she and Charles created. With a molded seat that seemingly floats in the air, this model has become one of the most celebrated chairs on the planet.

In 1946, the Museum of Modern Art exhibited the Eames DCM and the DCW (Dining Chair Wood), and reviews described them as "the finest chairs of modern design."[5] So great was their popular appeal that by 1951, the Herman Miller Furniture Company was selling two thousand units of the similar fiberglass model on a monthly basis. Over the next thirty-three years, the dynamic duo went on to create more than forty major furniture designs using new materials such as molded plywood, metal, aluminum, and wire mesh.

Due to their growing workload and commissions from large corporations such as IBM, Polaroid, Westinghouse, and Boeing, the Eameses set up a workshop at 901 Washington Boulevard in Venice, California. This creative space was "part museum, part funhouse, and part design and film studio,"[6] with objects, toys, masks, chairs, models, and plans scattered across the studio. Employees were expected to be inventive and resourceful. They tried their hands at the various projects stirring in the pot, from photography, to filmmaking, to research and development, to designing and scripting exhibitions, to making toys. It was an environment in which the Eameses learned not only from each other but also from their workers.

In general, the couple's partnership was easy, and they both seemed to flourish in it. Ray was an artist in her own right, but she also understood and added value to her husband's practice. Charles—who was raised in household of strong, smart women—appreciated Ray's sharp, creative mind. Throughout the years, Charles both privately and publicly recognized his wife's talents and encouraged her to express them freely. No doubt, his support enabled Ray to further cultivate her interests within their lifelong alliance.

Intensely curious and analytical, Charles and Ray were both preoccupied with how humans see and understand things, and their different skill sets complemented their exploratory work. Trained as an abstract painter, Ray approached design, furniture making, and filmmaking as if she were painting. In fact, in the documentary *Eames: The Architect and the Painter,* she

> "Anything I can do, Ray can do better. . . She is equally responsible with me for everything that goes on here."
>
> Charles Eames

emphasizes that she never left her primary art form, painting; composition, form, and color were of great importance to her. Charles, the architect, saw all that he did through the framework of architecture; structure, patterns, and functionality worked their way through his overarching vision. Since Ray did not enjoy the daily hassles of running and representing the firm, she happily relegated that responsibility to Charles and dove into the details of exhibition and furniture design and film editing. Charles, who was charismatic and outgoing, took on the natural role of interfacing with the outside world. He conducted the company's business dealings and spoke at engagements, which may have ultimately contributed to a general lack of acknowledgment of Ray's significant contributions.

However, in many ways, Charles regularly highlighted the important role his wife played in their work, as if he was embarrassed that his public profile might overshadow her. "She has a very good sense of what gives an idea, or form, or piece of sculpture its character, of how its relationships are formed," he once said. "She can see when there is a wrong mix of ideas or materials, where the division between two ideas isn't clear. If this sounds like a structural or architectural idea, it is. But it comes to Ray through her painting."[7] He often publicly celebrated Ray's talents, saying, "Anything I can do, Ray can do better,"[8] and, "She is equally responsible with me for everything."[9] In some of the films they directed, Charles made sure that her name preceded his, to suggest equality in their contributions.

Their sense of coupledom was a prominent feature of their relationship. Photographs of the pair frequently show them smiling at one another, with Charles's arm around Ray or both touching one of their creations. They even matched or contrasted their clothes to emphasize their connectedness. For example, their 1944 Christmas card shows the duo in black T-shirts and similar poses, and a photograph taken in 1947 features them in matching gingham shirts holding hands.

Their way of dressing, much like their lifestyle, was an example of studied simplicity. Understated and unconcerned with displaying wealth, they adopted dress styles that were essentially informal. It must have been hard for Ray to know where to pitch her image as a female in the workforce. Very few white, middle-class women without children worked at the time, and there was enormous cultural pressure on women to stay home and raise children. "Had she been too fashionable, she might have been labeled frivolous. Too 'arty' would have meant that she was insufficiently concerned with practicalities, while too conservative might have suggested that her design work was dull," their biographer, Pat Kirkham, has noted.[10] Thus, Ray opted for what would become her trademark unfussy uniform: the peasant-style pinafore dress paired with flats or low heels (even though she was only five feet tall). Charles cut a handsome figure with his handmade shirts, worn open-necked, and tweed or corduroy jackets. Few who met him escaped the captivating force of his charisma and good looks. And the fact that he enjoyed and felt comfortable in female company was not lost on Ray.

Charles was at the very core of Ray's life—so much so that she "regarded her life as only fully starting when they met," Kirkham wrote.[11] And her devotion and commitment to Charles was unwavering until the day he died. Charles, on the other hand, seemed to have the sort of personality that would pull others into his orbit. He had many female admirers and may have been involved in more than one serious extramarital relationship. It's unclear how much Ray knew about these alleged affairs and how they affected her, as she kept her feelings to herself. Regardless, Charles remained emotionally connected to his wife, and they managed to sustain a close and loving union over many decades.

Their mutual affection—along with their shared sense of humor, friends, work ethos, and visual aesthetic—was the cement that held the partnership together. These varying spheres of their lives intersected in the groundbreaking home they built together in 1949. The Eames House was conceived as a part of the Case Study House Program. In 1945, *Arts & Architecture* magazine, which was the premier platform for California avant-garde and modernist design, commissioned architects to create affordable, contemporary, high-quality housing solutions.

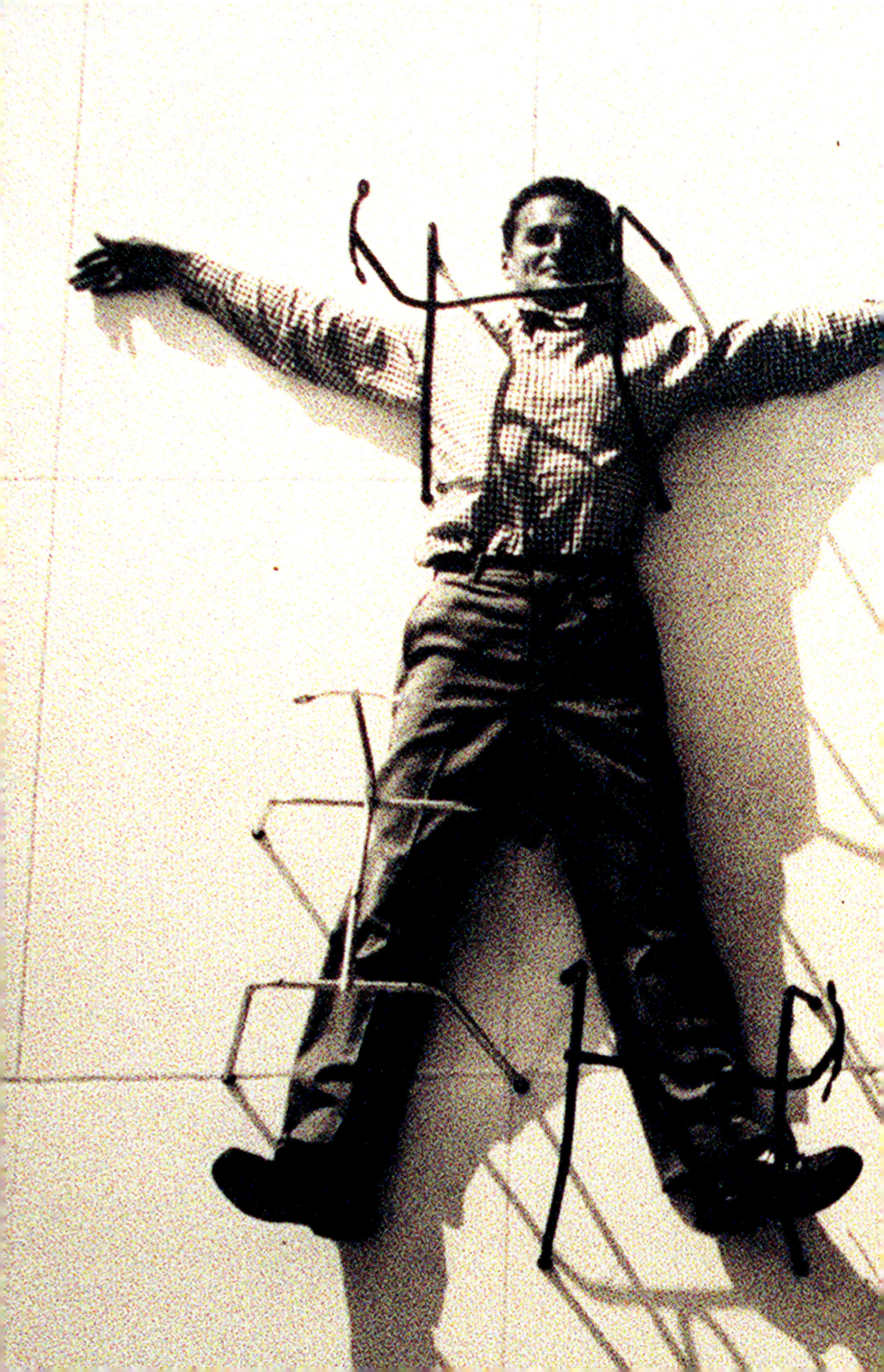

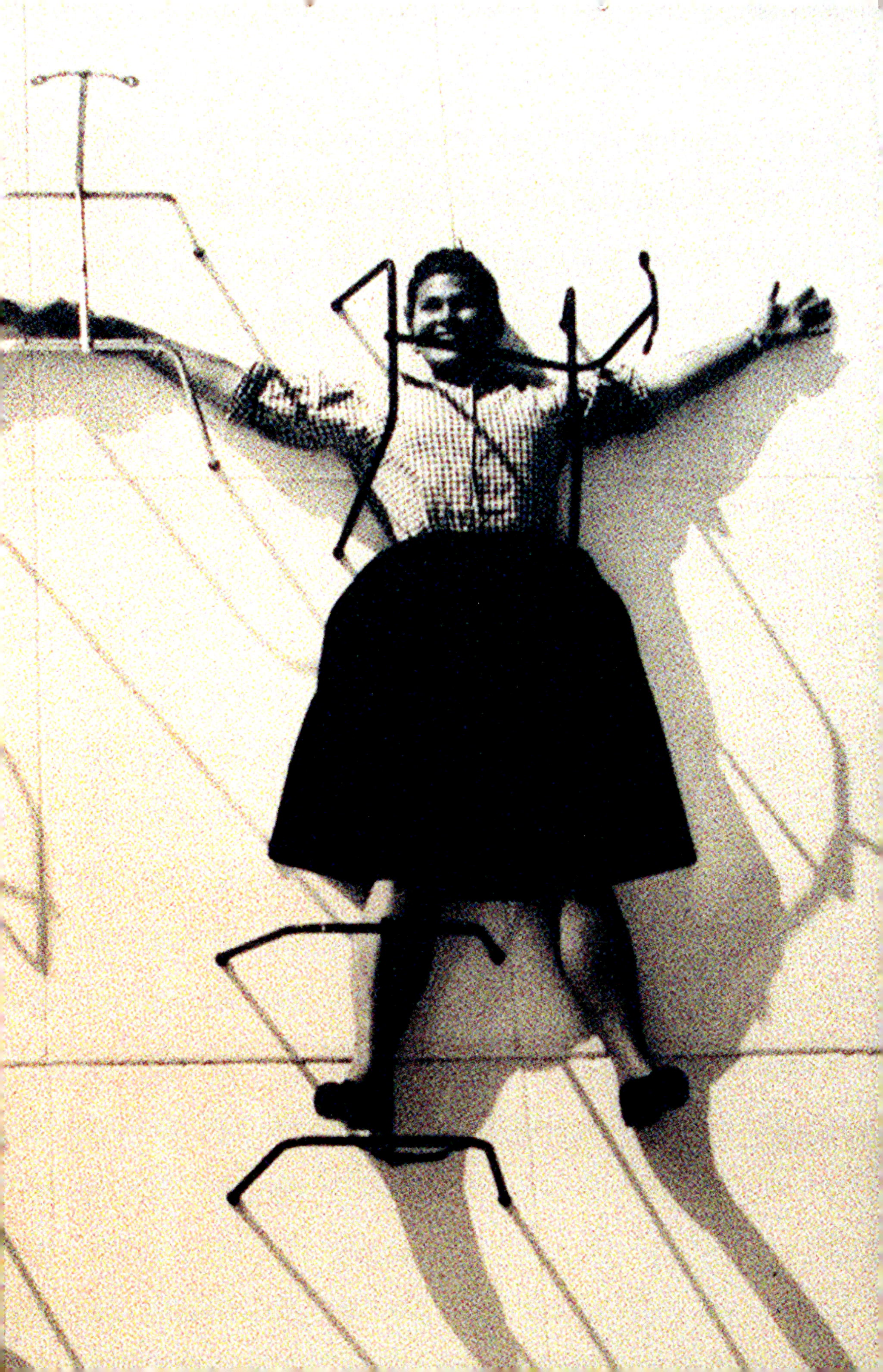

The husband-and-wife team's flair for the technologically and aesthetically innovative paid off. They achieved the perfect balance between the pragmatic and the poetic in a house that was hand-constructed in a matter of days from prefabricated industrial materials.

It is a treat to tour the home, as it has been preserved exactly how the couple left it. Set on a cliff overlooking the Pacific Ocean, the Eames House is a study of light and space, filled with whimsy and color, toys, kites, and Eastern wares. Sliding glass doors and windows open to a row of ten eucalyptus trees and an expansive meadow filled with wildflowers. By positioning this modern building in the midst of a wild landscape, the designers broke away from the traditional modernist mold, in which the natural environment is tamed and structured. But the most dazzling and unique feature of this house is the Piet Mondrian-style painted panels covering the facade.

The couple took on a few more architectural projects, including drawing the designs for the filmmaker Billy Wilder's house, but for the final three decades of their partnership, the Eameses primarily concentrated on their furniture and exhibition design, as well as filmmaking. Their strong aesthetic framework carried through their various projects in whatever medium they were working in at the time. Whether designing a chair, an exhibition, a multiscreen presentation, or a building, their primary concern was finding the most effective and pleasurable ways of conveying information within that medium.

An Eames exhibition was a multifaceted experience—additive and visually complex, with layer upon layer of text, illustrations, and objects. In 1955, Charles and Ray visited New York to help mount the *Textiles and Ornamental Arts in India* exhibition at the Museum of Modern Art. Their desire to communicate the show's message to a wider audience led them to create a short film about it. Perhaps because of their experience spotlighting Indian history and culture, Indira Gandhi hired the Eames Office in 1964 to plan an exhibition celebrating the life of her father, Indian Prime Minister Jawaharlal Nehru, who had recently passed away.

As usual, the couple went to great lengths to immerse themselves in all the necessary information for this important exhibition, even traveling to India and working closely with the National Institute of Design at Ahmedabad. They studied more than two hundred thousand photographs before selecting twelve hundred for display. The exhibition proved a resounding success, with an estimated ninety thousand people visiting it in New York before it moved on to London, Washington, D.C., and Los Angeles.

Charles and Ray were met with several other commissions throughout their careers. For a breakthrough cultural exchange between the United States and the Soviet Union, the U.S. Information Agency turned to the Eames Office to create a showcase that communicated ideas of American life to its hosts, the Soviets. *Glimpses of the U.S.A.* became the most famous of the Eameses' multiscreen presentations, where twenty-two hundred images of people and landscapes from across the U.S. were projected onto seven twenty-by-thirty-foot screens in a spectacular two hundred fifty-foot dome designed by the architect Buckminster Fuller. Nobody had seen this presentation before its public viewing. The Eameses had hand-delivered the precious cans of film themselves the night before the Moscow premiere and sat among the fifteen hundred guests (including Soviet Premier Nikita Khrushchev) during the screening.

In the compilation, some images provided context—the distinct, vast landscapes of America, such as the Rocky Mountains, the farmlands, and the cities and interlocking highways. But those photographs only served as a backdrop to the humanity of the people who occupied those places—snapshots of families kissing goodbye before work, kids going off to school, people eating meals. It was Ray's recommendation to end the show on a more intimate note: The last few images were of people saying goodnight, which produced a tender sense of closure for those watching

> "Eventually everything connects—people, ideas, objects. . . The quality of the connections is the key to quality per se."
>
> Charles Eames

the film. People left the pavilion visibly touched, and in the ensuing six weeks, three million Soviet citizens visited the exhibition. What the Eameses accomplished in that masterful twelve-minute presentation could not have been accomplished in any lecture or talk. It demonstrated the commonalities between the two rival countries through the language of everyday life.

The U.S. government went on to hire the Eameses to create another multiscreen presentation for the 1962 World's Fair in Seattle. But the most elaborate of their multiscreen presentations was *Think*—a piece that IBM commissioned for the New York World's Fair of 1964. In the 1960s and '70s, IBM gave the couple a generous budget and artistic latitude to design a series of exhibitions with scientific and mathematical themes. Both Ray and Charles were fascinated by technology and science, and were excited by the challenge of communicating these new and complex ideas. IBM tasked the Eames Office with designing a pavilion and an exhibition that would show the ways computers influence society, and the similarities between man and machine in terms of processing information for the World's Fair. This project became the duo's largest and most impressive undertaking to date. They were responsible for not only the exhibition, graphics, and signage, but also for directing a film that would convey all of these high-tech ideas. Everyone who stepped into the space was awestruck. The Eameses had built an ovoid theater, into which five hundred people would enter at a time via a hydraulic lift. An emcee greeted the audience and introduced the sequences that were projected onto twenty-two screens of varying shapes and sizes interspersed throughout the room.

The multiscreen presentations, the rapid cuts, and the sequences of still, moving, or even animated images that connected to ideas and emotions in a narrative way became hallmarks of their visual language and innovative filmmaking style. In the 1950s, California had emerged as one of the main centers of postwar experimental cinema, and the Eameses were part of a coterie of pioneering filmmakers such as James Broughton, Harry Smith, and Kenneth Anger. Ray and Charles had a great love for cinema and images—in fact, their fascination veered close to an obsession. The Library of Congress now holds an estimated seven hundred fifty thousand of their photographs (and this was not in the age of easy-to-carry and convenient smartphones). In filmmaking, collaborators such as Billy Wilder and the Indian writer Pupul Jayakar found that the couple worked symbiotically, with Charles's "creative vision"[12] grounded by Ray's discipline and editing skills.

> "Any time one or more things are consciously put together in a way that they can accomplish something better than they could have accomplished individually, this is an act of design."
>
> Charles Eames

All but one of the movies the couple made in their Venice workshop or their small Eames House studio can be classified as either "idea" films or "object" films. The work that best represents the duo's "idea" films is *Powers of Ten* (1977), which has been used as a teaching aid in many American schools and science museums. This film investigated the "relative size of things in the universe and the effect of adding another zero,"[13] as the Eames Office explained. The film opens on a man having a picnic by a lake in Chicago. He lies down, with the camera stationed one meter above him. From there, the camera zooms out, and the narrator (a physicist from the Massachusetts Institute of Technology) begins to explain the viewer's journey: "Now, every ten seconds, we will look from ten times farther away and our field of view will be ten times wider."[14] As the viewer's gaze moves out to the cosmos, having reached the height of ten meters to the twenty-fourth power, the lens begins speeding back to Earth, into the microcosmos, into the hand of the man having a picnic, and deeper—inside a proton of a carbon atom within a DNA molecule in a white blood cell. All of this is done in one continuous, seamless shot, which the design expert Michael Neault has called, "the most ambitious tracking shot in the history of cinema."[15]

Charles and Ray's innovative visual world reached millions of people. Not wanting to compromise their lofty standards of expression, they often invested a significant amount of their own capital into over-budget projects. But their commitment to such high benchmarks led them to produce aesthetically stunning films akin to "visual poems."[16] *Blacktop* (1952), *Parade, or Here They Come Down Our Street* (1952), *Toccata for Toy Trains* (1957), and *Tops* (1969) are but a few examples of their conceptually accomplished feats of rhythm and composition.

By 1978, many of the designers at the workshop would encounter Charles tired and cold, slouching at his desk. Clearly, the nonstop pace of production and the responsibility of running the firm were weighing on him. On August 21, 1978, Charles had a sudden, fatal heart attack while on a consulting trip in his hometown of Saint Louis. Ray was crushed. Charles had been a dominant force in the lives of many people, and his absence was deeply felt. Many wondered how Ray would carry on at the workshop without her life partner. Surprisingly, though, Ray approached her staff with new goals, and in a moving speech, asked for their help in moving the office forward into the future. Perhaps, in the last couple of years before Charles's passing, Ray had realized that she needed to forge a more independent persona for herself. She had been named Woman of the Year by the California Museum of Science and Industry in 1977; that same year, she sat on a number of panels and juries in Boston, Washington, and Tokyo. However, in the next decade, the work began to dwindle, and Ray spent the majority of her time putting together a comprehensive book about her joint work with Charles and cataloging their forty-year output for safekeeping at the Library of Congress.

In August of 1988, Ray was hospitalized due to complications from cancer. A few times during her hospitalization, she would awaken and ask friends for the exact date. An office associate shared that her last statement was about being with Charles. Then, on August 21—the same day Charles had passed ten years earlier—Ray also slipped away. This convergence of dates was the final way that Ray would be linked to her beloved husband.

It was the multifaceted nature of their shared career that made this partnership especially extraordinary. Were the Eameses designers, filmmakers, architects, or artists? No one job title fully describes their range of work. But one adjective does: curious. "Eventually everything connects," Charles once said.[17] Their joy and insistent curiosity for objects and ideas were the common threads that connected the wide breadth of their work. Combining inquiry and imagination with art and technology, Charles and Ray Eames crafted some of the most influential creative expressions of the twentieth century.

Lucille Ball & Desi Arnaz

The Pioneers

They were one of the most famous, beloved couples in Hollywood history: Lucille Ball and Desi Arnaz. But the two were polar opposites, which made their chemistry potent and palpable.

She was conservative, insecure, and shy. He, on the other hand, was unrestrained, extravagant, and savvy. However, they shared a few traits: Both were temperamental, confrontational, and stubborn—which only fueled their spirited fights.

They met while filming the RKO Pictures movie *Too Many Girls* (an apt title, since Desi was a known womanizer), and a romance bloomed on-set. Shortly after the film wrapped, the famed redhead summarily showed up at Desi's home, berating him and calling him a "Cuban sonofabitch."[1] It was early into their courtship, and Lucille had gotten wind that Desi had met up with his former lover while on tour with his band. And so, the pattern was set. After six months of escalating passion, accusations, and separations, they eloped on November 30, 1940. Lucille was twenty-nine and Desi, twenty-three.

"My friends gave the marriage six months," Lucille later said. "I gave it six weeks."[2] For his part, Desi offered, "It's amazing that two people from such different backgrounds and geographical

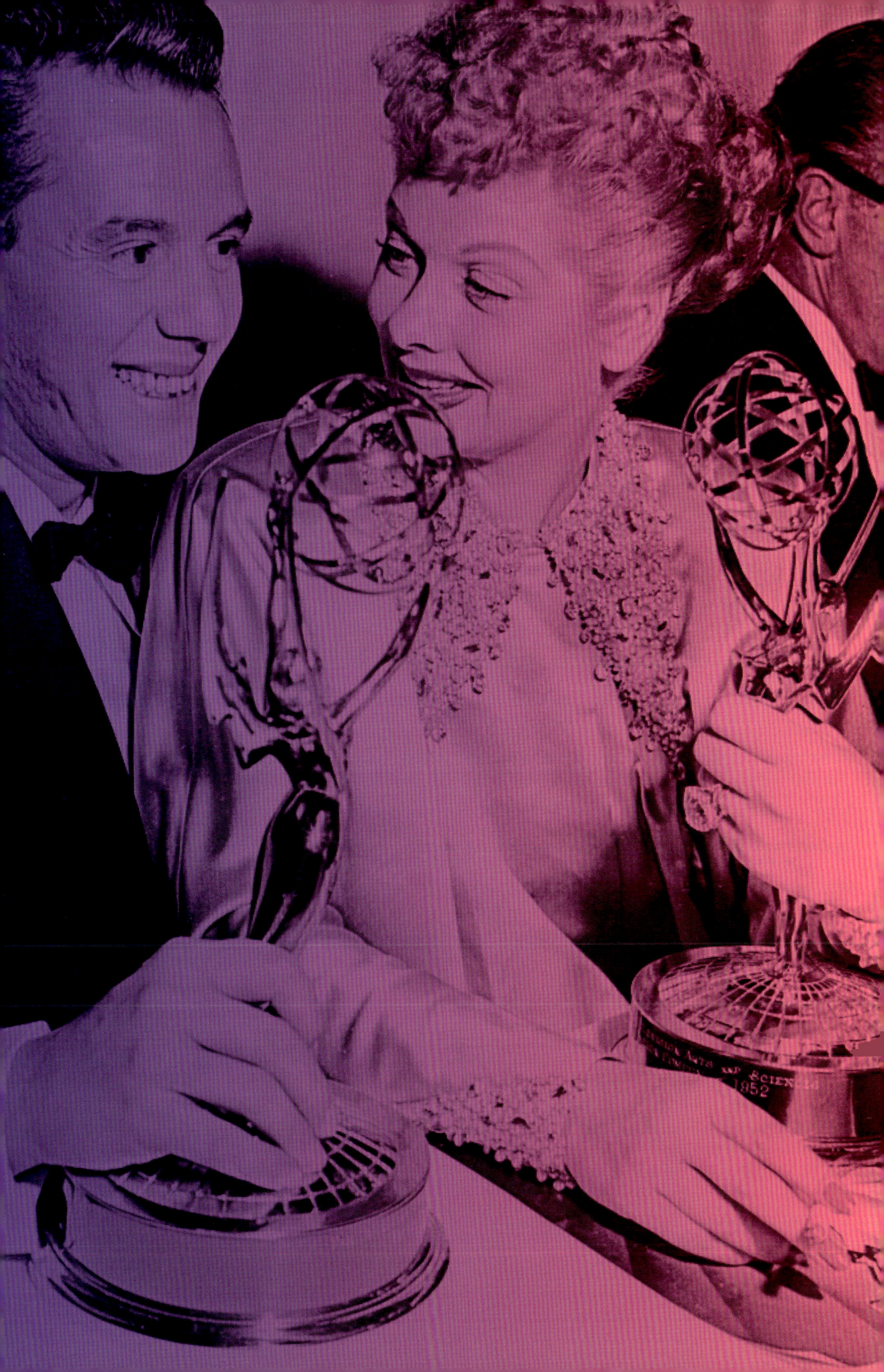

origins ever got together. That was perhaps part of our attraction, and also, I am sure, the cause of many of our arguments, fights, and other problems."[3]

Four years later, Lucille proceeded to file for divorce. She was convinced that Desi "was screwing everybody at Birmingham Hospital,"[4] where he was stationed with the United States Army Medical Corps during World War II. But tempers cooled, and they reconciled before the interlocutory decree became final. "We might have our ups and downs, just as many people have. But I'd rather quarrel and make up with [Desi] than anyone else in the world," Lucille said.[5]

This passionate, roller-coaster union went on to create a family unit with two children, an entertainment empire, and one of the most popular television series of all time. The couple essentially pioneered the TV situation comedy. Not only did they star in their own program, *I Love Lucy,* but they also founded Desilu Productions, the first-ever independent television-production company. Desilu (a moniker that combined their first names) was responsible for other hit shows such as *Star Trek* and *Mission: Impossible,* and became and remained the number-one independent production company until it was sold in 1967.

> "Once in his life, every man is entitled to fall madly in love with a gorgeous redhead."
>
> Lucille Ball

When they first met, Lucille had the bigger billing in the movies. Desi was a Cuban bandleader who had performed in the Broadway musical *Too Many Girls* before being cast in the film version. The war came along, and Desi enlisted in the U.S. Army. Lucille continued to act, but she was well aware that she was in danger of losing coveted roles to younger ingenues. Most prime opportunities had vanished for Desi upon his return from service.

Desi's constant on-the-road bookings with his band and Lucille's Hollywood commitments only prolonged their separations, which put a toll on their relationship. Desperately wanting to have a baby, a lonely and frustrated Lucille frequently lamented, "You can't have children on the phone."[6]

Then, an offer came along—one that Lucille considered not as a career move but instead as a means to save her marriage. CBS offered her a lead role in a television show called *My Favorite Husband,* a comedic portrayal of a marriage between two wildly different partners.

She actively campaigned to have Desi cast opposite her. This would have been an opportunity for them to work together and, with any luck, have a baby.

The executives at CBS were not convinced that Lucille and Desi would make a good onscreen pairing. "What do you mean nobody would believe it? We are married," retorted Lucille.[7]

"If no one will give us a job together, we'll find ourselves one," Lucille vowed to Desi.[8] That summer, the Arnazes developed a sketch-comedy act revolving around their real-life predicament: a married couple hurriedly meeting in between their separate professional commitments. They also formed Desilu Productions—with Desi acting as the company's president and Lucille as vice president—to help them mount a tour and handle the receipts. The tour was a resounding success, and CBS took a chance on casting Desi in the show.

It was agreed that the Arnazes would play "fictionalized, glamorized versions of themselves" in the series.[9] From the start, Lucy and Desi were dissatisfied with the scripts and suggested that Jess Oppenheimer become the head writer. Ever the savvy businessman, Desi negotiated a thousand-dollar cut in their salary in exchange for full ownership of the show, which enabled him to expand Desilu Productions into a full-fledged production company.

The year 1951 was momentous for Lucille. In July, she gave birth to their first child, Lucie Desiree Arnaz; in August, she turned forty; and in October, *I Love Lucy* debuted. It wasn't long before nearly thirty million viewers were tuning in each week to see what the wacky Lucy Ricardo and her Cuban, conga-playing husband, Ricky, were up to.

The writing team of Madelyn Pugh, Bob Carroll, Jr., and Jess Oppenheimer was tasked with churning out more than thirty episodes a season. Their scripts skillfully combined hilarious physical comedy, quick-witted dialogue, and tender, emotional moments.

Lucille was a gifted actress whose comedic instincts enabled her to take what was on the page and extract every ounce of laughter from it. On the show, her character's harebrained schemes often landed her in rowdy and hilarious situations. Who could forget the iconic episode where Lucy and her best friend, Ethel Mertz, find themselves working in a candy factory: Unable to keep up with the increasing speed of the conveyor belt, they rush to stuff the chocolates in their mouths and shirts to hide their incompetence from their boss. Or the time when Lucy schemes her way onto Ricky's television show to do a commercial for a vegetable drink with a high alcoholic content and gets hilariously tipsy during the many retakes. Her spellbinding physical comedy and whip-smart timing made her what one reviewer called the "undisputed sassy and silly redheaded queen of comedy."[10]

Desi, meanwhile, served as the perfect foil for his wife's screwball antics, which made them a genuine comedy team, rather than Lucy being a one-woman tour de force. Desi was

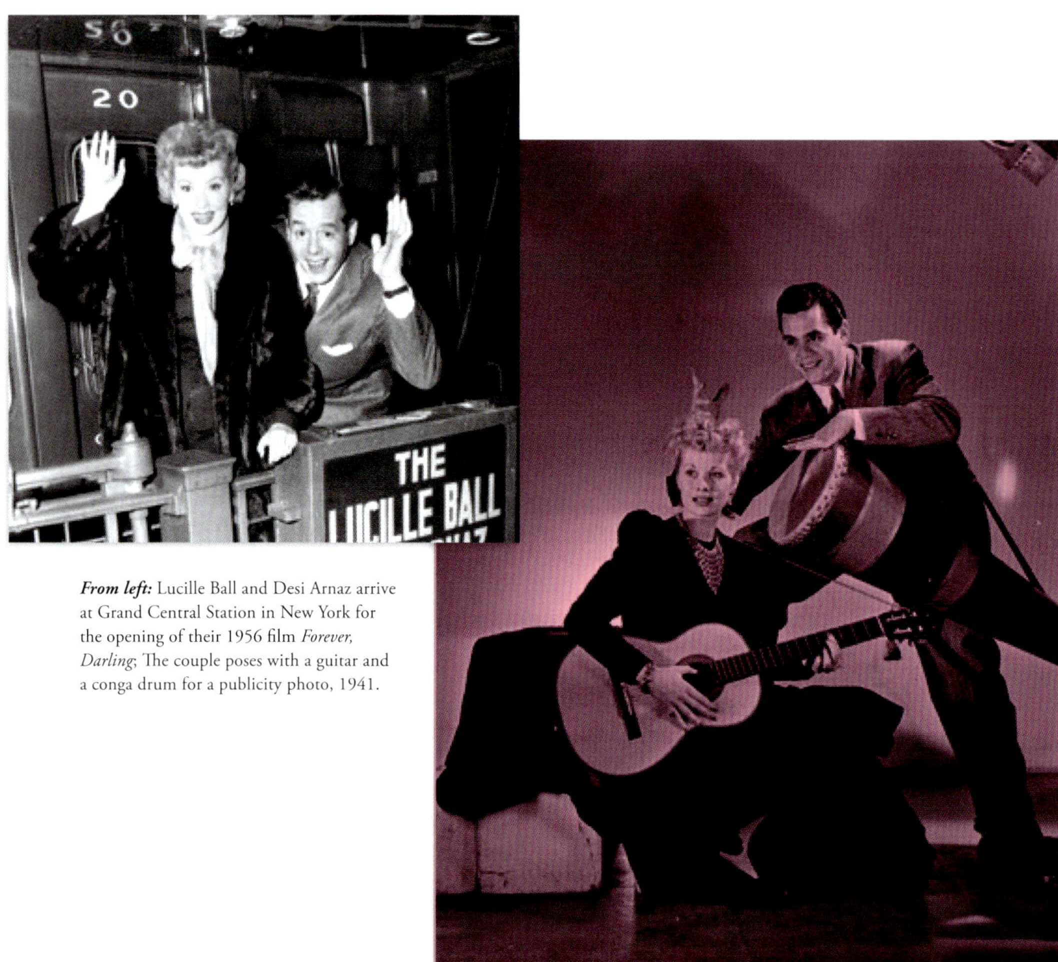

From left: Lucille Ball and Desi Arnaz arrive at Grand Central Station in New York for the opening of their 1956 film *Forever, Darling*; The couple poses with a guitar and a conga drum for a publicity photo, 1941.

savvy enough to insist on using the most innovative recording and filming methods, including the three-camera filming technique—a setup that became synonymous with sitcom television for decades to come. In this method, programs were shot on film, rather than kinescope, in front of a live studio audience, thus creating popular and very lucrative rerun deals.

In fact, Lucy was in awe of her husband's astute business sense. Even after their high-profile divorce, she said, "They talk about my business acumen. They're wrong. It was all Desi. He built Desilu into an empire."[11] Desi's sharp business maneuvers paid off handsomely. In 1957, the couple sold CBS the syndication rights to the first 180 episodes of *I Love Lucy* for $5 million; by 1961, Desilu's profits had reached another $5 million.

However, the fact remains that both brought their own unique talents to the partnership, and neither could have gone nearly as far without the help of the other.

By 1952, *I Love Lucy* was solidly installed as television's top-rated series when Lucille became pregnant again. The producers decided to integrate her pregnancy and the birth into the show. It appeared that the Arnazes' real life and that of their TV characters were mirroring one another. Lucille's actual birth to Desi Arnaz, Jr., by cesarean section took place on the same evening that the episode of her delivery aired on television. "Lucy Goes to the Hospital" was watched by 44 million viewers, surpassing the viewership of President Dwight Eisenhower's inauguration. News of the birth created nothing short of worldwide hysteria. It has been estimated that the couple received more than one million letters, telegrams, gifts, and telephone calls. Flowers filled not only Lucille's room, but also the entire hallway of her floor, the stairway leading to the floor below, and its corridor.

Lucy and Desi were an unbeatable team. *I Love Lucy* won Emmy Awards for Best Situation Comedy in 1953 and 1954, Lucille earned Best Actress honors in the comedy category in 1957, and *I Love Lucy* merchandise was sold in the marketplace. Lucille and Desi also starred in a movie together *(The Long Long Trailer)* and filmed and produced other TV projects.

With a million-dollar infusion of cash from CBS, Desilu leased the Motion Picture Center (later renamed Desilu Cahuenga Studios), and offices were created for their employees on the seven-acre lot. But the stress of their daily grind was wearing on their relationship. The Arnazes were seen publicly feuding, and rumors of marital woes circulated.

Cleo Morgan, Lucy's cousin, had shared that when the Arnazes quarreled in pre-Desilu days, Lucille would remind Desi that she was the one earning the money. Desi, in turn, had confided in Cleo that his wife's jabs hurt him deeply. Indeed, even after they were financially well-off, Lucille held Desi accountable for his half of the household expenses. It appears that Lucille's concepts of money and frugality were affected by her childhood experience of growing up poor, and her fear of getting older and being victimized by men. Martin Leeds, a key Desilu executive, had suggested that Lucille viewed her wealth as "a source of power over men."[12] This kind of imbalanced relationship between two very strong and hotheaded characters may have been one of the reasons Lucy and Desi would fall into a recurring pattern of arguments. Both did not know how to deal with their intense emotions and wounded one another deeply.

By 1954 and 1955, Desi's drinking, philandering, and gambling had become a serious problem. Perhaps, for him, it was a way to rebel or find release from the pressures of his work and relationship. One could only speculate why Lucille and Desi remained together, given all the problems they were facing. Some believe it was their dependence on one another, both in their private lives but even more so in their business life. Lucille attempted to downplay the embarrassing situation with her characteristic humor. "How *I Love Lucy* was born? We decided that instead of divorce lawyers profiting from our mistakes, we'd profit from them," she once told a reporter.[13]

According to Desi's autobiography, the couple had come to a crossroads in the mid-fifties. They once discussed whether to retire and work on interesting projects at their own pace, or expand Desilu Productions's reach and capability. Without hesitation, Lucille chose the latter.

By February 1956, industry trade papers reported that Desilu had eight hundred employees on payroll. The company projected a total production of more than two hundred television episodes for the upcoming season. The following year, the business had acquired RKO Studios's physical lots in Culver City and Hollywood for about $6 million. Things had somehow come full circle. A few years back, Lucille was on RKO's payroll for $50 a week; now she was the studio's rightful owner.

> "It's really amazing that two people from such different backgrounds and geographical origins ever got together. That was perhaps part of the attraction."
>
> Desi Arnaz

Between the Motion Picture Center and the RKO properties, Desilu had a total of thirty-five soundstages at its disposal. By the 1958–1959 season, Desilu was the industry's leader in television-film production, generating some $32 million from all of its programs. Despite its impressive growth, however, the Lucy-Desi combination remained the company's cornerstone.

Privately, Desi was suffering from serious health problems. Doctors had asked him to cut back on his work. Fearing that CBS might sue him if he disclosed his health issue, Desi instead pitched that the show switch to a one-hour format and a monthly production schedule. And thus, in 1957, *I Love Lucy* became *The Lucy-Desi Comedy Hour.* Celebrities such as Tallulah Bankhead, Danny Thomas, Red Skelton, and Milton Berle made guest appearances on the new series. Ratings were solid, but critics commented on the dull scripts and the subpar performances. The chemistry between Desi and Lucy, a major element of the original program's success, was absent; the pair's real-life marriage was unraveling, and their lack of intimacy was reflected onscreen.

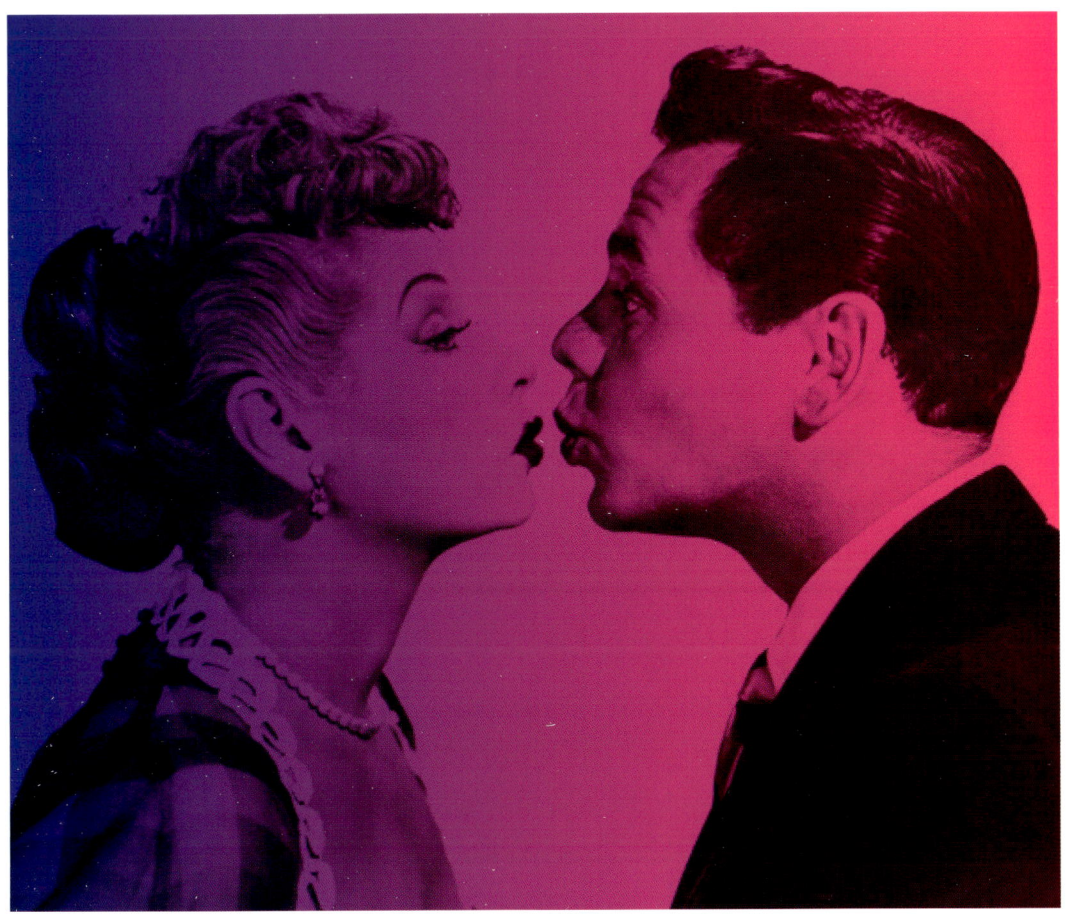

Lucille Ball and Desi Arnaz kissing in *The Long, Long Trailer,* 1953.

Lucille found it increasingly difficult to uphold the façade of a happy marriage. Desi's alcoholism had taken an irrevocable turn. Colleagues later shared that he would begin drinking at ten o'clock in the morning, and those around him were concerned about his erratic behavior. Desi was ejected from a Las Vegas casino for acting rowdy, and he was discovered to be drunk at work.

The pair decided to go on vacation to Europe with the kids to patch up their strained relationship. "It was a nightmare. . . Desi was falling-down drunk everywhere," Lucy's cousin Cleo later shared.[14] The final nail in the coffin came when a package arrived for Desi at a hotel in Rome addressed to "Mister Ball."[15] Everything went further downhill. Shortly after they returned, Desi was caught leaving a house of prostitution, which made front-page news in the *Los Angeles Herald Examiner.*

"When I look at my marriage now and ask myself what went wrong," Desi once reflected, "I think that one of the problems was that we were both working too hard and were together too much—all day and all night. Little arguments became big arguments. There was really no chance to be away from each other and let things cool off."[16]

As the pair's biographers, Coyne Steven Sanders and Tom Gilbert, put it: "Ironically, the very reason that *I Love Lucy* was developed—allowing the Arnazes unparalleled domestic and professional intimacy—had become a major source of problem in their marriage."[17]

As it goes with roller-coaster relationships, the extreme cycles of highs and lows don't stop unless you force yourself to get off the ride. The first week of March 1960 was perhaps Lucille's most painful: She filmed the final episode of *The Lucy-Desi Comedy Hour* and filed for divorce the next day. "After Desi and I went into the final clinch and the lights dimmed, there were no laughs, no smiles. The marriage, after nineteen years, had also ended that day," Lucille later recalled. "There is something about an ending—even when it is something you wanted to end—that hurts inside."[18] To her, the divorce was the number-one failure in her life. She shared that neither she nor Desi was ever the same, physically or mentally, after they parted.

Despite their divorce, Lucille and Desi maintained a strong personal bond and reportedly got along better than they did during their marriage. Lucille would call Desi for professional advice; when she took up residence in New York to star in the Broadway musical *Wildcat,* she put framed pictures of Desi in her living room and bedrooms. She clearly missed him. "I even missed the fighting. It was something. I had the kids and I had my work, but I didn't have a rock. I didn't have that one person I could lean on," she confided to her friend Jim Brochu.[19]

During her stay on the East Coast, she met the stand-up comedian Gary Morton, who was thirteen years younger than her. Theirs was a slow and steady relationship, where Lucille gradually fell in love with him. The pair married in 1961. Even after she wed Gary, though, Lucille continued working with Desi. For her next TV series, *The Lucy Show,* Desi occasionally served as a producer, and Gary warmed up the audience with his comedy act before the show.

As Desi's alcoholism grew worse, his interest in Desilu Productions steadily diminished. Lucille felt that she needed to step in and take the reins. They had originally agreed that each would be able to buy the other out, and Lucille invoked this option in 1962. "I never wanted to be an executive, but when my marriage to Desi broke up after nineteen years, I couldn't just walk away from my obligations and say 'forget it,'" Lucille said. "We were an institution. Life takes guts. If you don't take chances, you'll never bathe again because you might get dirty again."[20]

With the purchase of Desilu Productions, Lucille became the first woman to head a major studio. In doing so, she tapped into resources she never knew existed, and indeed, she had an impressive business acumen. By 1967, the production company had released

> *I Love Lucy* was never just a title.
>
> Desi Arnaz

a number of lucrative television hits such as *Star Trek* and *Mission: Impossible,* garnering fourteen Emmy nominations that year alone. Lucille decided to sell the company to Gulf and Western Industries for a reported $17 million (approximately $128 million today) that same year. Gulf and Western, in turn, rebranded the company Paramount Television.

While Lucille's marriage to Gary lasted for more than a quarter of a century, for countless fans, America's greatest couple remained the TV duo of Lucy and Ricky. Indeed, neither stopped loving the other.

After the death of Desi's second wife, Edith, in 1985, Lucille even insisted that he temporarily move into the Beverly Hills home she shared with Gary, so she could keep an eye on him. The very next year, when Lucille called Desi on his birthday, she was devastated to hear the news: Desi had been diagnosed with lung cancer.

Their devoted daughter, Lucie, cared for her ailing father until his very last day. She was there when Lucille saw Desi for the last time. Lucie had been playing an *I Love Lucy* episode to keep her dad occupied. Lucille and Desi sat together reminiscing, praising one another, laughing, and joking. "And I just shut the door to let them have their time together. . . like two kids on their first date," Lucie remarked.[21]

Lucille and Desi spoke one last time, on December 2, 1986. Desi had not eaten for days and was barely speaking. Lucille had asked her daughter if she could talk to Desi. Lucie was not even sure if he was lucid enough to understand the impending conversation, but she held the receiver up to his ear. Lucie could hear her mom's cracking voice, saying the same message over and over again: "I love you. I love you. Desi, I love you."[22] He summoned the energy to mutter back, "I love you too, honey. Good luck with your show."[23] Those were Desi's final words before his passing two days later.

Lucy and Desi have gone down in history as the pair that brought joy—hour after hour, country after country, generation after generation—through their portrayal of coupledom in the dawn of the television era.

Joan Didion & John Gregory Dunne

The Literary Mavericks

When the acclaimed writer John Gregory Dunne asked his dying mother for advice on how to cope with marital problems, she uttered two words: "Drink. Drugs."[1] Neither worked. At the height of their difficulties, Dunne's outrageously talented, more-famous-writer wife had gone out to publicly share their marital woes. In the December 5, 1969 issue of *Life* magazine Joan Didion wrote: "I had better tell you where I am, and why. I am sitting in a high-ceilinged room in the Royal Hawaiian Hotel in Honolulu watching the long translucent curtains billow in the trade wind and trying to put my life back together. . . [My husband and I] are here on this island in the middle of the Pacific in lieu of filing for divorce."[2] It was true: John Dunne and Joan Didion were going through a rough patch. Dunne had half-jokingly told his friends at parties that his marriage was always on the brink of collapse. Didion's rather detached reaction didn't help matters, either. "I don't know of many good marriages," she shared. "I don't know of many not-good marriages, either."[3] She was practical and levelheaded. She described marriage as an "exercise in self-improvement."[4]

What the stunned readers of *Life* magazine did not know was that Dunne had not only read and edited Didion's notorious piece, but he had also accompanied her to file the essay at the Western Union office before its deadline. Regardless of whatever arguments they were having, the couple would never turn in a written piece without running it by the other for a final edit. They were each other's most-trusted reader. As for Dunne, he ended up spending close to eighteen months in a motel near the Las Vegas Strip among hookers, druggies, and cardsharps, drafting a memoir about his despair. Didion was pleased to see that his efforts had given fruit to a wonderful book.

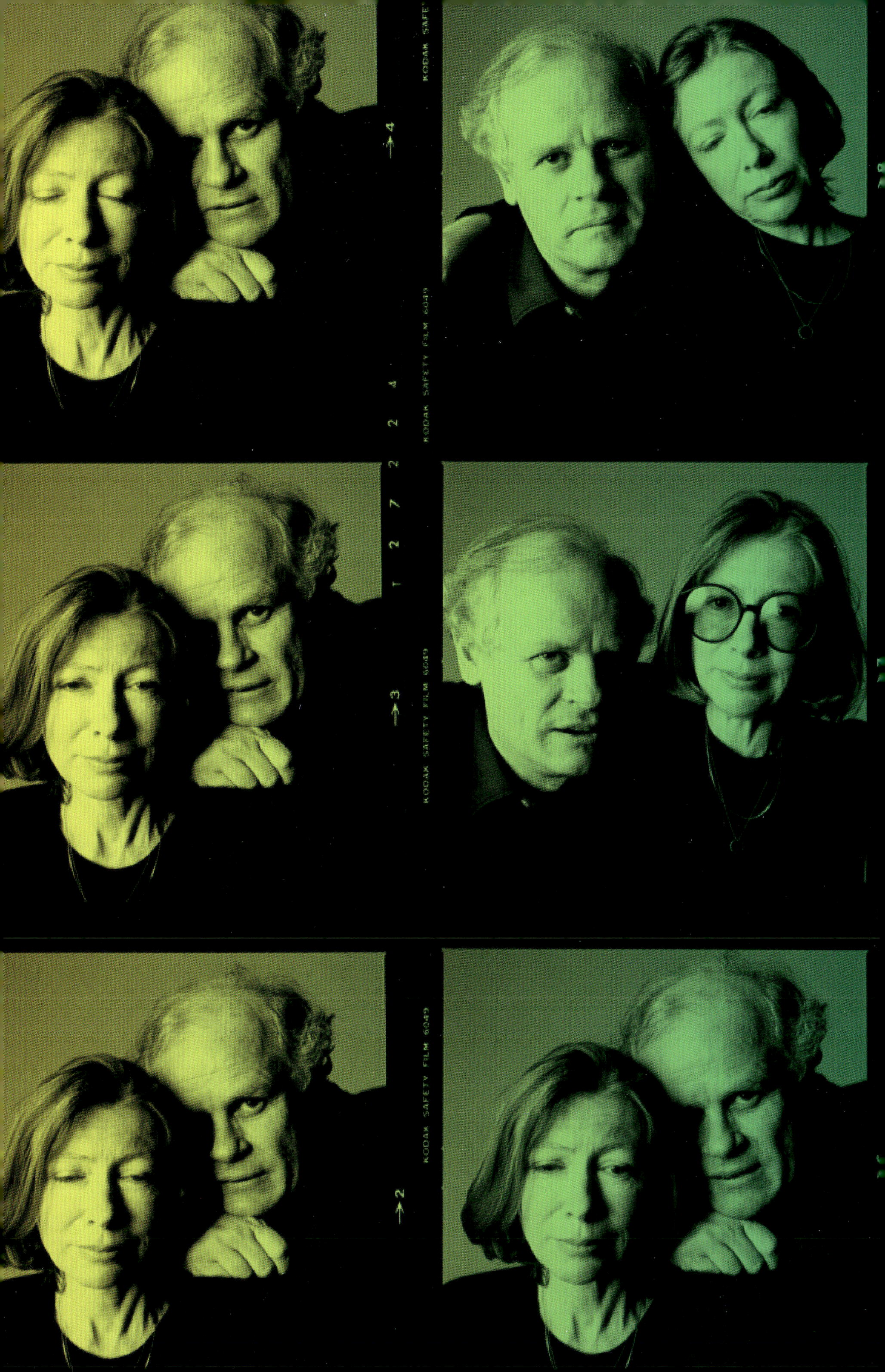

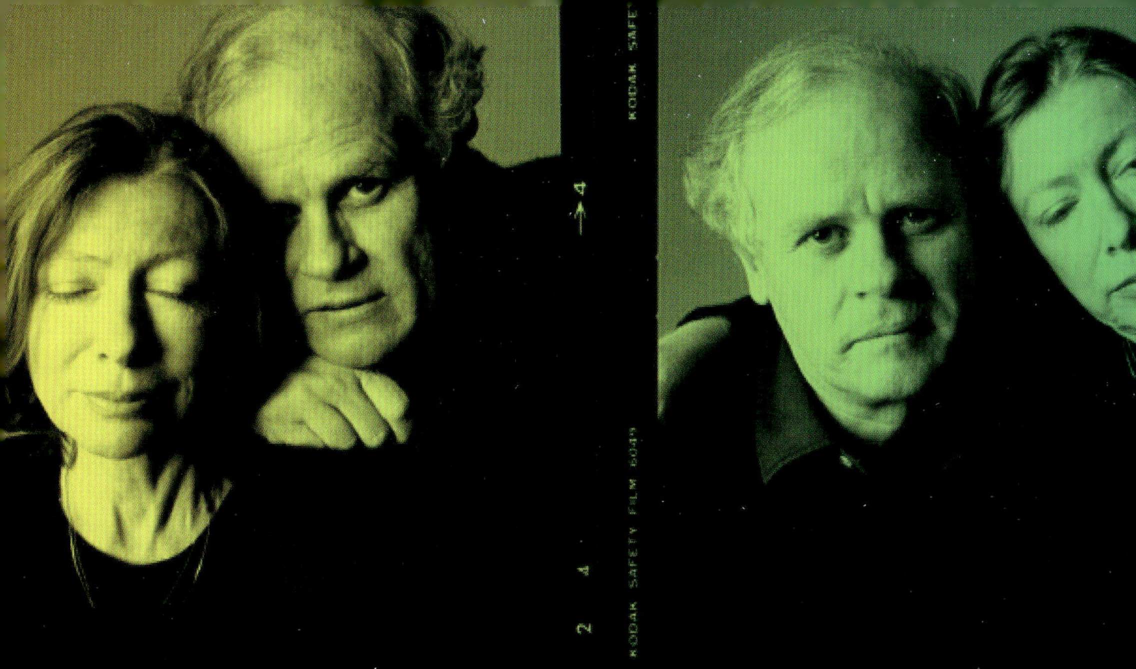
KODAK SAFETY FILM 6049
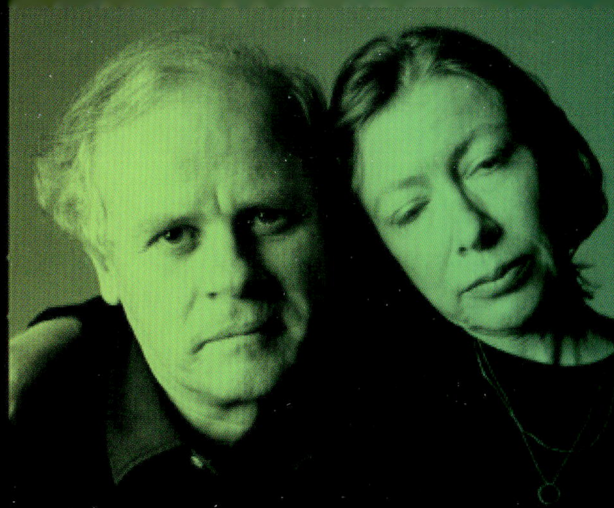

The two could not have been more different. She was small, frail-looking, and rail-thin; he was an imposing figure, tall and broad-shouldered. She was quiet, socially awkward, anxious, and prone to migraines; he was a loud, funny, natural raconteur with a volatile temper. She was raised Protestant in California; he was from New England, the grandson of an Irish immigrant. Didion spoke from experience when she noted, "[W]e are fatally drawn toward anyone who seems to offer a way out of ourselves."[5]

Didion and Dunne were an unlikely but inseparable duo that, over their forty-year marriage, helped each other become what Richard Severo of the *New York Times* called, "America's best known writing couple."[6] They were the rare triple threat, succeeding in journalism, fiction, and screenwriting. Didion was, arguably, the most talented pioneer of New Journalism, the movement that infused reportage with literary technique and permitted the writer to inject himself or herself into the narrative. The couple traveled together constantly for the better part of four decades, uncovering the undercurrents of change within politics and culture. Between them, they published twenty-seven books, collaborated on five feature films, and contributed essays to a wide variety of publications, including *Time, Life, Esquire,* and *The Saturday Evening Post.* Writing regular columns forced them to become piercing social observers, zeroing in on overlooked subjects that inadvertently carried the zeitgeist of the sixties and seventies. Through their shared passion, they developed an uncommon symbiosis. They were, in Didion's words, "terrifically, terribly dependent on one another."[7]

Didion grew up in Sacramento, where the open vistas and flat horizons were more reminiscent of the Wild West than the laid-back beach towns of Southern California. When she was five, her mother handed her a journal so she could start writing down her thoughts instead of complaining. This early coping mechanism became a lifelong habit that served as an early training ground for her illustrious career. From an early age, she was cognizant of style and authenticity, and in an effort to capture realistic dialogue, she practiced the fine art of social espionage. Clutching her notebook, the young Didion tiptoed behind trees and lingered in hallways and doorways to eavesdrop on people's conversations.

A sense of unfulfilled longing and nostalgia permeates Didion's work. "Every real American story begins in innocence and never stops mourning the loss of it," she once wrote.[8] While studying at UC Berkeley, Didion discovered that the French philosopher Jean-Paul Sartre's existentialist writing registered with her nascent worldview. Maybe it was her temperament, or the fact that she was born in the Depression era and raised during World War II, but Didion found herself drawn to the darker, more anxiety-ridden currents of life. She understood, from Sartre's work, that humans yearn for safety, permanence, and meaning,

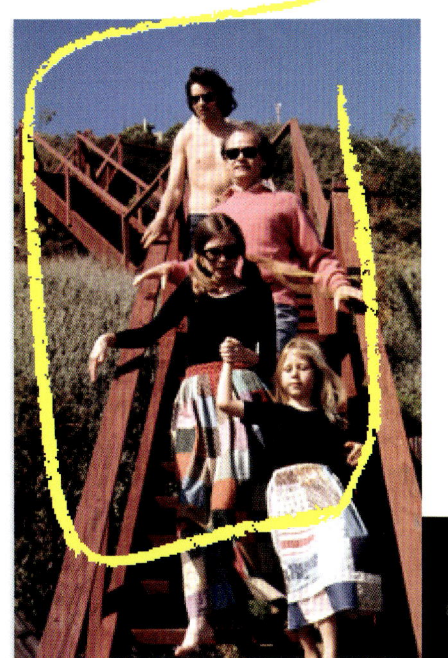

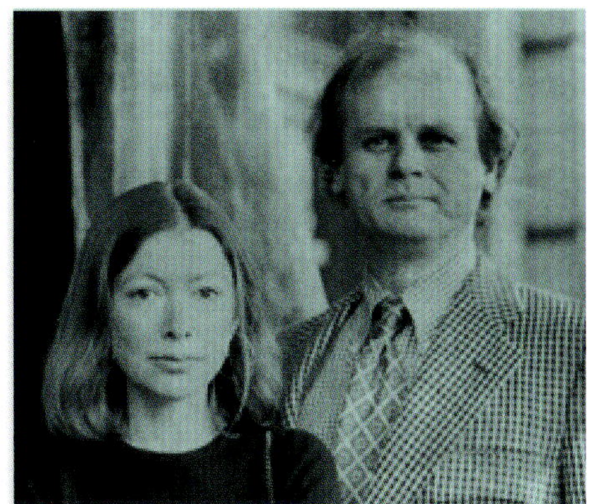

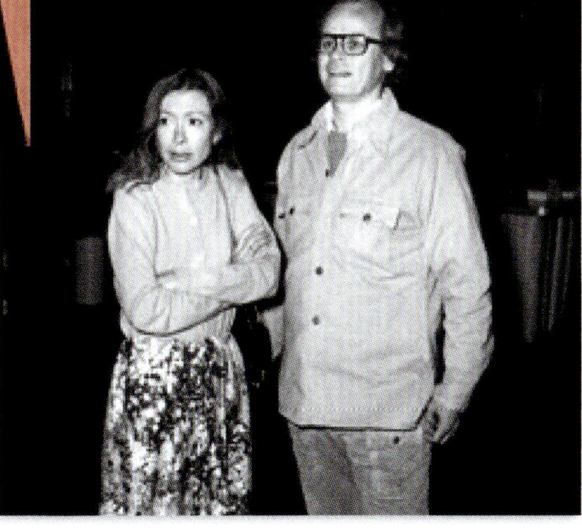

Clockwise from top left: Dunne and Didion with their daughter, Quintana Roo Dunne, and Dunne's nephew Anthony Dunne, walking down the stairs near their Malibu beach home, 1972; Didion and Dunne, February 28, 1974; Didion and Dunne attend a party for the movie *Play It As It Lays,* based on Didion's novel of the same name that the couple adapted for the screen together, at the Directors Guild of America in Los Angeles, October 1972.
Pages 131: Didion and Dunne work together in their Malibu library, 1972.

but that life itself can be random, unpredictable, and absurd. Confronted by this destabilizing dichotomy, she wondered how people coped with despair, failure, and an ever-present sense of emptiness. These complicated emotional responses would fuel Didion's imagination and her subsequent writing.

After graduating from Berkeley, Didion landed a job at *Vogue* and moved to New York. During her time at the magazine, she published her enduring essay "Self-Respect: Its Source, Its Power" (later retitled "On Self Respect"). As legend has it, Didion wrote the gripping piece on a moment's notice, after another writer had failed to submit an article. In the evenings, after a full day at *Vogue,* she would work on crafting her first novel.

She dated men, but none captivated her like the confident *Time* staff writer John Gregory Dunne. What most people did not know was that Didion's father, a veteran of World War II, had suffered from depression when she was young. His withdrawn emotional state had left his daughter exposed and vulnerable, and their frequent moves as a family only deepened her feelings of alienation and natural reserve. Dunne, with his exuberance and prodigious energy, gave her the sense of grounding and protection that she so craved. "People always say that

John would finish my sentences—well he did," Didion would reflect many years later. "He was the buffer between me and the world at large."[9]

Dunne was born in West Hartford, Connecticut, and was the second-youngest of six children in his well-off Irish Catholic family. While growing up, he felt ashamed of being an Irish American, as if he had been exiled to the fringes of high society. This sense of exclusion probably led to his writerly aspirations and his intense need to become an insider in Hollywood, a town that is renowned for its insularity and cliquishness.

At first, the young Dunne began writing because he had a stutter; putting words on paper was a means of expressing himself. But in time, writing became a habit. Dunne graduated from Princeton in 1954, and much to the dismay of his mother, who wanted him to be a businessman, he started his career as a journalist in New York.

Didion met Dunne at a dinner given by a mutual friend in 1958. That evening, her friend Noel Parmentel pointed at Dunne and said, "This is the guy you ought to marry."[10] In 1964, she did just that. The previous year, Didion had published her first novel, *Run River,* to tepid reviews, and the decade-long grind of working at *Vogue* had her itching for a reprieve. So, the couple soon set off for Los Angeles. There, they would not only have an opportunity to cover the social upheavals and protests erupting on the West Coast, but they would also be able to try their hands at making money by writing for the movies. Dominick Dunne, John's older, film-producer brother, became an important fixture in their social life. Los Angeles was a city that endeared itself to insiders, and every social occasion became a vehicle for the couple to network and learn the inner workings of their new social milieu. If they weren't having dinners at Dominick's house, they could be found at the hot industry hangouts in Beverly Hills, such as the Bistro on Canon Drive or the Daisy on Rodeo Drive.

During the day, the newlyweds sat in their rented Palos Verdes home and worked at their craft. The first issue they encountered was that neither knew anything about the mechanics of screenplays. In fact, they had never even seen a television script. Years later, Dunne recalled, "We were coming out of [the Daisy] one night. . . and some drunk actor was having a fight with his girlfriend, and he threw a script at her. And I picked up the script. It was a television script. It was the first script I'd ever read."[11] Dunne and Didion picked the script apart. They routinely went to screenings and began diagramming movie sequences. While still aspiring to write a screenplay, they turned in their monthly freelance contributions to their respective magazines.

The first couple of years in Los Angeles proved to be a transitional time for both of them. Besides grappling with work, Didion was trying to figure out her role as a wife. She wasn't a natural hostess, but she soon acquired the L.A. touch and began hosting parties.

Many days, they set about cruising through the city in search of a good story. They each kept a notebook and agreed on a policy: Whoever was the first to use a detail in their work could claim it. Dunne liked to uncover stories about the drifters and dreamers who passed their time inside dimly lit, seedy piano bars, while Didion preferred to study the elite. At galas and gallery openings, Didion would swiftly maneuver Dunne to mingle with the city's movers and shakers. Some of their finest essays about their observations of California subcultures—hippies, farm workers, and LSD experimenters—found their way to the pages of *The Saturday Evening Post.* The two would publish more than fifty pieces there, sharing a column between

> "I did not always think he was right nor did he always think I was right, but we were each the person the other trusted."
>
> Joan Didion

them called Points West. In 1967, Didion published "Slouching Towards Bethlehem," the essay that would make her into a literary celebrity—and an unexpected sex symbol of the sixties. The following year, the *Los Angeles Times* honored Didion with one of its Women of the Year awards. Didion may have given off the outward impression of an anxious and frail woman, but her work expressed confidence. She developed a writing style that became emblematically her own: detached, rhythmic, precise, and highly gripping.

Both members of the couple were adamant that they did not compete with one another. Dunne, whose reputation had grown more slowly than Didion's, basked in his wife's popularity. When they went to restaurants, he was noted to lean back in his chair to give the gawkers and fans a better view of his celebrity wife. He would frequently gloat about Didion's extraordinary talent to friends, producers, and anyone within earshot. But toward the late sixties, a kind of tension grew between them. Didion was immersed in writing her next novel, *Play It As It Lays,* and the dark mood of the novel enveloped her. Dunne was weary that his career aspirations had not unfolded the way he had envisioned. Much to his disappointment, Dunne's first book, *Delano: The Story of the California Grape Strike,* which he published in 1967, had not moved the needle on his career. His next book, *The Studio,* a hilarious exposé of Hollywood, earned lackluster sales. Adding to the couple's difficulties were money problems, heavy drinking, Dunne's temper, and Didion's withdrawal tactics.

By the time Dunne moved to Las Vegas to write his semiautobiographical 1974 novel, *Vegas: A Memoir of a Dark Season,* the couple's relationship felt frayed and was filled with verbal sparring. Dunne wrote about his restlessness, going to movies alone, driving the freeways for hours, and escape. In *Vegas,* the protagonist calls his wife from a temporary apartment and tells her he is about to go out with a nineteen-year-old, who is "supposed to suck me and fuck me." "It's research," the wife coolly responds.[12] The wife's aloofness and savvy reluctance to take the bait is all too similar to the signature "cool-bitch chic"[13] persona for which Didion was known.

Interestingly enough, once Didion finished *Play It As It Lays,* her doom-laden mood somehow lifted. The couple decided that they were stuck with each other, for better or worse; after all, who could understand the extended periods of self-absorption that writing required better than another writer? They both worked on their respective books in their home offices, often without speaking or sharing a meal for days.

When the couple lived in Hollywood, they hosted a mélange of film-industry elites along with rock and roll royalty. Dunne would work the room, chatting people up and refilling their drinks, while the more reserved Didion would replenish the food on the table. By the time they moved to Malibu in 1971, the Dunnes were firmly entrenched in L.A.'s film, music, and writing community. They were reverentially referred to as "the new voices of California literature."[14]

Film producers and studio heads would send many proposals and projects to the Dunnes throughout the seventies. In their screenwriting collaborations, the division of labor depended on each partner's schedule. Sometimes, one would write the draft and the other would act as the editor, or vice versa. Dunne and Didion's first joint screenplay was *The Panic in Needle Park* (1971), about young heroin addicts in New York City. Al Pacino was cast as the lead—his first starring role—and the film premiered at the Cannes Film Festival. The following year, the two adapted Didion's novel *Play It As It Lays* for the silver screen. Their blockbuster movie, *A Star Is Born* (1976), starring Barbra Streisand, went on to gross $80 million and won five Golden Globe Awards, including Best Motion Picture in the Comedy or Musical category.

It seems that their marriage eventually found some sort of equilibrium, largely thanks to the success of Dunne's bestselling 1977 book *True Confessions* and his increasing role in striking deals in Hollywood. Friends would note how, for years, Dunne had assumed the role of the "ideal writer's wife,"[15] guarding Didion from distractions, screening her calls, and supporting her during interviews, public appearances, and awards ceremonies. Once he

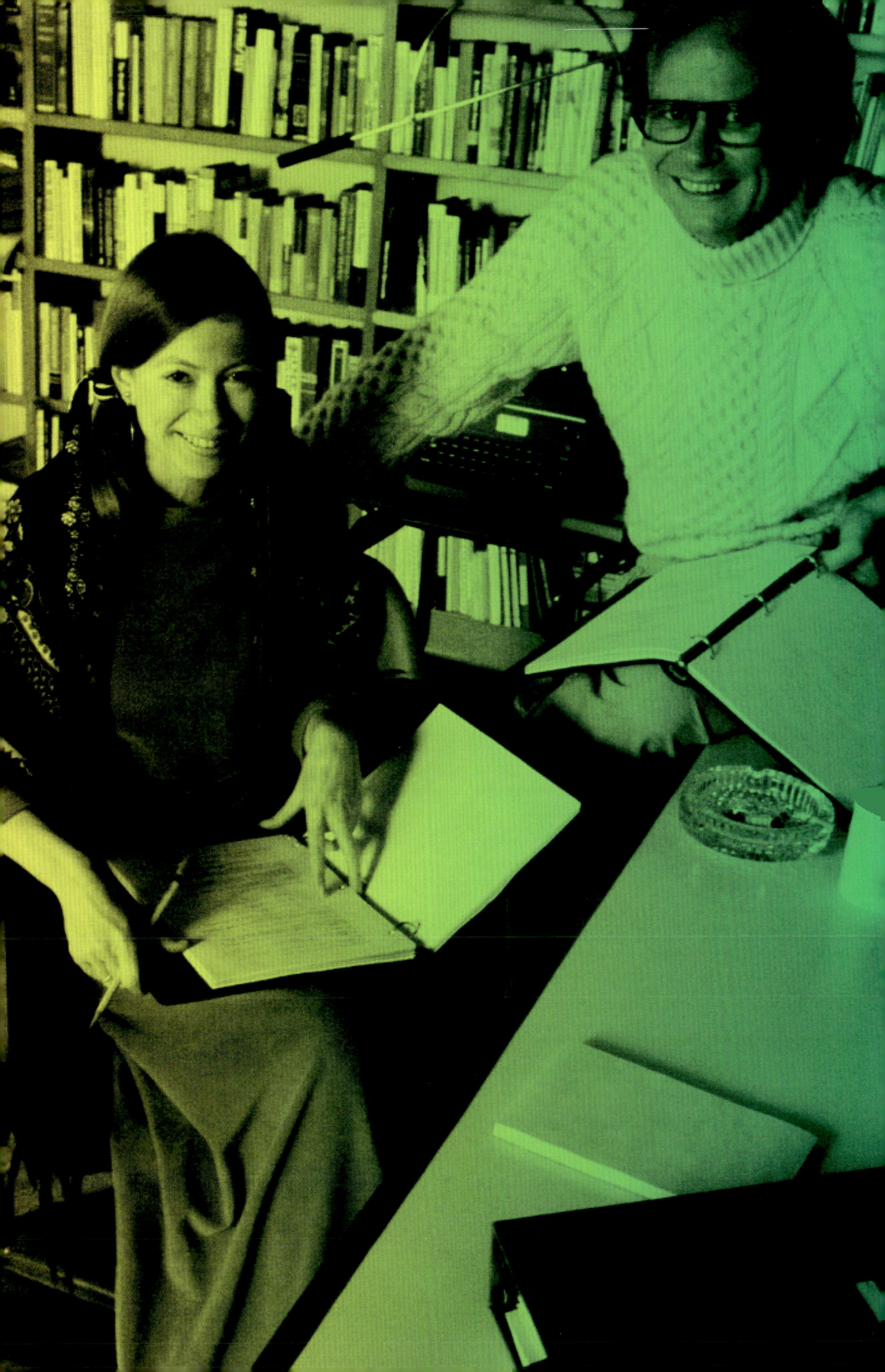

emerged from the shadow of being Mr. Joan Didion, Dunne not only carried on with those responsibilities, but was also able to carve out a literary identity of his own.

Stardom had its price for the Dunne family, however. Their writing commitments, coupled with their constant travel, impacted their young daughter, whom the Dunnes had adopted in 1966. The couple's difficulty conceiving a baby had led them to consult a doctor about adoption, and on March 3, 1966, they received a call inquiring if they wanted to adopt a baby girl who had been born that day. They accepted without hesitation and rushed to the hospital within the hour. Didion, who was aching for a baby, stood at the nursery window admiring the beautiful infant they would name Quintana Roo. The first words Didion would whisper to her newborn from the other side of the nursery's glass partition were, "You are safe."[16] "You are safe"[17] would be the same phrase she would utter to her daughter nearly thirty-eight years later, as Quintana emerged from a coma.

> "Marriage is memory, marriage is time. Marriage is not only time: It is also, paradoxically, the denial of time."
>
> Joan Didion

As Didion would later write in her book *Blue Nights,* she and Dunne were not prepared to make the traditional lifestyle changes that parenthood generally requires. The young Quintana became deft at ringing up room service during the family's extended hotel stays, often went to the courthouse with her parents to listen to people's dramas, and sat in on agent meetings. (Dunne wittily described his daughter as a child who "could pick an agent out of a police lineup."[18]) Growing up, Quintana played with Barbra Streisand's son and his pet lion cub, and lived in a rarefied world where the famous were never out of reach. Once, while traveling on a press junket for a movie, Didion took her child to see a Georgia O'Keeffe exhibition at the Art Institute of Chicago. Quintana gazed at the breathtaking *Sky Above Clouds IV* canvas, turned to her mother, and asked, "Who drew it?"[19] When Didion named the artist, the girl said, "I need to talk to her."[20]

In the late eighties, a doctor informed Dunne that he was a candidate for heart failure—an episode he would write about in his 1989 memoir, *Harp.* The diagnosis sent Dunne into an emotional tailspin. He would often tell Didion that he felt old, that he didn't want to drive after dark, and that he would rather stay in than go out to a party. These sentiments were not characteristic of Dunne before his health scare. In many ways, his growing medical concerns reoriented him toward envisioning another life for their family. Many years back, when they had been in Indonesia, Dunne and Didion had met a retired, vibrant couple. They were impressed by how this duo was going about the second half of their lives fully engaged, traveling and teaching around the world. Dunne would often tell Didion that he wanted them to live like the couple they'd met in Indonesia.

The familiar restlessness had set in, and Dunne began thinking that a move back to New York would reinvigorate them. Although Didion was at first reluctant about the move, she ultimately agreed, and they fell into a comfortable rhythm there once they were settled. They started most days with a walk in Central Park and breakfast at a deli near their Upper East Side apartment. Then they would go home, retreat to their adjoining offices, and begin work. In the evenings, they were found at their regular table at Elio's, sitting by the framed jackets of two of their books.

Perhaps Didion didn't want to believe that her once vivacious husband was having major health problems, but Dunne would often talk about his imminent death. He would tell her, over her objections, that when he died, she should keep the apartment and get remarried. Although money was tight, he persuaded Didion to travel to Paris with him, as he thought it would be the last time he could see the city. They stayed at their favorite hotel, Le Bristol, and walked through the magnificent Luxembourg Gardens in the rain. He told Didion that their joint epitaph should read, "They had a good time."[21] One can only imagine that for Didion, such declarations were both moving and disconcerting. The worst was when Dunne told Didion he no longer needed to keep detailed notes of his observations. One night, he asked her to write something down for him, but when she offered him the note the next day, he told her, "You can use it if you want to."[22] It was as though Dunne had given up completely.

The silver lining was Quintana's new life. She had suffered from a serious drinking problem and had gone through treatment, but she was back on her feet, newly married, and working as a photography editor for *Elle Decor* magazine. Then, on Christmas Day of 2003, Quintana was admitted to the hospital with flu-like symptoms that soon turned into pneumonia. Her condition deteriorated rapidly. She fell into septic shock, and unable to breathe on her own, she was sedated and intubated. It was after visiting Quintana in the intensive care unit that Dunne suffered a fatal heart attack. On their way home from the hospital, the worried father was thinking of his daughter's precarious state and told his wife, "I don't think I'm up for this." "You don't get a choice," Didion told him.[23] As they settled into their apartment for the night, John Gregory Dunne slumped in his chair and suddenly died.

Quintana recovered—for the time being—and Didion, consumed with overwhelming grief, turned to writing. How does one partner deal with the loss of the other? Certainly, grief is a universal experience, but very few have documented it as unflinchingly as Didion did in her most successful book, *The Year of Magical Thinking*. When the work won the 2005 National Book Award in Nonfiction, the judges called it "a masterpiece in two genres: memoir and investigative journalism."[24]

With this book, Didion's greatest feat was showing the reader the peaks and valleys of her unusual and successful marriage. We get glimpses into how she and Dunne talked to each other, worked together, and what they fought about. But above all, her arresting prose leads us into the most private, treasured aspect of their relationship: their love. In a particularly moving section, Didion shared that, on her birthday, just a few weeks before Dunne's passing, he read aloud a passage from her novel *A Book of Common Prayer*. "Goddamn. Don't ever tell me again you can't write," he said, closing the book. "That's my birthday present to you."[25] Didion was so moved that she began to cry.

In *The Year of Magical Thinking,* Didion also trod through the mountainous regions of her grief, pain, and the challenge of relinquishing her attachment to Dunne. In her mind, she still thought that he would walk through the door, answer the phone, or call out her name at any moment. She couldn't delete his e-mail messages, give away his shoes, or throw out his copies of *Princeton Alumni Weekly* magazine. To do so would mean acknowledging that he was never coming back. Didion also noticed that, in her husband's presence, she had never seen herself as old. "When John was alive, I saw myself through his eyes, and he saw me as how old I was when we got married," she later said in an interview.[26] Marriage, Didion had noted, was both a journey through time and a negation of time. Now, in Dunne's absence, she was seeing herself in a different light. Didion struggled to finish *The Year of Magical Thinking,* "because," she said, "for as long as I was writing it, I was in touch with him in some way."[27] But eventually, she came upon the hard, sweet wisdom of surrender. That didn't mean she was giving up; instead, she was giving in to the reality of her life. She finished her work a year after Dunne's passing and began planning for the book tour.

But, only a year and half after Dunne's death, Didion would be tested again. Just before the release of *The Year of Magical Thinking,* Quintana passed away of acute pancreatitis at

> In the early years, you fight because you don't understand each other. In the later years, you fight because you do.
>
> Joan Didion

age thirty-nine. Despite her heartbreak, Didion didn't cancel her book tour. "I mean, I was never in my whole life going to stop grieving for Quintana. . . [I]t was a question of are you going to live for the rest of your life," she later explained.[28] On the tour, Didion was greeted by hundreds of fans, many of them wishing to talk about their own experiences with grief. As years went by, Didion's status as a literary icon only grew. The National Book Foundation honored her with the Medal for Distinguished Contribution to American Letters; she was awarded an honorary doctor of letters degree from Yale University and a National Humanities Medal from President Obama. Aside from the acclaim and adoration she gleaned for her literary works, the octogenarian was chosen to represent the impeccably cool high-fashion house Céline in its spring/summer 2015 ad campaign. Members of what's been called "the cult of Joan"[29] can buy a sequined clutch bag designed to look like the cover of her book *The White Album,* or splurge on a leather motorcycle jacket with her face on the back for a cool $1,200.

In *The White Album,* Didion famously wrote, "We tell ourselves stories in order to live."[30] And she has continued to live and write stories to propel herself forward amid unthinkable personal tragedy. She went on to edit Dunne's last novel, *Nothing Lost,* which was published posthumously. She then set about writing Quintana's elegy in her powerful book *Blue Nights.* And, a few years later, she adapted *The Year of Magical Thinking* for the stage; it opened on Broadway in 2007. Recently, she was the subject of a documentary directed by her nephew Griffin Dunne. Even today, you can sometimes spot the literary giant in the streets of New York, crossing the sidewalk or having a meal near the Upper East Side apartment she once shared with her husband and partner, John Dunne.

Georgia O'Keeffe & Alfred Stieglitz

The Iconoclasts

Legend has it that when Alfred Stieglitz—then considered a key figure of the New York art scene—first laid eyes upon Georgia O'Keeffe's drawings in 1916, he dramatically declared, "At last, a woman on paper!"[1] He gazed at the abstract forms that leapt from the pages; they had a particular resonance that he had seldom seen. He was all the more intrigued to know the artist who had imagined them.

At the time, O'Keeffe was an unknown twenty-eight-year-old teaching art in Texas. For a while, she had wrestled with making art: Was it a means to express herself freely or to please others? In art school, a classmate had painted over her work to show how the Impressionists depicted trees. But she cared neither for the trees nor for the Impressionists. As the journalist Joan Didion once aptly wrote, from an early age O'Keeffe had "an immutable sense of who she was."[2] Spirited and unconventional, O'Keeffe went to Texas, "where there were no trees to paint and no one to tell her how not to paint them."[3] Since she couldn't say or do as she wanted, she felt that perhaps she could win back her freedom by painting as she wanted to paint. She would later recall that the act of painting seemed to be "the only thing I could do that didn't concern anybody but myself—that was nobody's business but my own."[4]

O'Keeffe may have been determined to forge her own path in art, but she was keenly aware of Stieglitz's esteemed reputation and craved his approval above all else. At fifty-two, Stieglitz had become an internationally acclaimed photographer and a well-respected gallerist who had given celebrated artists such as Constantin Brancusi, Paul Cézanne, Henri Matisse, and Pablo Picasso their first U.S. exhibitions in his Manhattan gallery. If anyone could understand modern art, it would be him, she thought.

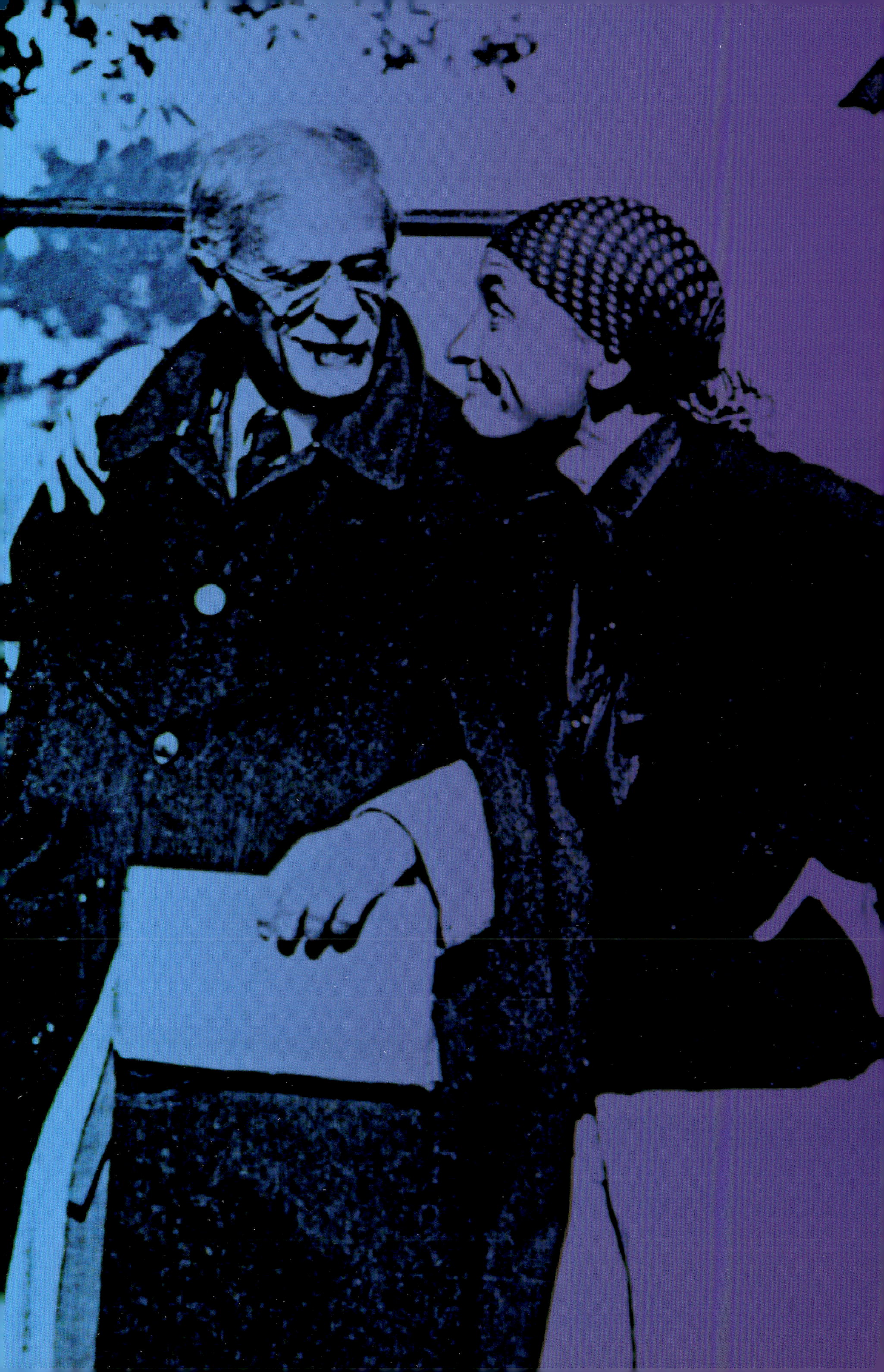

Stieglitz not only understood her art but proceeded to fall in love with her. They first began a cordial correspondence, discussing their daily struggles in creating art, but soon the formality gave way to intimate daily letters, sometimes twenty to thirty pages long. In fact, during their thirty-year relationship, some twenty-five thousand notes or letters were exchanged between these two influential twentieth-century artists. It quickly became apparent that they were intensely attracted to one another, intellectually, emotionally, and physically. When O'Keeffe finally moved to New York in 1918, Stieglitz became her mentor, agent, and lover. Eventually, the two wed in 1924. This is the story of a union between two of America's most celebrated and visionary artists—one, the godfather of modern art in the United States; the other, among the most legendary female artists of all time. Their partnership marks what some consider to be the first example of a modern marriage, where two independent, determined, and talented individuals tried to reconcile their desires for work and personal fulfillment together.

From their early letters, one can perceive their difference in temperament. O'Keeffe's writing is to-the-point, while Stieglitz's tone is more impassioned. O'Keeffe was a self-sufficient, practical countrywoman who felt revived by nature and quietude. Stieglitz was an intellectual New Yorker who loved to be surrounded by friends and family. He had come from a prosperous, close-knit, German Jewish family and had traveled extensively throughout Europe. He was a dashing figure with his graying hair and the shock of red vest he wore underneath his signature black cape. Twenty-four years older than O'Keeffe, he had been married for more than two decades to Emmeline Obermeyer, a dour and proper brewery heiress. By all standards, Stieglitz's first marriage was loveless, where neither had an interest or understanding of the other's needs and aspirations.

O'Keeffe, on the other hand, was born under modest circumstances on a dairy farm in Wisconsin; she was one of seven children. When she was a teenager, her parents left her and her brother with relatives and moved to Virginia in search of better opportunities. Her father was remote and unavailable, and her mother was overly concerned with her nonconformist daughter fitting in with the rest of society. With the exception of her feisty sister Claudia, who joined her in Texas, O'Keeffe did not enjoy a close relationship with her siblings. In Texas, the landscape was endlessly flat. The two sisters would walk toward the horizon, watch the glowing sunset, and wait to see the brightening of the evening star—a beacon and a personal symbol to the budding artist. When she first tried to capture that twilight sky, she painted the star as a mere dot on white paper. But then she encircled it with halos of yellow, red, and cooler colors, until its expansiveness reflected the way she felt inside. Ten sensuous watercolors made up that star. And when Stieglitz saw her work, he wanted to experience that pure white center of the artist.

As they slowly revealed their innermost feelings to one another, the two artists began to feel connected and fused to the other's innermost core. In his letters, Stieglitz described their relationship as "a contact of the souls,"[5] professing that O'Keeffe lived deep within him. She, in turn, validated the same connection. She wrote, "It seemed that I was nearer to you than I have ever been to anyone—So near that I almost seemed to touch the thing in you that is *real* life—call it soul if you want to."[6]

When Stieglitz gave O'Keeffe her first gallery show in 1917, she was still living in Texas. At the time, it was rare for a woman painter to have a solo exhibition. But Stieglitz believed that the female experience was spiritually distinct from that of the male, and he wanted to introduce that seldom-expressed viewpoint to the art world. Above all, he was convinced that

> "I'm getting to like you so tremendously that it sometimes scares me."
>
> Georgia O'Keeffe

he had found one of the geniuses of the modern age, and he was ready to devote himself to her advancement. In the early stages of their relationship, the smitten Stieglitz projected all the sensuality, mystery, and charm of an ideal woman onto her. "I wrote you this morning that you were a symbol to me—not a person. . . A symbol—Spirit—Woman," he told her.[7] Equally enamored but far more practical, O'Keeffe warned Stieglitz in her letter: "There little boy don't get so excited—don't bank too much on me—I'm only a woman—maybe I should say only a human creature."[8]

In previous romances, O'Keeffe had remained distant and ambivalent. She equated love with bondage—a lack of freedom. Besides, she wasn't after what other women typically wanted from men: security and fidelity. Stieglitz, however, displayed an understanding of her and her work that was uncommon in those days; in turn, she admired and trusted him. He was opening to an expanded life. When she wrote him that she wanted to stop teaching for a year to paint full-time, Stieglitz offered her a studio in New York. Once O'Keeffe moved to the city in 1918, they forged a relationship that centered on their all-consuming love and their art. He summarily moved out of the bedroom he shared with his wife and built his days around his new artist love. When Obermeyer caught him photographing O'Keeffe in their study, she gave him an ultimatum: either her or me. The decision was swift. Flouting convention, Stieglitz and O'Keeffe openly lived together for several years before they got married in December 1924. As later letters made clear, it was Stieglitz who wanted to wed,

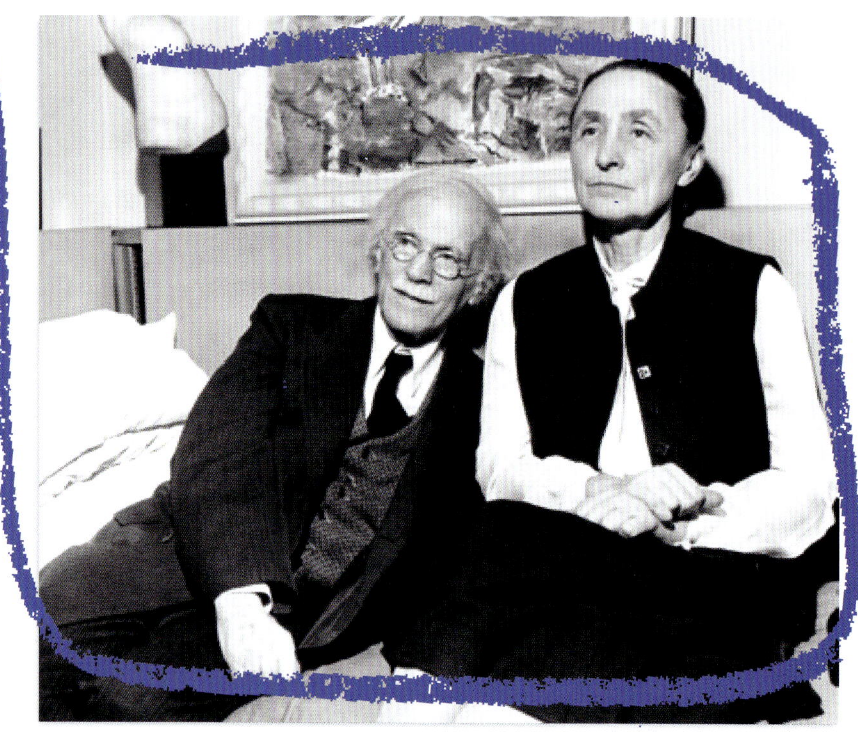

Alfred Stieglitz and Georgia O'Keeffe at Stieglitz's An American Place Gallery in New York, circa 1940.

not O'Keeffe. But even after marriage, she continued to assert her independence by steadfastly using her own surname, which Stieglitz also encouraged.

In many ways, Stieglitz was destined to fall for someone with O'Keeffe's style. She complemented him in many ways and yet shared the same visceral sensibilities in creativity and art. He was physically attracted to her lithe figure, grayish green eyes, and beautiful, long hands. At a time when women wore elaborate Edwardian dresses, O'Keeffe donned austere and elegant black clothing. Stieglitz was simply enamored with her unconventional beauty. Suddenly, after many years of hiatus, he picked up the camera and proceeded to document every fold and curve of her body: earlobes, neck, lips, nose, navel, buttocks, hands, and legs. "I was photographed with a kind of heat and excitement and in a way wondered what it was all about," she wrote at age ninety.[9] Stieglitz had never before photographed another woman in such a compulsive way. His photographic sessions became voyages of discovery, an effort to capture the essence of the woman who had brought him back to life both artistically and sexually. In less than three years, Stieglitz produced two hundred prints immortalizing his artist-heroine, making her one of the most photographed women of the century.

Three thousand visitors came to see those images at an exhibition in 1921. According to Benita Eisler, the couple's biographer, the photos documented "the most intense, passionate, and complex transaction between a man and a woman ever recorded by camera."[10] The heat of the lover's gaze blazed through each of the pictures, leaving the viewers viscerally affected. Stieglitz's newfound love had indeed raised his art to new powers of expression and catapulted him into his most prolific period. These electrifying photographs canonized O'Keeffe's image and influenced artists for generations.

Stieglitz also helped O'Keeffe translate some of her deepest artistic impulses onto the canvas. Because they both passionately sought out the best in everything, he demanded the finest photographic paper and the highest quality paints. Stieglitz's photography also influenced O'Keeffe's work, as she began incorporating his photographic techniques of space compression and extreme close-ups into her paintings. The author Laurie Lisle, who has written extensively about the couple, also notes that many of O'Keeffe's canvases steadily became approximately the same size as Stieglitz's eight-by-ten-inch prints. Inspired by the sharp lines and translucent surfaces of those prints, O'Keeffe gradually stopped painting with short, textured brushstrokes and began working primarily with oils. Her aesthetic shifted away from abstraction and grew more focused on the flowers and landscapes she encountered during their lengthy stays at Lake George, in upstate New York. Stieglitz's comprehensive studies of clouds, generally recognized as the first intentionally abstract photographs, may have also inspired O'Keeffe's iconic 1965 painting *Sky Above Clouds IV,* which now hangs in the Art Institute of Chicago.

> "I believe I would rather have Stieglitz like something—anything I had done—than anyone else I know."
>
> Georgia O'Keeffe

In the spring of 1921, Stieglitz was asked to help mount an exhibition at the Pennsylvania Academy of the Fine Arts. He balked at the stipulation that works by female artists would not be displayed. Stieglitz, who, according to Lisle, truly believed in "the integration of 'male' and 'female' qualities in people and liked to show paintings by men and women together rather than separately,"[11] insisted that O'Keeffe be included. "Take it or leave it," he retorted. "There'll be no show without her."[12] His obstinacy paid off, and O'Keeffe's work—along with that of two other female artists—was subsequently included.

Shortly thereafter, Stieglitz decided that the time was ripe for an O'Keeffe solo exhibition, which opened to great fanfare in 1923. This show firmly established her as a prominent artist in her own right. However, O'Keeffe was bothered by the increasingly overt sexual interpretations of her art, which likely stemmed from Stieglitz's exhibition of her nude photos and the gossip about his young lover. While O'Keeffe was annoyed by the chatter, Stieglitz seemed to secretly enjoy and even encourage it. For him, the photographs represented a display of his virility and further proof of his belief that theirs was "the perfect union of both a man and a woman and two intensely creative individuals."[13] He compared them to Adam and Eve in the presence of friends. Needless to say, O'Keeffe found her husband's promotional tactics and theories bothersome and counterproductive. In fact, throughout her illustrious career, she would correct anyone who categorized her as a *female* artist. In the 1940s, when she was firmly established in the art world, she confronted this idea head-on: "The men like to put me down as the best woman painter," she said. "I think I'm one of the best painters."[14] And she was.

From the start, O'Keeffe was bold and courageous in her style and practice. Her 1925 paintings that portrayed giant flowers were intended to make viewers stop and see a flower the way she experienced it. Yet people read all kinds of erotic symbols into the images. The unfurling flower petals, some said, looked like genitalia; the tone of her work was subliminally sexual. O'Keeffe would later write in protest, "[Y]ou hung all your associations with flowers on my flower and you write about my flower as if I think and see what you think and see—and I don't."[15]

By the mid-twenties, their marriage had begun to disintegrate. O'Keeffe wanted a child, but Stieglitz, in his sixties, was not up to the task. As her mentor, he advised her that motherhood would divert her from the trajectory he had set for her. Instead, Stieglitz said, her art would be her ultimate creation, their cherished offspring. When he moved into a new gallery, his priority was to make sure that O'Keeffe exhibited every year. And with each show, her stature and fame kept rising. But to paint, she needed space, quietude, and a clear head. The Stieglitz family home in Lake George, where she stayed in the summers, was a revolving door of visitors, family, and in-laws. For the sake of their privacy, O'Keeffe suggested they invest some of the proceeds from her art sales into building a lake house of their own. But Stieglitz, who thrived on having an audience, felt that moving to a private house was akin to social banishment. The curious O'Keeffe wanted to travel and discover fresh subjects for her painting, but an aging Stieglitz clung to New York and Lake George.

By 1928, O'Keeffe had cast her gaze on the West. Despite Stieglitz's complaints, she decided to visit her family in Wisconsin and felt revived by the beauty of the vast landscape. Memories of her childhood on the prairie flooded her mind. She wondered who she was, and who she was becoming. Nostalgic for those magical starlit nights in the wilderness, she wrote to Stieglitz: "I am learning something out here that I cannot quite define—but it is

“It seemed that I was nearer to you than I have ever been to anyone—so near that I almost seemed to touch the thing in you that is *real* life—call it soul if you want to.”

Georgia O’Keeffe

something very important to me—There is something very healthy for me in the feeling of this country."[16] Stieglitz, on the other hand, was increasingly concerned by her absence. He attempted to redirect her attention to their relationship. "We have both grown greatly—one thro' the other. Singly neither would have grown so strong," he wrote.[17] He urged her to come back. But in her customary direct and restrained tone, O'Keeffe responded that alone in Wisconsin, she was a "whole person. . . I seem to be only a very small fraction of a person when you are around," she said.[18] This transition period was what she called the "turning of a page" in her life.[19] She needed space to grow, as a woman and as an artist, outside the shadow of her famous and domineering husband. She knew things had to change, yet she was unsure of how.

When she returned to New York, their habitual power struggles began to peak. Adding to the mounting tension was Stieglitz's unusually close relationship with the doe-eyed, twenty-four-year-old Dorothy Norman. Her beauty and vitality, not to mention her readiness to worship the great artist Stieglitz, were hard for him to resist. Deeply wounded, O'Keeffe watched from the sidelines as Norman made daily visits to the gallery. By the early thirties, Norman had virtually become a permanent fixture in Stieglitz's life, not only as his lover but also as his gallery manager. The irony was not lost on O'Keeffe, who had to take care of Stieglitz through his many ailments, while he had numerous flirtations with women who were several decades younger than him. Finally, in 1929, O'Keeffe fell "into something," she wrote, "from which there is no return."[20] The conflict between woman and artist, between art and life had reached a tipping point. Torn between spending the summer with Stieglitz and his family or focusing on her work, she chose the latter. And when the arts patron Mabel Dodge Luhan invited her and fellow painter Rebecca Strand to stay with her in New Mexico, she accepted. When O'Keeffe got off the train and set her gaze on the light-washed mountains and the limitless landscape, she knew this was the world to which she belonged. The question was: How could she become a part of it? New Mexico's biomorphic, primeval shapes perfectly suited her simplified, abstract vocabulary, and the canyons' layers of orange, red, and yellow inspired her to paint with a new palette. The bleached desert bones; the dry, bald earth;

"We have both grown greatly—one thro' the other. Singly neither would have grown so strong."

Alfred Stieglitz

and the purity of her surroundings also encouraged her toward greater experimentation in composition. This land's subjects and colors would become emblematic of the O'Keeffe style.

Those first few months in the Southwest represented a homecoming for O'Keeffe—a journey toward that white, pulsing evening star of her youth. In the late afternoon, she would go up to a high mesa on horseback to watch the flaming sunset wash the valley below in shimmering hues. Then, at nightfall, she would slowly make her way back by moonlight and sometimes sleep under the star-filled sky. She recounted these experiences with a sense of wonderment in her frequent letters to Stieglitz.

Back in New York, Stieglitz read each letter and felt more abandoned. O'Keeffe was his muse, the creative force and spirit of his gallery, and without her he felt creatively sapped. Yet in his helpless state, he still did not want to join her on her travels. Meanwhile, O'Keeffe proceeded to have liaisons of her own in New Mexico, perhaps as retribution for the indignity she suffered from Stieglitz's public affair with Norman, or out of her need to explore and experiment, or maybe both. Biographers have suggested that her travel companion, the vivacious and striking Strand, became one of her lovers. Strangely enough, O'Keeffe was well aware that Strand had had a fleeting affair with Stieglitz only a few years back. Others have intimated that O'Keeffe had a short-lived affair with the impresario Luhan as well.

Fearing that he had lost her forever, Stieglitz deluged O'Keeffe with constant letters. "And I felt you were with me. . . [and] we worked as a team. . . But there was always your yearn for the Southwest—[and] I feared it. Was jealous of it. Knew it would win you from me," he wrote.[21] From afar, O'Keeffe countered: "My body couldn't live close to you without feeling loved—and I didn't *feel* loved."[22] A few days later, she continued: "I seemed to get back to what I had been before I gave up myself to you. . . to stretch something inside myself that had almost died."[23]

The summer of 1929 proved to be a turning point for the couple, as the now-middle-aged O'Keeffe struggled to find personal fulfillment, even at the cost of her partnership with her husband. What made their relationship so unique, however, was how these two independent, strong-willed individuals set about renegotiating their roles and expectations. Their battles would be hard-won, as O'Keeffe, following a severe depression in 1933, came to terms with Stieglitz's relationship with Norman and her inability to nurture herself and her art on the East Coast. She clearly cared for Stieglitz but wondered how much she could give him without feeling depleted and overwhelmed. Ironically, this precarious balancing act strengthened her resolve that painting stood at the center of her identity. After all, Stieglitz was devoted to her work, and whatever the price, he was committed to having her resume the life of an artist. So, in 1934, after her highly acclaimed retrospective at Stieglitz's gallery, O'Keeffe established a new arrangement, from which she rarely deviated until Stieglitz's passing. Each spring, with paint and canvas in tow, she would set out for New Mexico, and return to New York in the fall with breathtaking paintings that Stieglitz would exhibit and sell to the world.

O'Keeffe knew that she had never been a wife in the traditional sense. She was no longer a lover, either, but she could be a close friend and a part-time caretaker to her husband. Her leaving each year was difficult for both, but now Stieglitz would repeatedly reaffirm the wisdom of her decision. "How can I be jealous of a place?"[24] he reassured her. When he endured numerous ailments, people wondered why O'Keeffe was not there by his side. She would tell others, in her imperious tone, that she doubted he would feel any better if she were there nursing him. Part of the problem was that Stieglitz was a noted hypochondriac. But even more relevant was the fact that O'Keeffe had an overarching artistic agenda from which she seldom strayed.

In her book *The Second Sex,* the French philosopher Simone de Beauvoir said, "One is not born a genius, one becomes a genius,"[25] and noted that sadly, the lives of most women were not conducive to a search for excellence. This was not the case with O'Keeffe. Self-possessed and hardworking, she made a decision about the kind of artist she wanted to be and harnessed her great energy and talent to achieve that goal. Stieglitz once admiringly said that he would rather have six months with this extraordinary woman than twelve months with someone else.

While O'Keeffe's star was on the rise, Stieglitz's health was declining. In 1938, he suffered the first of six coronary attacks that left him for the most part bedridden and frail. Now it was O'Keeffe who supported her spouse financially until his passing eight years later. Although their physical passion had waned, O'Keeffe recalled all that she owed him, his efforts on behalf of her career, and the inspiration she drew from his constant innovation. She took his example to heart as she worked, becoming one of the country's most prolific artists until her passing at the age of ninety-eight. The biggest coup came in 1943, when the Art Institute of Chicago proposed an O'Keeffe retrospective; this was the first major museum to exhibit her work in a solo show. The ultimate accolade came three years later, when New York's Museum of Modern Art mounted a retrospective of her three-decade career. Stieglitz was too frail to participate in the glittering opening event, but O'Keeffe made sure to take him through the exhibition herself beforehand. After seeing it, he wrote to her: "Incredible Georgia—and how beautiful your pictures are at the Modern. . . Oh Georgia—we are a team—yes a team."[26]

As planned, she left for New Mexico shortly thereafter, but before going she hid messages for Stieglitz to discover while she was gone. In the summer, when doctors reached out to O'Keeffe to tell her that Stieglitz had experienced yet another angina attack, she decided not to return. She believed he would recover, as he always had. In fact, Stieglitz rallied to write her a final note: "I am sitting in your room. At your desk. . . As always read your letters first. . . kiss—another kiss. Tomorrow I will go to the Place [his gallery] for a while."[27] But he never did. His helper found him sprawled on the floor; the pen he was holding had rolled a few feet from his body. O'Keeffe rushed back and was with him as he passed away in the early morning hours of July 13, 1946. A few days later, the grieving O'Keeffe buried his ashes at the foot of a tall, old pine by Lake George. "I put him where he could hear the water," she said.[28]

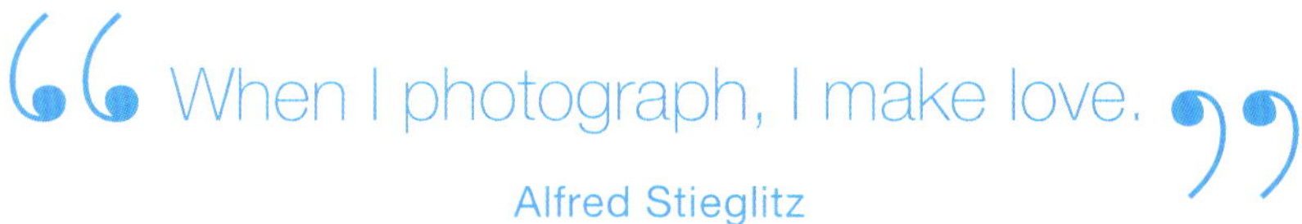

One would think that their years of prolonged separation would have made it easier for O'Keeffe to transition into being a widow. But she admitted that, especially during the first few years, she missed her longtime companion dearly. Stieglitz had always shielded her from the commercial side of the art world, and without him she had to learn to deal with the public and dealers on her own.

After Stieglitz's death, O'Keeffe moved to her home at Ghost Ranch, in New Mexico, and continued painting. Prices for her work continued to climb steadily, as did her reputation. Harvard and Columbia were among the many universities to bestow honorary degrees upon her, and she received the nation's highest civilian honor, the Presidential Medal of Freedom, in 1977. By then, her eyesight had deteriorated, and she was becoming increasingly dependent on a handsome young man who was helping out on the ranch and bore a striking resemblance to Stieglitz in his younger years.

In early March 1986, a few months after being awarded the National Medal of Arts, O'Keeffe's frail body gave out at a hospital in Santa Fe. That spring, her ashes were scattered not at Lake George like Stieglitz's but over Ghost Ranch—the place with which she will be forever identified. She had said she wanted to hear the wind instead.

Rei Kawakubo & Adrian Joffe

The Renegades

When Adrian Joffe would see Rei Kawakubo walking her dog in the streets of Tokyo, he wouldn't have the nerve to approach her. That is understandable. A tiny woman with taut cheekbones, Kawakubo exudes an aura of mystery and severity. Besides, it's intimidating to go up to a woman who is considered a legend and initiate small talk.

At the time, Kawakubo was already a preeminent designer in Japan—the shaman of chic, whose antiestablishment brand, Comme des Garçons (CDG), revolutionized the fashion industry. Even before meeting her, Joffe would spend a big portion of his paycheck on CDG garb. He was not living in Japan at the time but would travel there frequently to secure licensing deals for his sister Rose's London-based knitwear label.

By the time the two met in 1987, Kawakubo had made quite a name for herself on the international fashion scene. In the eighties, designers such as Thierry Mugler and Gianni Versace were the harbingers of women's style with their tailored, shoulder-padded power suits and glitzy, figure-hugging dresses. When Kawakubo's creations hit the Paris runways, they shook the fashion establishment to its core. A cadre of disheveled models stomped down the catwalk, wearing mostly black, oversize, unfamiliar clothing: trousers with sweater cuffs around the ankles, black maxi skirts and moth-eaten knitwear, large overcoats, and deconstructed garments. At first, Westerners, who were accustomed to gender-specific, body-conscious dress, found the creations absurd and nihilistic. But Kawakubo was unconcerned. Soon she garnered a cultlike following of artsy downtown women, which grew into legions of fans.

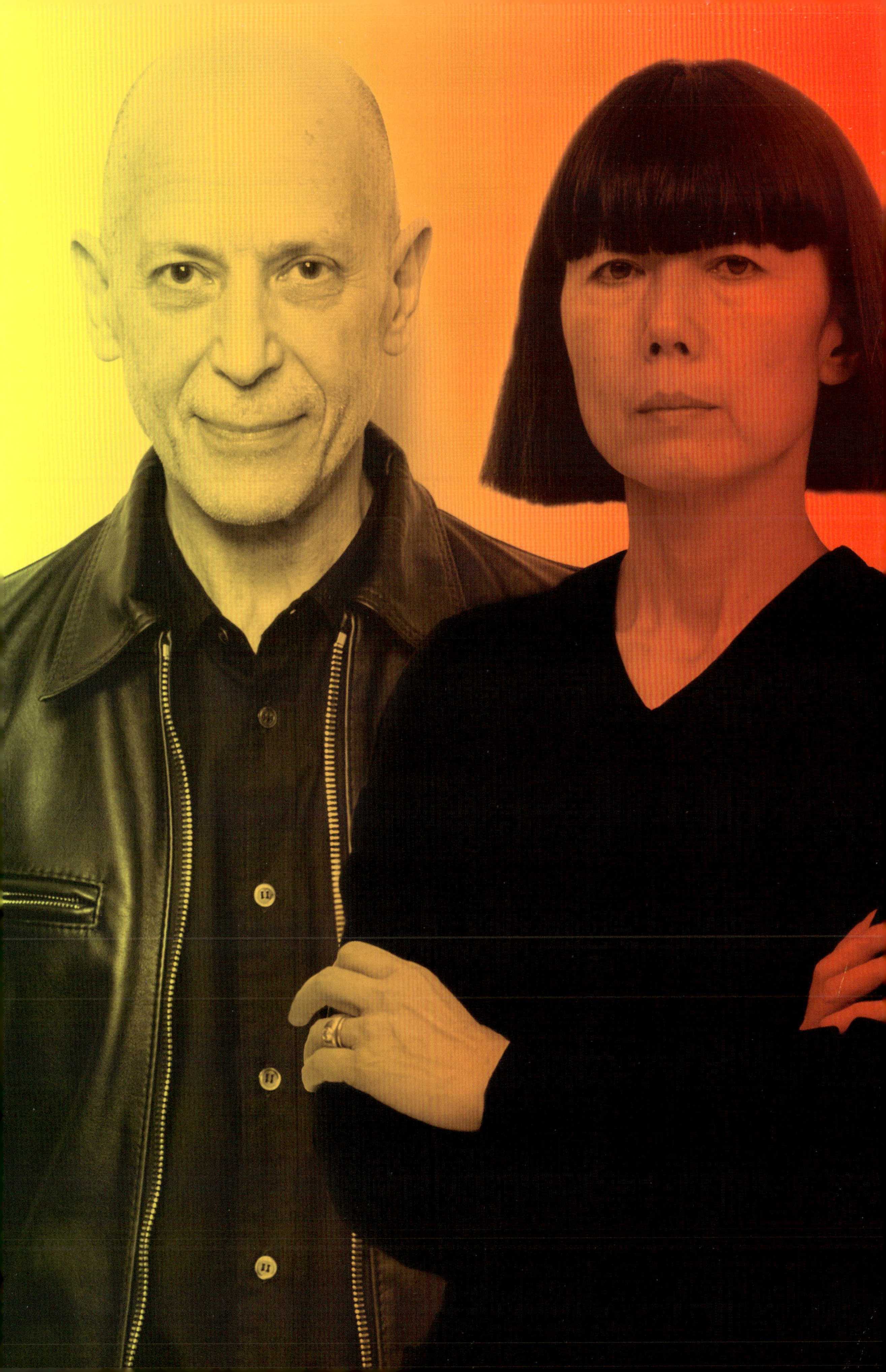

Presently, Kawakubo is, in the words of Thomas P. Campbell, the former director of the Metropolitan Museum of Art, "recognized as among the most important and influential designers of the past forty years."[1] In 2017, she became the second living designer to have an exhibition devoted entirely to her work at the Metropolitan Museum of Art's Costume Institute. Although it is a high honor to be chosen for a large exhibition at the prestigious museum, it took the curator, Andrew Bolton, thirteen years to convince the reticent designer to participate. Kawakubo's contribution to her field is especially significant because she has introduced a new visual vocabulary to fashion. As Campbell put it: "Since her Paris debut in 1981, she has blurred the divide between art and fashion and transformed customary notions of beauty, identity, and the body."[2] Figuring out new ways of doing things and breaking predetermined boundaries is central to Kawakubo's ethos—whether it is in her creative process, in the retail sector, or in her personal relationship with her husband and president of Comme des Garçons International, Adrian Joffe. The two have made CDG into a global fashion empire.

The dominant theme in their collaboration is reconciling what most perceive as opposites. How do two people who have had no formal training in fashion or business lead one of the world's most venerable fashion empires? How can a fashion house be creative, idiosyncratic, and independent and still enjoy such commercial success? How can clothing that refutes the traditional definitions of race and gender be deemed at once an anomaly and a mainstay of the fashion industry? And finally, how does a married couple that works together live separately on two different continents— Joffe in Europe (France) and Kawakubo in Asia (Japan)? So many facets of this duo's work are hedged by paradox, and yet this struggle to balance such contradictions has fueled Kawakubo and Joffe's creative power.

Kawakubo never trained as a designer. She studied fine arts and aesthetics and by happenstance stumbled into a career in fashion. To this day, she considers herself an outsider who dwells beyond fashion mores. "For more than forty years that I have been making clothes, I have never thought about fashion," she said in 2014. "In other words, I have almost no interest in it."[3] And it has been her detachment from such constraints that has led her to become one of the most significant players in the fashion industry. Because she lacks formal training, Kawakubo cannot sew or cut a pattern. Instead, she communicates her ideas to her patternmakers by simply offering them indicators like "a scribble, a crumpled piece of paper," or "inside-out pillowcase."[4] The job of her trusted patternmakers, in turn, is to muddle through her koan-like riddles and transform her ideas into blueprints for clothing.

The process of coming up with a new collection is fraught with anxiety and suffering for CDG's entire design team. Kawakubo starts from zero every time, with no preconceived

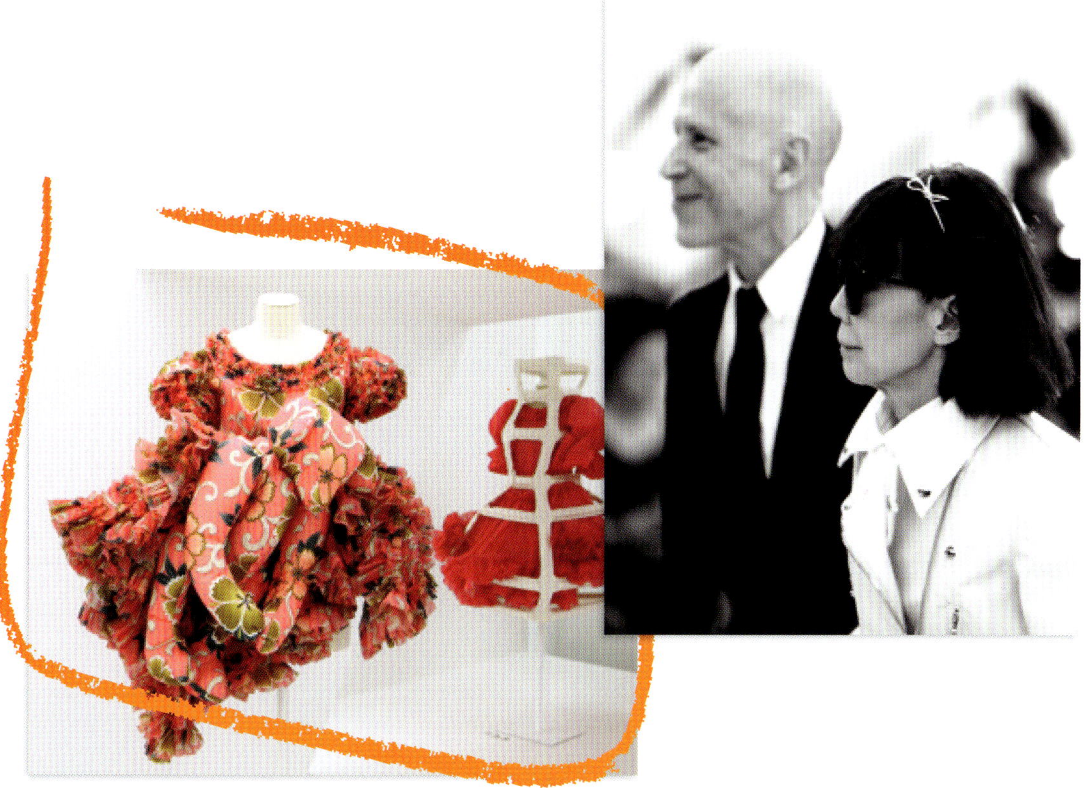

From left: Designs by Rei Kawakubo on display at the *Rei Kawakubo/Comme des Garçons: Art of the In-Between* exhibition at the Metropolitan Museum of Art's Costume Institute in New York, May 1, 2017; Joffe and Kawakubo arriving on the red carpet at the Metropolitan Museum of Art's Costume Institute benefit celebrating the opening of *Rei Kawakubo/Comme des Garçons: Art of the In-Between.*

notions about Western or Eastern cultural or dressmaking traditions. Take, for example, her spring/summer 2014 collection: Kawakubo baffled the fashion press by sharing, "I felt the only way to do something new was to try not to make clothes."[5] Indeed, one of the most famous pieces was a dress that had no openings. It should come as no surprise that Kawakubo's creations have been described as "wearable abstraction."[6]

The antiestablishment spirit of punk permeates through everything she does—even in the way she initially set out to sell her clothes. When she opened her first store in Tokyo, Kawakubo chose not to display the clothes in the window. Instead, she kept them in the back room and brought them out to clients as a means of interacting. In another act of subversion, Kawakubo dispensed with mirrors in her boutique, insisting that "one should buy clothes because of how they make you feel, not how they make you look."[7]

When Kawakubo became renowned on the global scene in 1981, she had nearly one hundred fifty franchised shops across Japan. She had also developed three new lines for the brand, including Tricot, Robe de Chambre, and her menswear label, Homme. Her legendary Paris runway show was followed by the opening of the first CDG boutique in the French capital, and two years later Kawakubo brought her clothing stateside by launching a CDG section in Henri Bendel, a high-end New York department store. Still, Kawakubo's business was almost entirely based in Japan, and she knew she had to hire a commercial director based in Europe in order to expand her reach.

Kawakubo met Joffe in 1987, when he interviewed for a key position in her company. His background was different from hers, which probably piqued Kawakubo's interest. Born in South Africa, Joffe moved to London with his family when he was eight years old. He majored in Asian studies in university and considered traveling to California or India but wound up in Osaka, Japan. While he was there, he spent a lot of time practicing Zen meditation, which led him to consider becoming a monk. By the time he returned to London to work on his Ph.D. in Tibetan and Zen Buddhism, he had also perfected his Japanese. This became extremely useful when his sister started her own knitwear company called Rose Joffe, and Joffe agreed to help her look for distribution in Japan. His entrée into the fashion business was, like Kawakubo's, serendipitous. Kawakubo probably viewed the fact that he didn't have a business degree as an advantage; the straight and narrow path has never been of interest to her. In 1987, Joffe moved to Paris from his London base to join CDG as a commercial director, but the two did not become romantically involved until 1991.

In the seventies and eighties, Kawakubo was linked to another pioneering Japanese artist: Yohji Yamamoto. Kawakubo was in her thirties when she met and fell in love with the iconoclastic designer. There was something glamorous about the two of them together—the golden couple that held the coveted positions of queen and king of the Japanese school of design. They made their Paris debuts the same year; both were challenging the status quo of Western couture. Yamamoto's friend and associate Irène Silvagni has referenced "the enormous competition between Rei and Yohji."[8] The assumption is that the two never collaborated but thrived on a mutual competition. Such are the pitfalls of partners who bump and rub against one another while vying to excel in the same field. The relationship ended in the early nineties amid rumors of Yamamoto's penchant for alcohol, gambling, and women.

Kawakubo uses words sparingly and dislikes explanation and extrapolation, especially on personal matters. But she has often noted in her rare interviews that the best way to know her is through her clothes. When asked about her men's clothing line, Homme, in 1983, she shared, "Homme is my conception of what a man is, subtle, not over-styled like so many men's collections. It's for the kind of man I like working with."[9] Indeed, Joffe appears to be the ascetic disciple of the brand, with a uniform consisting of a white Comme shirt and black Comme suit. His shaven head and slim frame complete the look. He is also often seen wearing a pair of graffitied Dr. Martens boots—a limited-edition Comme collaboration adorned with his wife's message: "My energy comes from my freedom."[10] (Freedom and independence represent another theme in both their relationship and their business.) Within a year of their involvement, Joffe and Kawakubo exchanged matching Cartier rings in the shape of nails during a wedding ceremony in Paris's Hôtel de Ville.

> "There're no borders between people in the mind."
>
> Adrian Joffe

What makes this partnership especially interesting is not only that they hail from different cultures but also that he is ten years her junior and still considered her employee. In a 2014 *Financial Times* interview, Joffe matter-of-factly acknowledged that his wife is his boss. To him, it seems logical: In order for Kawakubo to have autonomy in both her art and her business, she has made sure that she owns almost the entire company. This suits Joffe's temperament and vision just fine. "We have our own special place in the system," he has said.[11] From his point of view, he holds a great deal of responsibility without exposing himself to business risk.

Joffe has reigned as the president of Comme des Garçons International for more than twenty-five years. Relatively early in his tenure, he turned the global company to profitability, which allowed Kawakubo to focus on her work in Tokyo. This meant that she would live and work primarily in her native country, while her husband would reside in Paris, where CDG is headquartered. This is certainly a rare and unique arrangement. But shortly after she had gotten married, Kawakubo noted, "One's lifestyle should not be affected by the formality of marriage."[12] True to this vision, the two have formed a union that is both interconnected yet independent. Joffe visits Japan about ten times a year, and Kawakubo comes to Europe four or five times. In between, they talk on the phone several times a day.

Autonomy is a value that is deeply imbedded in Kawakubo's character—and one that Joffe appreciates and understands well. It is not an understatement to say that Joffe knows Kawakubo most deeply. Aside from being president and CEO of her company, he "acts as the bridge and the translator between the designer and the rest of the world,"[13] as the fashion critic Vanessa Friedman has put it. At her shows, the reclusive Kawakubo does not come onstage to take a bow, nor does she address the press directly. She has been dubbed the "silent oracle of fashion"[14] for a reason. She prefers to whisper her rare utterances to Joffe, who dutifully translates and relays the messages to the public. She knows more English than she lets on. But for the rebellious designer, this seems to be the most convenient way of not explaining herself or her work to anyone.

Kawakubo grew up seeing her mother struggle to express herself fully in a marriage where the husband made all the decisions. When the kids had grown, her mother wanted to work outside of the house, but her husband disapproved. For most Japanese families of that era, the husband's word was beyond reproach. But Kawakubo's mother became a model of defiance and autonomy when she divorced him and landed a teaching position at a high school. It comes as no surprise that Kawakubo's goal in early adulthood was to be self-sufficient. Her fashion business became the vehicle.

Her label, Comme des Garçons (which translates to "like boys"), set out to change fashion's perception of femininity when it launched in 1969. Kawakubo started making clothes, she said in 1982, for a woman "who is independent. One who is not swayed by what her husband thinks. One who can stand by herself."[15] That meant designing garments that were not overtly sexual but rather comfortable and discreet. She borrowed from the tradition of menswear: muted colors, pants, and constructions that were looser, not body-hugging. In recent decades, Kawakubo has also toyed with making her menswear line more androgynous. In one collection, she created a pair of trousers spliced into a skirt. Her refusal to follow the traditional definitions of women's- or menswear has challenged the rigidity of some of these dichotomies. Do women have to accentuate their body shapes to look attractive? Should men wear shoulder-padded suits to appear strong and powerful? She feels that the integration of feminine and masculine in her collections liberates the wearer "to express through clothes both sides of one's character."[16]

Likewise, much of Joffe's creative energy is spent striking a balance between ideals that may seem at odds with one another, such as juggling Kawakubo's extreme creative streak with necessary business strategies. This seems to be par for the course within a brand that, in his own words, "breaks all the rules—but also is part of the industry."[17]

As chief executive officer, Joffe emphasizes innovation in both product design and shopping experience. His innate, out-of-the box retail ingenuity has steered CDG to the pinnacle of success. The brand has grown to encompass several lines and multiple designers, and grosses more than $260 million in annual sales. One of his early strategies was to launch spin-off brands such as Comme des Garçons Shirt, paving the way for a casual-luxury line called Play (known by its logo depicting a heart with eyes). The brand is beloved by many, from teenagers to celebrities such as the actress Diane Kruger and musicians Justin Timberlake, Drake, and Kanye West.

Joffe's main task is to employ Comme's rule-breaking philosophy in creating additional revenue streams. At a time when most luxury brands were building ever more lavish flagships and outposts, Joffe came up with an inventive alternative-retailing model that required very

"I have always been interested in collaboration and [the] potential synergy that could derive from different people."

Rei Kawakubo

little capital investment. A series of pop-ups, called guerilla stores, sprang up in various locations around the globe between 2004 and 2011. According to Joffe's guidelines, these shops had to be run by non-fashion partners who would be permitted to sell dead stock that had been locked up in CDG's warehouses. No more than $2,000 could be spent renovating the spaces, and each of these stores would remain open for only a year. It is amusing to think that fashion fans can't even buy a seasonal "It" bag for $2,000; still, the brand's creative partners made their decoration budgets work. The Berlin store, for example, featured raw cinder blocks and peeling wallpaper, but the unfussy, urban decor gave the ephemeral outpost a chic, edgy appeal. This groundbreaking venture generated robust sales for the company, but when others started to copy the model, Joffe and Kawakubo decided to move on to another concept.

> "Collaborations have no meaning if one plus one does not equal much more than two."
>
> Rei Kawakubo

In 2004, the pair sent ripples across the fashion industry by cofounding one of the world's most forward-thinking retail concepts, Dover Street Market (DSM). In no time, the London outpost had become a must-visit retail destination for many. The space resembles an art installation, but on closer view, one notices that it is actually a store that presents merchandize in artful and whimsical ways. Far from a typical brand flagship, DSM sells CDG products alongside those of emerging designers and established luxury houses. As Joffe said in an interview with *AnOther Magazine,* "It's true that we don't distinguish between men and women, cheap and expensive, new, strong creation and timeless tradition, and we don't dumb down to the lowest common denominator in terms of the desires and aspirations of our customer."[18]

Kawakubo designs all of DSM's common areas, as well as its CDG spaces and some of the art pieces, which include a black skeletal figure of a dinosaur that greets patrons on the second floor. Some of the market's permanent brands also have creative freedom to design their areas on a biannual basis. The founders have once again found a way to straddle the line between their ideas and fashion consumers by throwing out the rule book that dictated how a retail space should look. DSM has come together with the likes of Frieze art fair, the Michael Hoppen Gallery, and the Institute of Contemporary Arts in order to display artworks in the store alongside the merchandise. This concept shop has been so well received that it has expanded to other locations, including Tokyo, Singapore, Beijing, New York, and Los Angeles.

"Collaborations have no meaning if one plus one does not equal much more than two," Kawakubo has said.[19] Indeed, she and Joffe have significantly expanded their reach by working alongside one another. For example, Kawakubo was never interested in fragrance, as she "didn't like the idea of putting on a perfume to seduce somebody," Joffe has said.[20] Besides, there is not a strong perfume culture in Japan. At Joffe's insistence, the pair began exploring different scents. Staying true to their antiestablishment ethos, in 1998 they launched CDG's first "anti-perfume," called Odeur 53, whose notes included "oxygen," "nail polish," "flash of metal," and "wash drying in the wind."[21] Later came a series of fragrances that evoked the smells of "dry clean," "tar," and "garage."[22] In 2014, the musician Pharrell Williams, who is a devotee of CDG, signed on as a collaborator and created his own woodsy scent, called Girl—but, in keeping with the company's gender-fluid philosophy, the fragrance was unisex. By getting into the perfume business, Joffe created an additional $10 million revenue stream for CDG.

Kawakubo and Joffe believe that collaboration, when done with integrity and sincerity, strengthens the brand and keeps moving the business forward. To that end, they have teamed up with other designers and brands such as Nike, Supreme, Converse, Hedi Slimane, Junya Watanabe, and Tao Kurihara over the past couple of decades. At a time when blending creativity and commerce becomes a daunting balancing act for so many design houses, Kawakubo and Joffe have been able to successfully juggle both, inspiring numerous designers along the way.

Who would have thought that an aspiring monk and an aesthetics major, living on different ends of the globe, would one day come together to build one of the most enduringly innovative fashion brands of all time? Perhaps the answer comes from the thoughtful and deliberate CEO of the company himself. Joffe, who is a practicing Buddhist, credited the runaway success of their business to the fact that neither him nor Kawakubo has concerned themselves with boundaries. "There're no borders between people in the mind. We are all together as human beings, as humanity," he said. "Retail should be the same. We don't want to be categorized into one box."[23]

Lou Reed & Laurie Anderson

The Harmonists

This is a love story. This is a love story between two people who found each other during midlife, two adults who were well established in their fields of work, bringing their own history and experience into each other's lives.

Lou Reed has been called one of the most influential figures in rock and roll. First with his group, the Velvet Underground—arguably the most seminal American art-rock band of the twentieth century—and then as a solo artist. The songs "Take a Walk on the Wild Side," "Sweet Jane," and "Heroin" represent a sampling of his gripping lyrical honesty, covering unexplored topics such as domestic abuse, drug addiction, sexual deviance, and the dark underbelly of the New York nightlife scene. As David Bowie once remarked, "[T]he verbal and musical zeitgeist that Reed created—the nature of his lyric writing that had been hitherto unknown in rock. . . gave us the environment in which to put our more theatrical vision."[1] And Reed's influence reached different genres of music, from punk in the seventies, to glam rock in the eighties, to alternative rock in the nineties. He loved sound—not just metal music or rock and roll, but also "nature sounds," he said. "The sound of wind. The sound of love."[2] He loved them all. "Ordered sound," he explained, "is music. . . and my life is music."[3]

But if you were to ask Laurie Anderson, his partner of twenty-one years, she would describe Reed as a writer. In fact, she called him "a writer who sang his words."[4] Some would say that Reed's goal was to marry literature to the vivacity of rock and roll. Indeed, in 1987, he told a *Rolling Stone* reporter, "I've always felt that if you thought of [my work] as a book, then you have the Great American Novel, every record as a chapter. . . It tells you all about me, of growing up in the sixties, seventies, and now the eighties. That's what it was like

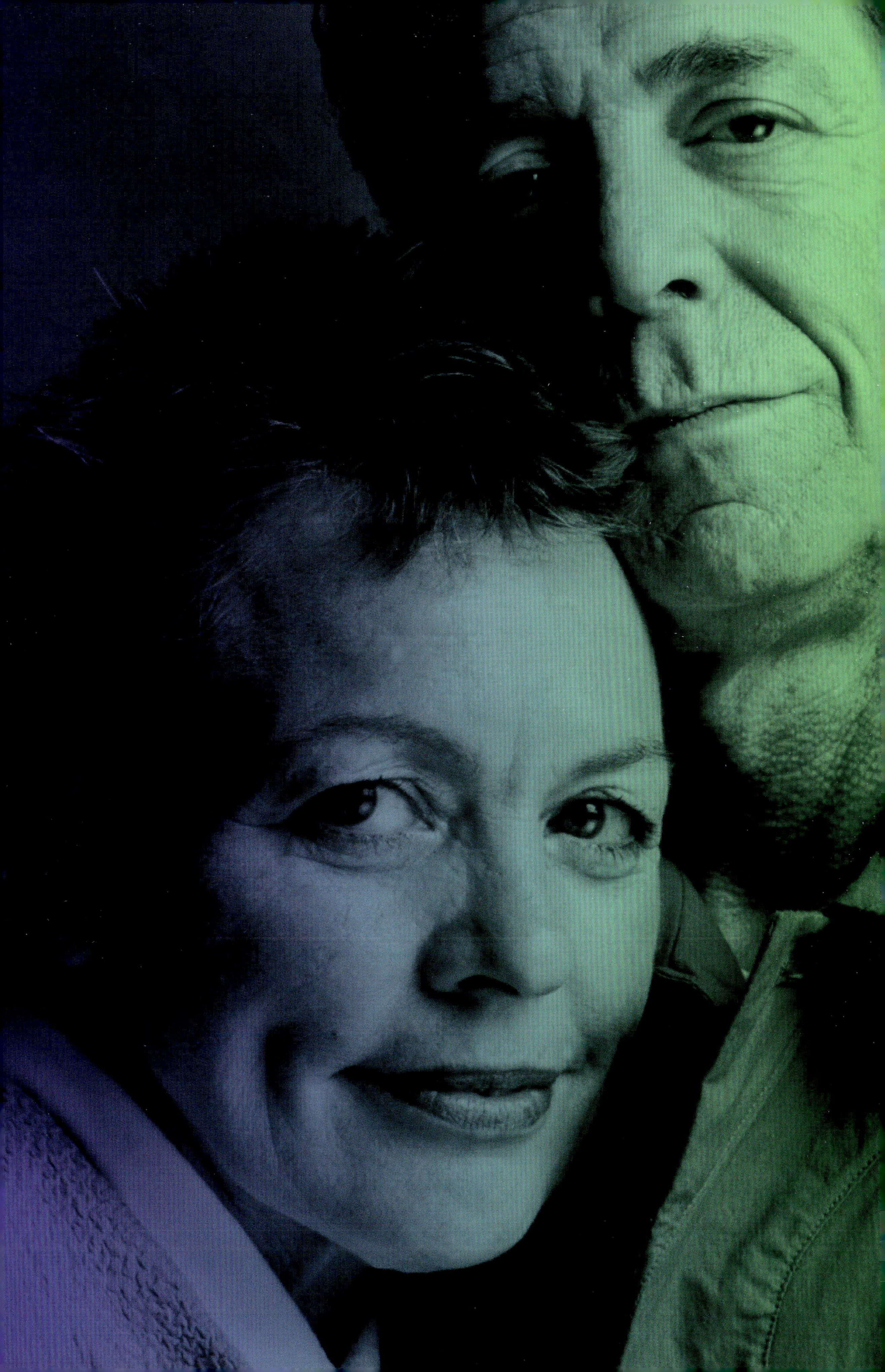

for one person, trying to do the best he could, with all the problems that go along with everybody. Except mine took place in public."[5]

Laurie Anderson also knows a thing or two about writing. She has published six books and, like Reed, has a deep interest in exploring sound. For her debut performance in 1972, she organized some of the locals in Rochester, Vermont, and had them harmonize by honking car and motorcycle horns. Another experiment in sound involved her filling her violin with water so it would "weep" a Tchaikovsky concerto.

When Anderson was honored at the 2016 Hammer Museum gala in Los Angeles, she put on a mesmerizing performance. She drew her bow over a synthesized violin and a whole range of hauntingly beautiful sounds (not necessarily tones you would expect out of a violin) washed over the space. Her calm and perfectly pitched voice cut through the night. She, too, is a master storyteller. She deceptively spins simple, satirical tales: how she wrote a letter to President John F. Kennedy when she was in grade school, or hitchhiked to the North Pole, or stayed in bed for a year. Anderson, as one writer described her, "is deliberate about mixing myth and reality."[6] In her performance art, she is known for electronically distorting her voice to create multiple personalities—some seductive, some robotic, and some menacing. Anderson was the second of eight children, reared in a household full of clamor and noise. It is no accident that in her performances she often chooses to speak in dozens of voices rather than one.

Some of her literary "teachers" included the Beat writer William S. Burroughs and the filmmaker Jean-Luc Godard. The former taught her how to write in the second person, while the latter passed on the lesson that, in his famous words, "a story should have a beginning, a middle, and an end—though not necessarily in that order."[7]

After reading through the transcripts, interviews, and biographies, one begins to question the true sequence of Anderson and Reed's incandescent relationship. Perhaps Reed's passing in 2013 did not mark the end of their union, but rather a transformation to another kind of connection. Perhaps what most people view as a story's conclusion is just the middle. Perhaps bonds can grow deeper, or subtler, in spite of a partner not being physically present.

Reed and Anderson met the way two people do in the best love stories: by chance. Although both were artists living in New York, they met in Munich in 1992 while collaborating on a performance. They were invited to play in John Zorn's Kristallnacht festival, commemorating the 1938 Night of the Broken Glass, and Reed had asked Anderson to read something with his band. Afterward, he told her, "You did that exactly the way I do it!"[8]

Anderson instinctively liked Reed but was not blown over by him in any way. Reed suggested they get together. "Yes! Absolutely! I'm on tour, but when I get back—let's see,

> No kinds of love are better than others.
>
> Lou Reed, "Some Kinda Love"

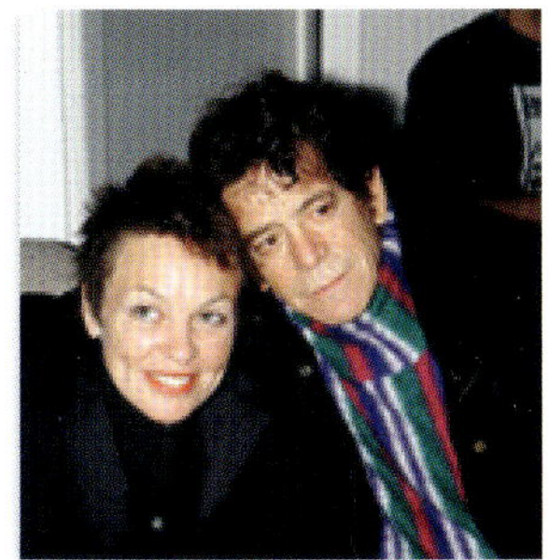

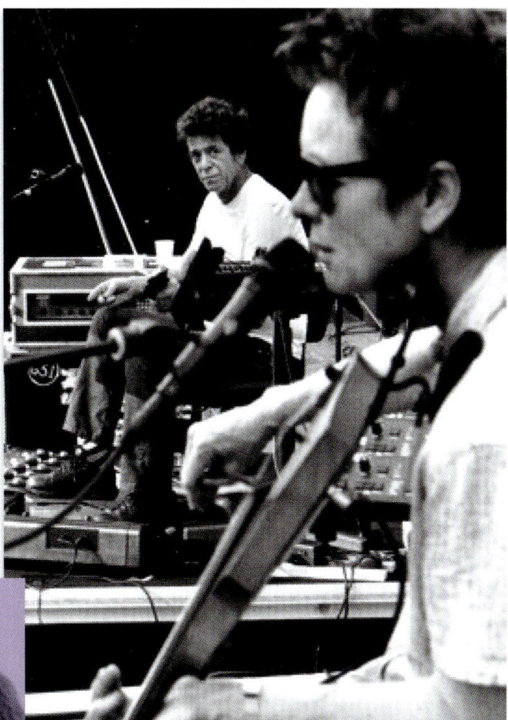

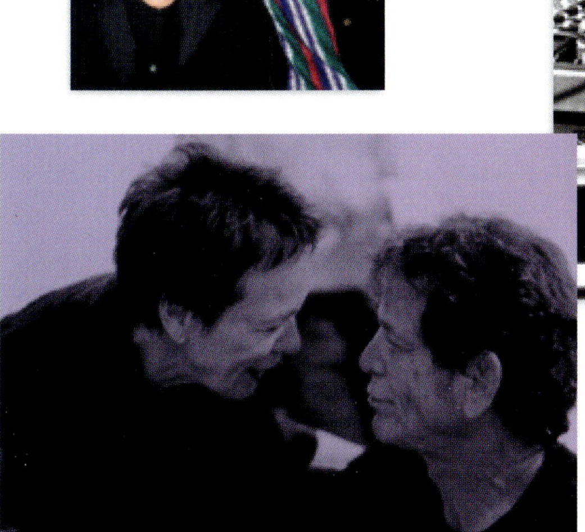

Clockwise from top left: Anderson and Reed backstage at Arts on the Highwire, a benefit concert for the New York Arts Recovery Fund at the Hammerstein Ballroom, January 11, 2002; Reed and Anderson in concert on San Giorgio Maggiore island in Venice, Italy, June 15, 2002; The couple attends an event celebrating Reed's album with the artist Julian Schnabel, *Berlin,* at Steven Kasher Gallery in New York, June 25, 2009.

about four months from now—let's definitely get together," she replied.[9] That she was not hurriedly trying to establish a connection probably made her even more desirable to Reed.

On their first date, they met at the Audio Engineering Society Convention in New York, by the microphones section. They "geeked out,"[10] as she put it, looking at amps, cables, and electronics. Of course, Anderson was not under the impression that they were on a date at all. It was only after they went to a movie, and dinner, and then on a walk that evening that she caught on. Shortly thereafter, the pair became inseparable, collaborating and performing together, while also engaging in civic and environmental activism.

At Reed's memorial in 2013, Anderson shared glimpses into their relationship in her speech. "We talked about love and work, and ambition and sorrow, and vacations and dog training. . . We talked about how to make something beautiful, what to do when you fail, and about how to make something supremely ugly. . . Lou and I talked about music and songwriting. . . We looked for magic, and we went on pilgrimages and went swimming. And we cared for each other when we were sick, and we raised our dogs, Lolabelle and Will. And we invented private worlds with countless crazy characters. We built houses, played music together, did tours," she recounted.[11]

For twenty-one years the two forged a creative partnership that drew from great love and intimacy. "I was a partner in both work and love," Anderson said at the memorial. "I never had a single doubt that we loved each other beyond anything else from the time we first met until the moment he died."[12]

Music entrepreneur Michael Dorf witnessed the early days of their courtship and was struck by Reed's tenderness and the way he always made sure Anderson was taken care of. In his 2017 biography of the rocker, author Anthony DeCurtis expressed a similar sentiment. "In public, Reed was unusually deferential to Anderson, almost boyish in his efforts to be pleasing, like a high school kid trying to learn how to properly behave with his first girlfriend," he wrote.[13] Clips of the couple in a 2003 interview with Charlie Rose show Reed doting on Anderson and gushing, "She does everything: She writes, she paints, she does photography, she sculpts, she's a tech head—there's nothing she can't do."[14]

This kind of behavior was a far cry from Reed's younger years—this wild creature who once dragged a female fan by her hair and pushed her off the stage; this rebellious, confrontational musician from Andy Warhol's Factory. Warhol produced the Velvet Underground's debut album, in which lyrics carry countless references to drug culture and sadomasochism. Reed essentially fired him and released three subsequent records with the band. At the time, the works were not met with commercial success, and Reed left the group in August 1970.

He met David Bowie right after breaking from the Velvet Underground. Bowie produced Reed's second solo album, *Transformer,* and the album's success catapulted Reed into glam-rock stardom. Then came a brief falling out with Bowie, as well. You could say that Reed spent the better part of the seventies shocking and defying expectations. He sported bleached hair, a black muscle shirt, black leather pants, a spiked dog collar, and studded black leather cuffs onstage. The persona he adopted was that of a gender-bending, tough, smart, bad boy.

"Glam rock, androgyny, polymorphic sex—I was right in the middle of it," he said. "Some say I could have been at the head of the class."[15] Rumor had it that his parents had sent a seventeen-year-old Reed to a psychiatric ward to receive twenty-four treatments of electroconvulsive shock therapy (ECT), partly to discourage his homosexual feelings. However, after Reed's passing, his sister, Merrill Reed Weiner, disputed these rumors, sharing that the doctors had recommended ECT to treat his anxiety and other mental health issues.

Well-documented, though, is his four-year relationship with Rachel, a transsexual whom he had met at a club. Reed had been in a methamphetamine haze when he took her to his place. "At the time, I was living with a girl, a crazy blonde lady, and I kind of wanted us all three to live together, but somehow it was too heavy for her. Rachel just stayed on and the girl moved out," he later told the photographer Mick Rock. "Rachel was completely disinterested in who I was and what I did. Nothing could impress her. He'd hardly heard my music and didn't like it all that much when he did."[16]

Reed had true affection for his lover and dedicated his album *Coney Island Baby*—which contains some of his deepest and most sentimental lyrics—to her. Rachel accompanied Reed virtually everywhere. However unconventional the pairing appeared, their life together followed a conventional domestic script: In this and his previous, short-lived first marriage, the role of the other was that of a caretaker and attentive listener. That dynamic was also evident in his relationship with his second wife, Sylvia Morales. They had met in the late seventies, when Morales was in her twenties. Before long, she had moved into the apartment Reed had shared with Rachel.

> "I had gotten to walk with him to the end of the world. Life—so beautiful, painful, and dazzling—does not get better than that."
>
> Laurie Anderson

By the time the eighties rolled around, Reed wanted to extricate himself from his previous life. He married Morales, joined Alcoholics Anonymous, bought a home in rural New Jersey, and recorded the album *Growing Up in Public*—a redemptive tale, with salvation coming through the guise of a female lover.

Morales, he said, "helped me so much in bringing things together and getting rid of certain things that were bad for me, certain people. I don't know what I would have done without her."[17] Indeed, she provided the grounding, support, and stability that Reed had been searching for. But after thirteen years of filling this role, Morales felt exhausted and the marriage suffered.

Transformation. That was a theme in Reed's work. Curious and restless, he experimented, and when he felt ready he would move into another territory. This pattern carried over to his music, as well. And when the sound of his music changed in his ensuing albums, his longtime fans couldn't help but compare it to the standards of the Velvet Underground. Asked about his feelings regarding his fan base's ambivalence toward his musical evolution, he responded, "It's not that I resent it, but I can't pay any attention to that. I mean, there's got to be more to life and more to me than that."[18] Clear-eyed and thoughtful, Reed did not want to get trapped into looking, behaving, or sounding like anyone that Lou Reed didn't want to be.

Hence, one can understand the depth of Reed's attraction to Anderson. She crossed artistic boundaries as a writer, musician, performance artist, and filmmaker and was unconcerned with her work fitting into any known system. As an artist, she has long been admired for her impeccable avant-garde credentials and her signature singularity. In 1980, the runaway success of her song "O Superman" propelled Anderson into mainstream culture. Her recognizable and somewhat androgynous image (a beautiful, fine-boned face framed by cropped, spiked hair) graced popular music magazines and MTV. The eighties brought her recognition in various ways. She was awarded an honorary doctorate from the San Francisco Art Institute and a prestigious Guggenheim Fellowship for Creative Arts in Film. Such honors have only continued throughout her prolific career.

Well established in her own life, Anderson had no interest in assuming the role of a savior or nursemaid to anyone, even Lou Reed. "We didn't have the kind of relationship where the other person has the qualities that you lack, and you try to make a complete person by combining the two of you," Anderson has said.[19] This was a relationship between two adults who wanted to share their most valued attributes with one another.

As evidenced in their duet of "Hang On to Your Emotions," Reed pulled Anderson toward his love of rhythm and blues; likewise, she would nudge him into the avant-garde, experimental scene. They sometimes toured together, with Anderson playing the violin and Reed on the guitar. Their joint performance of Reed's song "I'll Be Your Mirror" is a fitting example of the role each played in holding space for the other. The musician Sarth Calhoun, who toured with the couple, commented on their unusual bond. "It was intense hanging out with them every day, going to lunch with them and then being onstage between them," he said. "It was so delicate, where the slightest breath would affect the music. They understood each other very well, and they both had this great ability to be succinct, so in conversations with them I would always feel like I was rambling on. It was like hanging out with two poets."[20]

"Keep it simple."[21] That was the advice Reed often gave Anderson when critiquing her work. And when she had trouble finishing a record, he would go into the studio and work on it with her. One would think that two artists meddling in each other's work would be a recipe for disaster. But Anderson claimed the process was "so much fun and so intuitive, and it was like it was his own work, because in many ways it was. And the boundaries could be just so fluid."[22]

In 2010, the pair served as the artistic ambassadors to a cultural event in Sydney called Vivid. At a press conference there, a reporter asked how it felt to work together as a married couple. With a deadpan expression, Reed told the reporter that they had been clear about each other's identities for eighteen years, since they met. Pressed to disclose if they would do an album together, he responded, "Laurie does what she does; I do what I do. And when they cross each other, that's a really good thing, but it shouldn't be what we do."[23] His candid response shows how the two consciously maintained certain artistic and personal boundaries.

Of course, like any real love story, there were moments of frustration, especially when one partner acted too needy or felt abandoned. A woman with her own serious ambitions and goals, Anderson was the least compliant of any of Reed's lovers. During their relationship, she kept her Canal Street loft, while he maintained an apartment on West Eleventh Street. That they often lived apart and both traveled extensively was painful for Reed, who clearly felt a need to spend more time with Anderson. Her independence was not meant to unnerve him. And if it ever did, that didn't discourage her from exercising it. Anderson's firm but gentle determination and emotional restraint both unsettled Reed and made him value and respect her. Ultimately, they bought a weekend home in East Hampton, New York, that they regarded as theirs, and joined one another on tours from time to time. With all the traveling, they became each other's home. With all the inevitable pushes and pulls of coupledom, they learned to forgive each other.

One day in the spring of 2008, Anderson was in California, speaking with Reed on the phone. She had been in a reflective mood and began enumerating things she'd always wanted to do but had never done. One was marriage. Reed suggested they get married immediately. So, they both booked flights and met each other the very next day in Boulder, Colorado, where they were wed in a friend's backyard.

With each passing year, their relationship deepened and found new dimensions. Inspired by Anderson's artistic versatility, Reed became interested in photography and published three books of photos. He had been practicing tai chi since the early eighties and introduced

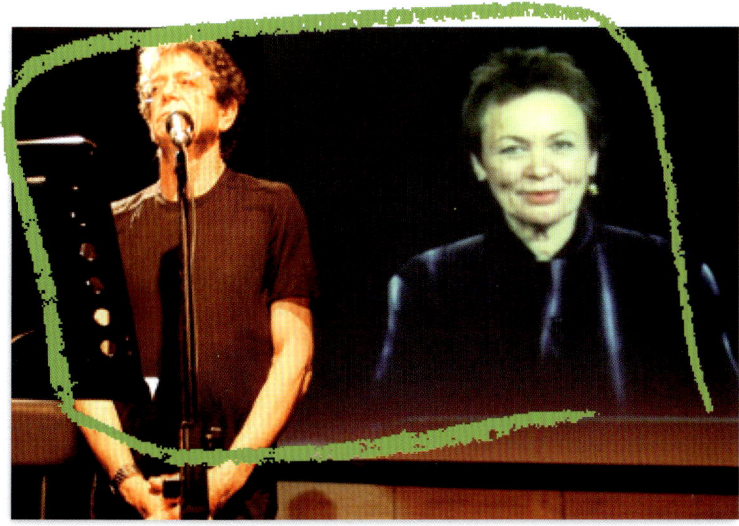

Anderson appears onscreen from Berkeley, California during one of Reed's performances in Barcelona, Spain to read "Amèrica," a poem by Enric Casasses, October 24, 2008.

Anderson to his spiritual discipline, which he was drawn to due to the way in which this martial art explores the relationship between extremes. "When I saw that combination of grace and power, the fast and the soft, the yin and the yang, that's what I'd been looking for," he said.[24] Anderson, a meditator and a Buddhist, introduced Reed to Yongey Mingyur Rinpoche, a renowned Tibetan Buddhist master. Both became Mingyur Rinpoche's students, and Reed would go on to release an ambient album of electronic mediation music titled *Hudson River Wind Meditations* in 2007.

As Reed grew older, he began exploring Judaism—the faith he was born into. In the seventies, Reed would walk onstage with a swastika shaved into his hair and hurl anti-Semitic comments at others. "I've certainly been really difficult in the past, in a lot of ways, or extremely temperamental," he later reflected. "But that's because I was beset, and I didn't have it together."[25] By the 2000s, Reed would take part in Seders to celebrate Passover and once visited his relatives in Israel while on tour with Anderson.

During Reed's final years, when his health was deteriorating, Anderson canceled her projects and stopped traveling so she could take care of him. At first, it was the treatments for hepatitis C that made him ill. But then he was diagnosed with liver cancer. He received a liver transplant that had him feeling better at first, but soon his body failed. The night before his death, the couple stayed up talking. "Take me into the light," Reed said to Anderson[26]—an apt request for his final journey with his partner of twenty-one years. Those would be his last words.

What is striking about Anderson is that she is reflective by nature; she digs deeper to understand even the unknowable. What does death mean, and what is replaced in the absence of a life partner? In a poignant tribute she penned for *Rolling Stone,* Anderson shared that watching Reed pass away in her arms, his eyes open as his hands did the water-flowing twenty-one form of tai chi, was a life-changing experience. "So much of life can't be captured. . . [Y]ou can't hold on to a lot of things," she wisely said.[27]

"I had gotten to walk with him to the end of the world," Anderson wrote. "Life—so beautiful, painful, and dazzling—does not get better than that. And death? I believe that the purpose of death is the release of love."[28]

And what comes next, following the death of a loved one? According to Tibetan Buddhists, those who have recently died spend forty-nine days in a transitional realm called the bardo, through which the living can still communicate with them. For forty-nine days, Anderson gathered friends to share their thoughts about Reed, and by the end of the ceremony, she felt that she had learned more about life, energy, and transformation than she had in her

> How strange, exciting, and miraculous that we can change each other so much, love each other so much through our words and music and our real lives.
>
> Laurie Anderson

previous sixty-six years. "Living in the present, I see him everywhere—and the way his life has turned to energy everywhere I look," she said. "I see it in nature, and I see it in the things he loved. I see his exuberance, and sometimes I hear his over-the-top, insane laugh. . . And I finally see how people turn into light, and into music, and eventually into other people, and how fluid boundaries are."[29] Transformation—that was Reed's gift.

Even three years after Reed's passing, Anderson still felt him as a living presence. "I learn from him every day now," she said. "I have since he died. Every single day I see something in my house that he put there for me, a note or a piece of paper or a book that he had written in, or one of his shirts. He's very, very present for me. It's not like, 'Oh, my dead husband.'"[30] Sometimes she felt as if he were looking out through her eyes. It may sound strange, but to Anderson it made perfect sense "Ah. Of course," she said. "You become so much a part of someone else, and they're a part of you."[31]

In a touching tribute to her lost love, Anderson propped up several of Reed's guitars against a group of amps in a conceptual musical-art piece entitled *Lou Reed Drones,* letting the sound resonate for days. And she has painstakingly gone through Reed's extensive personal archive and arranged for it to be available for free at the New York Public Library.

"It's inspiring that you can't hold on to a lot of things—you can't hold on to the most important things," Anderson conceded.[32] Even the memory of a loved one only "lives in the mind and dies with it," she added.[33] Feeling the utter transience and fragility of life, Anderson said there is only one thing to do: "Make something beautiful."[34] She continues making films and art, performing, and working on books. The virtual reality film she made with the mixed-media artist Hsin-Chien Huang, *La Camera Insabbiata (Chalkroom),* won an award at the Venice Film Festival in 2017.

Alejandro & Pascale Jodorowsky

The Alchemists

In 2013, the legendary filmmaker Alejandro Jodorowsky learned that the International Astronomical Union had named an asteroid after him. The three-mile-wide celestial rock, known as 261690 Jodorowsky, orbits between Mars and Jupiter, and serves as an apt metaphor for Alejandro's otherworldly career.

The extraordinary life of the Jewish, Chilean-born artist has led him down various paths: Alejandro has directed plays, acted, and written comic books, poetry, and novels. He has explored psychology and alchemy, and he studied under a Zen Buddhist monk for five years. He also invented the concept of "psychomagic"—a form of psychotherapy that proposes to treat the unconscious—and dispenses life advice to his nearly two million followers on Twitter. He once remarked that people often reverentially refer to him as "a master." "No, I am not a master," he said. "I am an eternal disciple."[1]

If you wish to meet Alejandro in person, you can venture to a café near his Paris apartment on Wednesdays and find him giving free tarot readings. He uses the Tarot de Marseille deck and follows the method of Philippe Camoin, a descendent of the family that printed and preserved the traditions of that deck for centuries. Camoin's readings take into account the mysterious web of synchronicity—a concept first developed by the psychologist Carl Jung, who maintained that events that seemingly have no causal relationship can be meaningfully related. So, was it synchronicity that Alejandro would meet the love of his life, Pascale Montandon, at one of his tarot readings? "He looked at me, and I understood immediately that he knew me, my soul, and I felt like my life was changed," Pascale later said of the experience.[2]

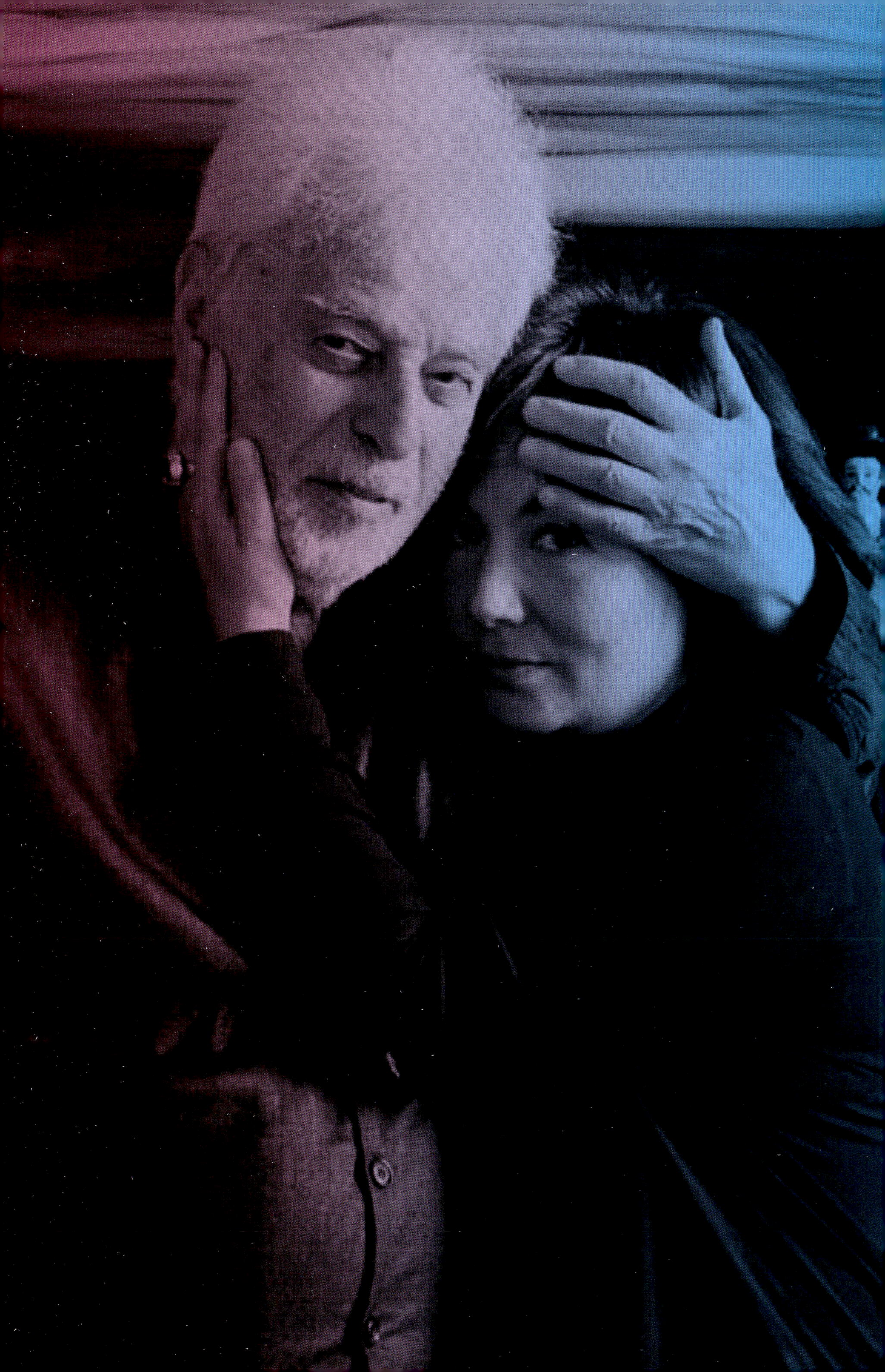

Alejandro had been married twice before. His prior unsuccessful relationships, he believes, were due to him repeating and reliving his emotionally arid, primal relationship with his mother. "My specialty was to be a lover of women whose neuroses prevented them from loving me," he said in an interview.[3] He had prophetically told his children, "Today I suffer with your mother, but later, perhaps at the beginning of my old age, I will find the woman of my dreams, a Vietnamese with whom, full of happiness, I will finish my lifetime."[4] When, at seventy-six, he began a relationship with Pascale, who was Vietnamese and forty-three years his junior, his children were not the least bit surprised.

It is as if Alejandro's life and experiences conspired to find him a partner with subtle Eastern sensibilities and a shared commitment to creativity. He has called Pascale his "immense love" and "the half of my soul"[5]—descriptions that this whimsical metaphysician doesn't take lightly. "I spent many years of my life immersed in esoteric mysticism. Torah, gospels, Hinduism, Sufism, Taoism, Buddhism, etc. In all these disciplines I found priests and sacred men who, like my father, excluded women from their spiritual life. But I, because of that lack of emotional relationship with my mother, had a torturous thirst for love," he said in an e-mail. "One day, in an alchemy book I could see something that liberated my soul. . . In *The Silent Book of Alchemy* it is affirmed that an alchemist does not perform the Great Work if he does not work accompanied by a woman who is at the same spiritual level."[6]

After their fabled tarot-card meeting, the two maintained a friendship for over a year while Alejandro waited for his ex-wife to move out. Only then did Alejandro and Pascale officially begin their relationship, and five years later they married. "I was not a half anymore," Alejandro later said of their union. "I was two who were one."[7]

Many psychologists believe that similarities in background breed familiarity and attraction within couples. Pascale and Alejandro, at first glance, cannot be more different than one another. They share few commonalities in terms of age, experience, family situation, native language, culture, gender, race, nationality, and religion. However, they forged a union out of something much stronger: a deep love for one another, and a mutual desire to live for—and through—their art.

Ever since Pascale was a child, she had a precise and unwavering vision for her artistic and personal life. "For me, art was my religion—it still is. . . I wasn't interested in seduction, but I was guided to find true love with Alejandro in order to completely realize myself," she shared in an e-mail.[8] She was born in France to two Eurasian parents: One grandmother was Cambodian, the other Vietnamese, and her grandfathers were both French. When she studied art, she found herself removed from the typical Western style; instead, she used her

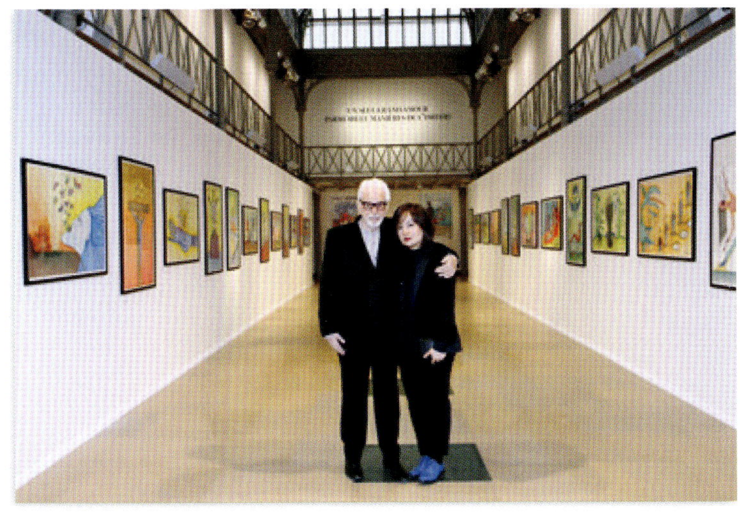

Alejandro and Pascale Jodorowsky attend the *pascALEjandro: L'Androgyne Alchimique* exhibition opening at the Galerie Azzedine Alaïa in Paris, April 27, 2017.

creativity as a vehicle to discover her true identity. Through that search, she has developed her talents as a photographer, painter, and stage and costume designer.

Alejandro was born to Ukrainian Jewish parents in Tocopilla, Chile, in 1929. The reorientation of identity has also been a part of his life's journey. "In Bolivia I was a Russian. In Chile I was a Jew," he has said. "In Paris I was a Chilean. In Mexico I was French. And, in America, I am a Mexican."[9] Alejandro's father was an abusive, authoritarian man who ran a shop with his emotionally stifled wife. It is said that Alejandro's mother became pregnant when her husband beat and then raped her, suspecting she had been flirting with a customer. His parents wanted him to become a doctor, and when he strayed from that path, he was racked with anxiety. However, he felt that being an artist was in his blood. In his early twenties, he sought refuge in the theater and led an avant-garde performance group with thirty members. He left for Paris at the age of twenty-three and trained under the legendary mime Marcel Marceau. Less than a decade later, he traversed the Atlantic again to settle in Mexico, where he studied with a Buddhist monk. In addition to his Zen practice, he directed more than one hundred plays and stirred up controversy, both with a comic strip that he wrote and with his first feature film, *Fando y Lis,* which instigated riots and was banned in Mexico.

Alejandro's psychedelic and ultraviolent Western, *El Topo,* released in the early seventies, blended Eastern spirituality and European surrealism. It was this film that solidified him as a countercultural icon. Dennis Hopper was so bowled over by *El Topo,* he asked Alejandro to recut his next film. John Lennon saw the movie several times and persuaded his manager, Allen Klein, to buy its distribution rights. Alejandro's subsequent friendship with Lennon and his partner, Yoko Ono, helped him immeasurably in getting his next film, *Holy Mountain,* financed. For that project, the iconoclastic filmmaker cast a cadre of gender-fluid actors whom he had discovered at the New York nightclub Max's Kansas City. The 1973 movie—considered a surrealist masterpiece—still exerts an influence on pop culture. The video for Beyoncé's song "Formation" and the set design for Kanye West's *Yeezus* tour both drew inspiration from *Holy Mountain*'s imagery. However, Alejandro had a falling out with Klein that led to his two most famous films disappearing from circulation for thirty years. Many people thought they were lost forever. Alejandro is not bitter, though. "[Klein] didn't kill my pictures," he told Tara Brady of *The Irish Times*. "*Avatar* makes hundreds of millions of dollars and after three months no one can remember it. People can remember things from my pictures forty years after they've seen them."[10]

Alejandro would get burned again trying to make a film adaptation of Frank Herbert's science-fiction novel *Dune*. He spent two years in preproduction, creating more than three thousand storyboards; he signed on Pink Floyd and the French prog-rock band Magma to provide the soundtrack; he assembled an all-star cast consisting of Mick Jagger, Orson Welles, and Salvador Dalí (who insisted on a salary of $100,000 per minute of screen time). However,

> "When you find love, real love, it's like a catastrophe, like a tsunami. Like an earthquake, because all your individuality, all what you believed you are, it's breaking. And you are completely another person. You never know what you were."
>
> Alejandro Jodorowsky

the film was never made. Alejandro has no regrets about that, either. "[I]f I had made *Dune*, I would have been trapped in big movies," he has said. "Instead, I get to make comic books. I am very happy about what I did."[11] In his wildly prolific career, Alejandro has produced forty books and eighty comics, various live-theater performances and exhibitions of his drawings, and has conducted tarot courses. But his biggest and most profound work came later in his life. According to esoteric texts, an alchemist can't accomplish the magnum opus without having known true love.

For more than twenty years, Alejandro did not make any movies; he says that the industry's commercial goals were a major deterrent. He credits his relationship with Pascale—"the one that arose in me the miracle that is love," as he has called her[12]—for his recent return to filmmaking. "I don't remember my mother touching me, and not even my father. They didn't touch me," Alejandro said in 2014. "I think I learned to be happy with caresses at seventy years old. I find a woman I love now and I make a movie with feelings."[13]

He took a leap and created *The Dance of Reality* in collaboration with his wife. The film represented the first in his proposed trilogy of cinematic memoirs. Alejandro wrote and directed it, while Pascale designed the costumes and photographed the shoot. Through making a film about his childhood in Tocopilla, Alejandro was attempting to practice "psychomagic" on himself by reconciling his wounded parental relationships and his difficult past. The movie he wrote reimagined his early childhood through the eyes of his older self. As he sees it, memory is a point of view that can be altered by retelling the stories from a different perspective. That shift in viewpoint can, in turn, empower and heal us in unexpected ways.

In the case of *The Dance of Reality,* Alejandro set out to give his stifled mother a voice, both literally and figuratively. She had dreamed of becoming an opera singer, so Alejandro cast a Chilean soprano to play her and sing her lines. As a child, he had always been terrified of his bullying father. Yet as an adult looking back, he was able to inject his father's character—who was played by his son Brontis—with a sense of humanity. For Alejandro, this endeavor was not about making cinema; in fact, on the movie's set, he told his crew, "This is not a film. This is the healing of my soul."[14] Brontis conceded that the process healed their "family psyche."[15] Through his role and his on-camera interactions with the young Alejandro character, Brontis came to understand how much his father had grown over the decades. Interestingly, Alejandro seemed to have gained a deeper understanding of Brontis through the experience, as well.

Knowing all too well that working on the film would be a challenging and emotional venture for her husband, Pascale made herself available as a steady source of support. What was Alejandro like on the set? "With me in the private life, I know the very delicate person that he is," Pascale has shared, "but in shooting, he's terrible! Terrible! Everybody scares. He knows what he wants and says it very clearly, so people who are not secure take this like an aggression."[16]

After completing the movie, Alejandro was unsure of how the public would respond to it. Nothing could have prepared the silver-haired filmmaker for the reception he received following *The Dance of Reality*'s premiere at the Cannes Film Festival: He was greeted with one of the event's longest-lasting standing ovations. Nor had he ever expected that Tocopilla would honor him with a Distinguished Son of the City award.

Alejandro picked up the story of his youth again to make his next psycho-memoir, *Endless Poetry.* He wanted someone close to his heart to play a youthful version of himself, and he didn't need to look far: His youngest son, Adan, took on the role. The eighty-seven-year-old filmmaker appears onscreen as well, to offer insight and console his younger self. The effect is as touching as it is mesmerizing. During a tense moment in the film, when the young

> "An alchemist does not perform the Great Work if he does not work accompanied by a woman who is at the same spiritual level."
>
> Alejandro Jodorowsky

Alejandro confronts his tyrannical father, he finally experiences a sense of healing for the first time. "What I never could say in eighty, eighty-six years of my life: 'I forgive you.' I did it there, crying," he explained in 2017.[17] Adan also observed that, once Alejandro had cleared his unresolved feelings toward his father, he as a son was also able to forge a deeper connection to Alejandro. "After the movie, I was another person," Adan has shared. "In fact, I shaved my hair and I went to the desert in Tacoma and I buried my hair in the desert, and then I started to do a lot of ceremonies, and then I had a kid, and my life changed completely."[18]

This powerful series of psycho-memoirs has indeed been Alejandro's magnum opus, where he slowly peeled away the pain and the societal and childhood conditionings that had kept him at bay, away from his most essential self. Indeed, the driving force of Alejandro's journey has been the search for himself—and showing others that life's biggest lesson is to learn how to connect with one's soul. Pascale pays the highest tribute to their relationship by calling it a vehicle for her to become a deeper version of herself. When he released *Endless Poetry* at age eighty-eight, Alejandro still had that vitality and intense curiosity about discovering the infinite universes within him. "I'm searching. I am beginning. I feel, really, I am beginning," he declared.[19]

At a 2017 screening of *Endless Poetry,* the trim and debonair filmmaker, with his full head of white hair and his lively disposition, didn't seem eighty-eight. Alejandro is clearly happy to share the spotlight with Pascale. Onstage, throughout the night, he held his artist wife close and recognized her contributions. Pascale had designed the costumes for this movie, but more importantly, she collaborated closely with her husband in rendering the film with color tonalities that had rarely been seen in cinema. The two artists painstakingly reviewed every image and worked with a technician to add hyper-saturated colors (and, in some cases,

Pascale and Alejandro Jodorowsky arrive for a screening of the film *Only God Forgives* presented at the Cannes Film Festival, May 22, 2013.

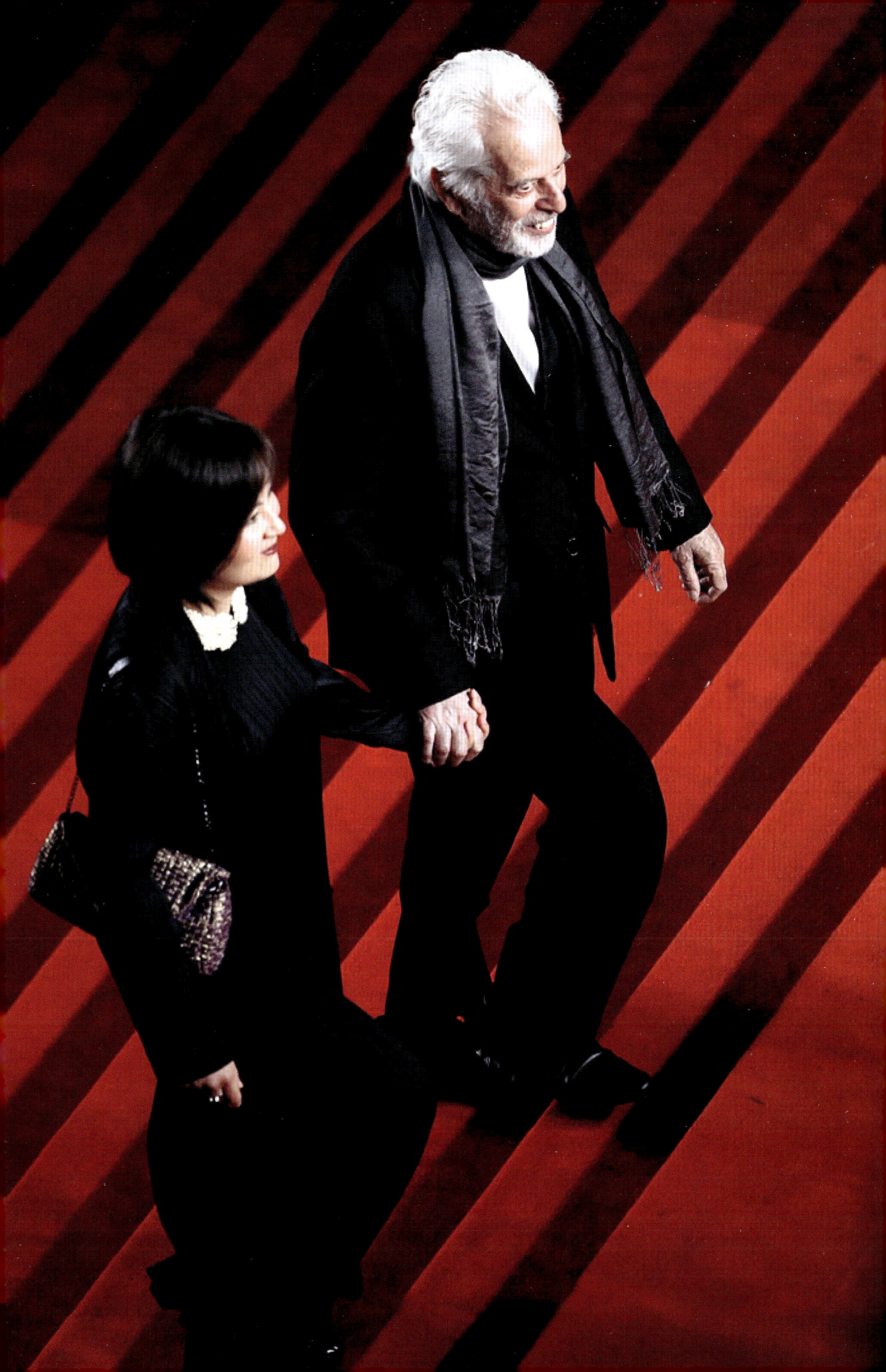

light and shadows) to each frame. The result is striking and poetic, but the approach served a symbolic purpose, as well. "I really like to see that we can color the past," Alejandro said. "I started to do that in my memories."[20]

Pascale, an experienced painter, took the lead in coloring the images to bring Alejandro's vision to a higher level. In an interview, she described their collaboration as intuitive, spontaneous, and harmonious, saying, "It's complete trust; there is no hierarchy and there is no dichotomy."[21] "And no discussion," Alejandro chimed in, comparing their artistic process to the act of conceiving of a child. "When you make love, a man gives a part of his body and a woman receives it in her body, but you don't tell the parts what to make."[22] This collaborative effort they credit to their creative entity, which they call pascALEjandro.

The couple views pascALEjandro as a union of two fertile minds whose unique identities vanish in favor of a third being. They consider pascALEjandro to be one, single artist—the fusion of their feminine and masculine selves. It is under this moniker that they have shown their paintings. It started by chance. Alejandro had never thought of himself as an illustrator, but with Pascale, his drawing became a means of seduction. "I draw only for her," he has said. "I always had fear a young lover would come and take her, so I said I need to seduce her with something."[23] After his wife discovered his graceful drawings, Alejandro continued to do more and asked her to color them. Pascale had previously painted in black and white, but through pascALEjandro she discovered a color scale that she never would have used in her personal work. In this shared imaginative space, both have harnessed their uncharted talents to produce art. Their first body of work, aptly called *Yin and Yang/Yin,* started as a mere exploration. Friends encouraged them to exhibit, and the duo ended up presenting their paintings at the Museum of Modern Art in Paris.

Their collaborative paintings express a powerful symbolic nature. One particular image, called *The Essential Point,* shows a man and a winged woman floating in midair against a blue background, their tongues meeting and generating a spark—almost mimicking the spark seen in Michelangelo's *The Creation of Adam.* PascALEjandro's works are strange, otherworldly, magical, and pack an emotional charge. The art critic Donatien Grau has written that pascALEjandro uses art as "a tool to improve our awareness of things."[24] The goal of this unique collaboration is to create meaningful art that goes beyond the couple's independent selves, yet finds its way to the heart of one another.

Time is precious for this couple: Alejandro is now ninety years old and filming the third installment of his autobiographical film series with his wife by his side. There is no denying that there lies a great difference in age between the two, but that apparently does not bother either of them in the least. Alejandro believes that, in our innermost cores, humans don't have names or ages. Consequently, aging does not seem to upset him much. Through his

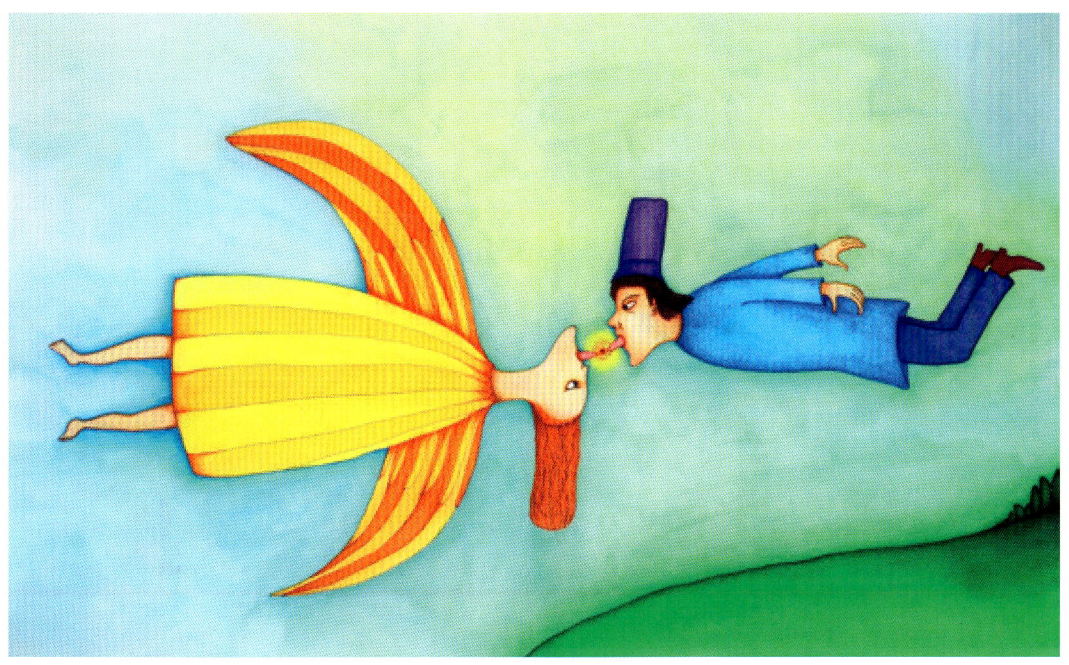

The Essential Point, 2016, by pascALEjandro, a collaborative artistic entity formed by Pascale and Alejandro Jodorowsky.

spiritual practice as a Buddhist, he appears to have gained a healthy perspective toward the passage of time. "In a certain essential way, progress in life is learning to die, for which it is necessary to grow old," he explained in an interview. "Old age allows one to let go of personal selfishness in order to arrive at the transpersonal. Old age is not a disease, it is an advance toward freedom."[25]

One quickly realizes that this couple's profound connection transcends nationality, religion, and age. Pascale has said that, even before knowing Alejandro, she had a clear vision of falling in love with a wise, older man. "It's as if all the time I were living with an empty seat by my side, knowing that one day I would recognize sitting in it the object of my love," she said in 2014.[26]

For Pascale, it was of utmost importance to be with a man who expressed the highest level of artistry and who possessed a depth and spirituality that she had always yearned for in a partner. Such qualities, she knew, could only be present in a man who had many decades of life experience. Pascale is grounded enough not to paint an overly romantic or rosy picture of their coupledom. By no means does she feel that Alejandro is perfect; he is possessive, he has a fiery temperament, and he can sometimes be intense and excessive. Yet she claims that, even with all these attributes, he is perfectly suited to her.

She feels herself to be lucky beyond measure. A love like theirs, Pascale believes, happens once in a lifetime. "For me, this is him and this is forever," she insisted in an e-mail.[27] Alejandro, in turn, said in his typically casual but poignant manner: "I'm Pascale's first man, and she's my last woman: That's the truth of it."[28]

“Many ideas grow better when transplanted into another mind than the one where they sprang up.”

Oliver Wendell Holmes, *Former Associate Justice of the U.S. Supreme Court*

“No matter how brilliant your mind or strategy, if you're playing a solo game, you'll always lose out to a team.”

Reid Hoffman, *co-founder, LinkedIn*

“What counts in making a happy marriage is not so much how compatible you are, but how you deal with incompatibility.”

Leo Tolstoy, *author*

"It is not a lack of love, but a lack of friendship that makes unhappy marriages."

Friedrich Nietzsche, *philosopher*

"In my mind, marriage is a spiritual partnership and union in which we willingly give and receive love, create and share intimacy, and open ourselves to be available and accessible to another human being in order to heal, learn and grow."

Iyanla Vanzant, *inspirational speaker*

"Shared joy is a double joy; shared sorrow is half a sorrow."

Swedish proverb

Bibliography

INTRODUCTION

Bazelon, Emily. "The Place of Women on the Court." *New York Times Magazine,* July 7, 2009. https://www.nytimes.com/2009/07/12/magazine/12ginsburg-t.html.

Healy, Nan Savage. *Toni Wolff and C. G. Jung: A Collaboration.* Los Angeles: Tiberius Press, 2017.

"HeForShe." *Wikipedia,* last modified November 26, 2018. https://en.wikipedia.org/wiki/HeForShe.

Myers, Jack. *The Future of Men: Masculinity in the Twenty-First Century.* Oakland: Inkshares, 2016.

Sanford, John A. *The Invisible Partners.* Mahwah, NJ: Paulist Press, 1980.

LOU ANDREAS-SALOMÉ AND RAINER MARIA RILKE

Andreas-Salomé, Lou. *The Erotic.* Translated by John Crisp. Oxford: Routledge, 2017.

Corbett, Rachel. *You Must Change Your Life: The Story of Rainer Maria Rilke and Auguste Rodin.* New York: W. W. Norton, 2017.

Lobo, Carmen. "Letters to Lou Andreas Salome—Rainer Maria Rilke." *Art and Thoughts,* November 11, 2013. https://artandthoughts.fr/2013/11/11/letters-to-lou-andreas-salome-rainer-maria-rilke.

Popova, Maria. "Rilke's Love Letters." *Brain Pickings,* June 6, 2012. https://www.brainpickings.org/index.php/2012/06/06/rilke-salome-love-letters.

"Rainer Maria Rilke and Lou Andreas-Salomé: The Correspondence." Briefly Noted, *The New Yorker,* July 31, 2006. https://www.newyorker.com/magazine/2006/07/31/rainer-maria-rilke-and-lou-andreas-salome-the-correspondence.

Rilke, Rainer Maria. *Letters of Rainer Maria Rilke 1892–1910.* Translated by Jane Bannard Greene and M. D. Herter Norton. New York: W. W. Norton, 1945. Accessed online as "Full Text of 'Letters of Rainer Maria Rilke 1892–1910.'" https://archive.org/stream/lettersofrainerm030932mbp/lettersofrainerm030932mbp_djvu.txt.

Rilke, Rainer Maria, and Lou Andreas-Salomé. *Rilke and Andreas-Salomé: A Love Story in Letters.* Translated by Edward Snow and Michael Winkler. New York: W. W. Norton, 2008. Excerpted in "13 December (1926): Rainer Maria Rilke to Lou Andreas Salomé." *The American Reader.* theamericanreader.com/13-december-1926-rainer-maria-rilke-to-lou-andreas-salome.

Vickers, Julia. *Lou von Salomé: A Biography of the Woman Who Inspired Freud, Nietzsche, and Rilke.* Jefferson, NC: McFarland, 2008.

TONI WOLFF AND CARL JUNG

Bair, Deirdre. *Jung: A Biography.* New York: Back Bay Books, 2003.

Healy, Nan Savage. *Toni Wolff and C. G. Jung: A Collaboration.* Los Angeles: Tiberius Press, 2017.

"The Red Book." W. W. Norton and Company product page, accessed April 25, 2019. https://books.wwnorton.com/books/detail.aspx?ID=12004.

SALVADOR DALÍ AND GALA

Ansen, David. "The Death of Shock Cinema." *Newsweek,* October 15, 2009. https://www.newsweek.com/death-shock-cinema-80945.

Dalí, Salvador. *50 Secrets of Magic Craftsmanship.* Translated by Haakon M. Chevalier. New York: Dover Publications, 1992. First published 1948 by Dial Press, New York. Apple e-book.

———. *The Secret Life of Salvador Dalí.* Translated by Haakon M. Chevalier. New York: Dover Publications, 1993. First published 1942 by Dial Press, New York. E-book.

Gibson, Ian. *The Shameful Life of Salvador Dalí.* London: Faber and Faber, 1997.

Mann, Jon. "How the Surrealist Movement Shaped the Course of Art History." *Artsy,* September 23, 2016. https://www.artsy.net/article/artsy-editorial-what-is-surrealism.

McGirk, Tim. *Wicked Lady: Salvador Dalí's Muse.* London: Hutchinson, 1989.

Stanska, Zuzanna. "Dali and Gala—The Love Story." *Daily Art Magazine,* February 14, 2017. www.dailyartmagazine.com/dali-gala-great-love-story.

Thurlow, Clifford. *Sex, Surrealism, Dalí, and Me: The Memoirs of Carlos Lozano.* London: Yellow Bay Books, 2011.

SERGE GAINSBOURG AND JANE BIRKIN

Adams, Tim. "A Charmed Life." *The Guardian,* October 28, 2007. https://www.theguardian.com/music/2007/oct/28/worldmusic.paris.

Anderson, Darran. *Serge Gainsbourg's Histoire de Melody Nelson.* London: Bloomsbury Academic, 2013.

Kaplan, Ilana. "Jane Birkin Brings Serge Gainsbourg Back to the New York Stage." Vanities, *Vanity Fair* online, February 1, 2018. https://www.vanityfair.com/style/2018/02/jane-birkin-birkin-gainsbourg-le-symphonique.

Morse, Erik. "How Jane Birkin Became the Muse to France's Coolest Man." *Esquire* online, January 26, 2016. https://www.esquire.com/entertainment/movies/news/a41491/jane-birkin-serge-gainsbourg.

Robinson, Lisa. "The Secret World of Serge Gainsbourg." *Vanity Fair,* November 2007.

Sethi, Anita. "Jane Birkin: My Family Values." *The Guardian,* January 18, 2013. https://www.theguardian.com/lifeandstyle/2013/jan/18/jane-birkin-my-family-values.

Simmons, Sylvie. *Serge Gainsbourg: A Fistful of Gitanes: Requiem for a Twister.* London: Helter Skelter, 2001.

Skidmore, Maisie. "The Secret Stories of Jane Birkin and Serge Gainsbourg." *AnOther* online, November 5, 2015. www.anothermag.com/fashion-beauty/7996/the-secret-stories-of-jane-birkin-and-serge-gainsbourg.

Verlant, Gilles. *Gainsbourg: The Biography.* Translated by Paul Knobloch. Los Angeles: TamTam Books, 2012.

JEAN-PAUL SARTRE AND SIMONE DE BEAUVOIR

Appignanesi, Lisa. "Did Simone de Beauvoir's Open 'Marriage' Make Her Happy?" *The Guardian,* June 10, 2005. https://www.theguardian.com/world/2005/jun/10/gender.politicsphilosophyandsociety.

Colman, Dan. "Lovers and Philosophers—Jean-Paul Sartre and Simone de Beauvoir Together in 1967." *Open Culture,* January 24, 2013. www.openculture.com/2013/01/jeanpaul_sartre_and_simone_de_beauvoir_together_in_1967.html.

De Beauvoir, Simone. *Force of Circumstance.* Translated by Richard Howard. Harmondsworth, U.K.: Penguin, 1985. English translation first published 1963 by Putnam.

———. *The Second Sex.* Translated by Constance Borde and Sheila Malovany-Chevallier. New York: Vantage, 2011. First published 1949 by Éditions Gallimard, Paris. PDF e-book.

Jameson, Frederick. "Sartre in Search of Flaubert." *New York Times,* December 27, 1981. https://www.nytimes.com/1981/12/27/books/sartre-in-search-of-flaubert.html.

Menand, Louis. "Stand by Your Man." *The New Yorker,* September 18, 2005. https://www.newyorker.com/magazine/2005/09/26/stand-by-your-man.

Moorehead, Caroline. "A Talk With Simone de Beauvoir." *New York Times,* June 2, 1974.

O'Doherty, Gemma. "Simone de Beauvoir Was the Mother of Feminism. . . and on Her Centenary, All They Write About Is Her Scandalous Love Life." *Independent.ie,* January 12, 2008. https://www.independent.ie/woman/celeb-news/simone-de-beauvoir-was-the-mother-of-feminism-and-on-her-centenary-all-they-write-about-is-her-scandalous-love-life-26344054.html.

Rowley, Hazel. *Tête à Tête: The Lives and Loves of Simone de Beauvoir and Jean-Paul Sartre.* Chatto and Windus, 2006. Apple e-book.

Sartre, Jean-Paul. "Sartre on the Nobel Prize." Translated by Richard Howard. *New York Review of Books,* December 17, 1964. https://www.nybooks.com/articles/1964/12/17/sartre-on-the-nobel-prize.

Seymour-Jones, Carole. *A Dangerous Liaison: A Revelatory New Biography of Simone de Beauvoir and Jean-Paul Sartre.* Century, 2008.

Sigal, Clancy. "The Torrid Affair Between Nelson Algren and Simone de Beauvoir." *Los Angeles Times,* October 18, 1998. https://www.articles.latimes.com/1998/oct/18/books/bk-33545-story.html.

"Simone de Beauvoir, Author and Intellectual, Dies in Paris at 78." *New York Times,* April 15, 1986. https://www.nytimes.com/1986/04/15/obituaries/simone-de-beauvoir-author-and-intellectual-dies-in-paris-at-78.html.

Smith, Dinitia. "Beauvoir and Sartre, and a Book in Dispute." *New York Times,* September 29, 2005. https://www.nytimes.com/2005/09/29/books/beauvoir-and-sartre-and-a-book-in-dispute.html.

BILL MASTERS AND VIRGINIA JOHNSON

Maier, Thomas. *Masters of Sex: The Life and Times of William Masters and Virginia Johnson, the Couple Who Taught America How to Love.* New York: Basic Books, 2009.

Thomas Maier, author of *Masters of Sex.* Interview by Terry Gross. *Fresh Air,* National Public Radio, July 30, 2013. Transcript accessed online. https://www.npr.org/templates/transcript/transcript.php?storyId=206704520.

RUTH BADER AND MARTIN GINSBURG

Carmon, Irin, and Shana Knizhnik. *Notorious RBG: The Life and Times of Ruth Bader Ginsburg.* New York: Dey Street, 2015.

De Hart, Jane Sherron. *Ruth Bader Ginsburg: A Life.* New York: Knopf, 2018.

Dodson, Scott, ed. *The Legacy of Ruth Bader Ginsburg.* Cambridge, U.K.: Cambridge University Press, 2015.

Frontiero v. Richardson, 411 U.S. 677 (1973). https://caselaw.findlaw.com/us-supreme-court/411/677.html.

Gibson, Katie L. *Ruth Bader Ginsburg's Legacy of Dissent: Feminist Rhetoric and the Law.* Tuscaloosa: University of Alabama Press, 2018.

Ginsburg, Ruth Bader. "Ruth Bader Ginsburg's Advice for Living." Opinion, *New York Times,* October 1, 2016. https://www.nytimes.com/2016/10/02/opinion/sunday/ruth-bader-ginsburgs-advice-for-living.html.

Ginsburg, Ruth Bader, with Mary Hartnett and Wendy W. Williams. *My Own Words.* New York: Simon and Schuster, 2018.

Hunt, Helena, ed. *Ruth Bader Ginsburg: In Her Own Words.* Evanston, IL: Agate B2, 2018.

Izadi, Elahe. "Ruth Bader Ginsburg's Advice on Love and Leaning In." *Washington Post,* July 31, 2014. https://www.washingtonpost.com/news/post-nation/wp/2014/07/31/ruth-bader-ginsburgs-advice-on-love-and-leaning-in.

Justice Ruth Bader Ginsburg. Interview by Irin Carmon. *The Rachel Maddow Show,* February 16, 2015. MSNBC television. Transcript accessed online. www.msnbc.com/msnbc/exclusive-justice-ruth-bader-ginsburg-interview-full-transcript.

Mathews, Jay. "The Spouse of Ruth." *Washington Post,* June 19, 1993. https://www.washingtonpost.com/archive/lifestyle/1993/06/19/the-spouse-of-ruth/a57e6536-3e1b-4c30-8bab-1f2c629cf172/?utm_term=.e790d3aab72c.

McClure, Emily. "All of Ruth Bader Ginsburg's Jabots, From Her Statement-Making Dissent Collar to Her Sassy Beaded Accessories." *Bustle,* May 6, 2015. https://www.bustle.com/articles/81407-all-of-ruth-bader-ginsburgs-jabots-from-her-statement-making-dissent-collar-to-her-sassy-beaded-accessories.

Rafei, Roya. "Ruth Bader Ginsburg: The Former Rutgers Law Professor Led the Legal Campaign for Gender Equality." *Rutgers Today,* February 29, 2016. https://news.rutgers.edu/feature/ruth-bader-ginsburg-former-rutgers-law-professor-led-legal-campaign-gender-equality/20160228#.XL1OWc9KhmB.

Ruth Bader Ginsburg. Interview by Angella M. Nazarian. E-mail. August 8, 2017.

"Ruth Bader Ginsburg Exclusive Interview | Rachel Maddow | MSNBC." YouTube video, posted by MSNBC, February 17, 2015. https://www.youtube.com/watch?v=jq3c9ESnZwI.

"Ruth Bader Ginsburg on Integrity." Video posted on Academy of Achievement website, accessed April 21, 2019. https://www.achievement.org/video/gin0-int-020.

Steinmetz, Katy. "How Ruth Bader Ginsburg Found Her Voice." *Time* online, accessed April 21, 2019. time.com/ruth-bader-ginsburg-supreme-court.

"The Burger Court, 1969–1986." Supreme Court Historical Society website, accessed April 21, 2019. https://supremecourthistory.org/timeline_court_burger.html.

Totenberg, Nina. "Martin Ginsburg's Legacy: Love of Justice (Ginsburg)." *Weekend Edition Saturday,* National Public Radio, July 3, 2010. https://www.npr.org/templates/story/story.php?storyId=128249680.

Valente, Joanna C. "Ruth Bader Ginsburg's Love Story Will Basically Melt Your Heart." *Kveller,* November 13, 2015. https://www.kveller.com/ruth-bader-ginsburgs-love-story-will-basically-melt-your-heart.

Vrato, Elizabeth. *The Counselors: Conversations With 18 Courageous Women Who Have Changed the World.* Philadelphia: Running Press, 2002.

QUEEN ELIZABETH II AND PRINCE PHILIP

"An Address by the Queen to Parliament, 2012." Royal.uk, March 20, 2012. https://www.royal.uk/queens-address-parliament-20-march-2012.

"A Speech by the Queen on Her Golden Wedding Anniversary." Royal.uk, November 20, 1997. https://www.royal.uk/golden-wedding-speech.

Brandreth, Gyles. *Philip and Elizabeth: Portrait of a Royal Marriage.* London: Arrow, 2004.

Hennessy, Patrick, and Roya Nikkhah. "Diamond Jubilee: Queen Voted Favourite Monarch of All Time." *The Telegraph,* June 3, 2012.

"Royal Wedding: Prince Harry, Meghan Markle Marry at Windsor Castle—As It Happened." CBS News online, May 19, 2018. https://www.cbsnews.com/live-news/royal-wedding-2018-watch-live-stream-follow-live-updates-today.

Smith, Sally Bedell. *Elizabeth the Queen.* New York: Random House, 2012.

———. "Love and Majesty." *Vanity Fair,* January 2012. https://www.vanityfair.com/style/society/2012/01/queen-elizabeth-201201.

CHARLES AND RAY EAMES

Amelar, Sarah. "Two Eames Grandchildren on Charles and Ray's Living Room." *New York Times,* October 5, 2011. https://www.nytimes.com/2011/10/06/garden/the-eames-house-living-room.html.

Cohn, Jason, and Bill Jersey. *Eames: The Architect and the Painter.* Documentary film. First Run Features, 2011.

"Everything Is Connected." Eames Office website. http://www.eamesoffice.com/scholars-walk/everything-is-connected.

Filler, Martin. "Prisoners of the Fun Factory." *New York Review of Books,* November 22, 2011. https://www.nybooks.com/daily/2011/11/22/prisoners-fun-factory.

Folkart, Burt A. "Ray Eames, 73; Member of Noted Design Team." *Los Angeles Times,* August 23, 1988. https://www.latimes.com/archives/la-xpm-1988-08-23-mn-806-story.html.

Harrison, Kay. "Charles and Ray Eames: The World Through Their Eyes." *60 Reservoir* blog, May 18, 2014. https://blog.zanui.com.au/charles-ray-eames.

"IBM Pavilion NY World's Fair." Eames Office website. http://www.eamesoffice.com/the-work/ibm-pavilion-ny-worlds-fair.

Kirkham, Pat. *Charles and Ray Eames: Designers of the Twentieth Century.* Cambridge, MA: MIT Press, 1998.

Office of Charles and Ray Eames. *Powers of Ten.* Film. 1977. From Eames Office website. http://www.eamesoffice.com/education/powers-of-ten-2.

Pavlus, John. "The Eames Studio's Inspiring History and Unknown Dark Side." *Fast Company* online, November 9, 2011. https://www.fastcodesign.com/1665403/the-eames-studios-inspiring-history-and-unknown-dark-side.

Richard, Pascale. "The Beauty of Simplicity: The Films of Charles and Ray Eames." *Images and Views of Alternative Cinema,* 2014. Posted by Christopher Zimmerman on the blog *View From the Corner: Reflections on Contemporary Culture,* June 30, 2014. http://cmzimmermann.blogspot.com/2014/06/ivac-2014-beauty-of-simplicity.html.

"The Timeline of a House and a Household Name." Eames Foundation website, 2013. http://www.eameshouse250.org/timeline.html.

The World of Charles and Ray Eames. Edited by Catherine Ince. London: Barbican Art Gallery, with Thames and Hudson Ltd., 2015. Exhibition catalog.

Woodward, Daisy. "Ten Things You Might Not Know About Charles and Ray Eames." *AnOther Magazine* online, October 23, 2015. http://www.anothermag.com/design-living/7945/ten-things-you-might-not-know-about-charles-and-ray-eames.

LUCILLE BALL AND DESI ARNAZ

Arnold, Roxane. "From the Archives: Lucille Ball Dies; TV's Comic Genius was 77." *Los Angeles Times,* April 27, 1989. https://www.latimes.com/local/la-me-lucille-ball-19890427-story.html.

Brooks, Marla. *The American Family on Television: A Chronology of 121 Shows, 1948–2004.* Jefferson, NC: McFarland, 2005.

Carter, Maria. "A Look Back at Lucy and Desi's Turbulent Love Story." *Country Living* online, March 1, 2017. https://www.countryliving.com/life/entertainment/a41926/lucy-and-desi-love-story.

Percoco, Michael. "Remembering Pioneering Comedian Lucille Ball and *I Love Lucy.*" *Geeks of Doom,* April 26, 2014. https://www.geeksofdoom.com/2014/04/26/remembering-pioneering-comedian-lucille-ball-and-i-love-lucy.

Sanders, Coyne Steven, and Tom Gilbert. *Desilu: The Story of Lucille Ball and Desi Arnaz.* New York: William Morrow and Company, 1993.

Smith, Cecil. "They Still Love Lucy 30 Years Later." *San Francisco Examiner,* October 11, 1981.

JOAN DIDION AND JOHN GREGORY DUNNE

Adams, Michael. "Sin and Guilt in the Fiction of John Gregory Dunne." *CUNY Academic Works.* Critique 25.3, 1984: 154–159. https://academicworks.cuny.edu/cgi/viewcontent.cgi?article=1117&context=gc_pubs.

Anolik, Lili. "How Joan Didion the Writer Became Joan Didion the Legend." *Vanity Fair,* February 2016. https://www.vanityfair.com/culture/2016/02/joan-didion-writer-los-angeles.

Ardeljan-Braden, Alexa. "How Joan Didion Gave Los Angeles Its Voice." *Culture Trip,* updated October 11, 2016. https://theculturetrip.com/north-america/usa/california/articles/joan-didion-los-angeless-preeminent-voice.

Brockes, Emma. "Q: How Were You Able to Keep Writing After the Death of Your Husband? A: There Was Nothing Else to Do. I Had to Write My Way Out of It." *The Guardian,* December 16, 2005. https://www.theguardian.com/film/2005/dec/16/biography.features.

Daugherty, Tracy. *The Last Love Song: A Biography of Joan Didion.* New York: St. Martin's Press, 2016.

Didion, Joan. "A Problem of Making Connections." *Life,* December 5, 1969.

———. *The White Album.* New York: Simon and Schuster, 1979.

———. *The Year of Magical Thinking.* New York: Knopf, 2005.

Didion, Joan, and John Dunne. Lecture, Portland Arts and Lectures series, September 23, 1992. *The Archive Project* podcast, Literary Arts. https://literary-arts.org/archive/joan-didion-john-dunne.

Dunne, Dominick. "A Death in the Family." *Vanity Fair,* May 2003. https://www.vanityfair.com/news/2004/03/dunne200403.

Dunne, Griffin. *Joan Didion: The Center Will Not Hold.* Documentary film. 94 min. Netflix, 2017.

Dunne, John Gregory. *Quintana and Friends.* New York: Dutton, 1978.

Garis, Leslie. "Didion and Dunne: The Rewards of a Literary Marriage." *New York Times,* February 8, 1987. https://www.nytimes.com/1987/02/08/magazine/didion-dunne-the-rewards-of-a-literary-marriage.html.

"*Harp* by John Gregory Dunne." Book review. *Kirkus Reviews,* 1989. https://www.kirkusreviews.com/book-reviews/john-gregory-dunne-2/harp.

Hoby, Hermione. "From Literary Heavyweight to Lifestyle Brand: Exploring the Cult of Joan Didion." *The Guardian,* August 17, 2015. https://www.theguardian.com/lifeandstyle/2015/aug/17/joan-didion-literary-heavyweight-lifestyle-brand-celine.

"Joan Didion, Writing a Story After an Ending." Interview by Terry Gross. *Fresh Air,* National Public Radio, October 13, 2005. Transcript accessed online. https://www.npr.org/templates/story/story.php?storyId=4956088.

Severo, Richard. "John Gregory Dunne, Novelist, Screenwriter and Observer of Hollywood, Is Dead at 71." *New York Times,* January 1, 2004. https://www.nytimes.com/2004/01/01/arts/john-gregory-dunne-novelist-screenwriter-and-observer-of-hollywood-is-dead-at-71.html.

Syme, Rachel. "Their Love Letter to Aunt Joan (Didion)." *New York Times,* October 24, 2017. https://www.nytimes.com/2017/10/24/movies/joan-didion-documentary-the-center-will-not-hold.html.

"The Joan Didion Documentary." Kickstarter campaign, created by Griffin Dunne, October 22, 2014. https://www.kickstarter.com/projects/867987830/the-joan-didion-documentary.

Van Meter, Jonathan. "When Everything Changes." *New York Magazine,* September 29, 2005. nymag.com/nymetro/arts/books/14633/.

GEORGIA O'KEEFFE AND ALFRED STIEGLITZ

"Carl Jung and Taos, New Mexico." Beezone Library, accessed March 25, 2019. https://www.beezone.com/jung/jung_pueblo.html.

De Beauvoir, Simone. *The Second Sex.* Translated by Constance Borde and Sheila Malovany-Chevallier. New York: Vintage Books, 2011.

Didion, Joan. "Georgia O'Keeffe." Third essay in section 3 of *The White Album.* New York: Simon and Schuster, 1979. Excerpted in "In Praise of Hard Women: Joan Didion on Georgia O'Keeffe." *Reading Is Therapy,* February 15, 2018. http://www.readingistherapy.com/praise-hard-women-joan-didion-georgia-okeeffe.

Eisler, Benita. *O'Keeffe and Stieglitz: an American Romance.* New York: Doubleday, 1991.

Foerstner, Abigail. "O'Keeffe Was No Saint, Tell-All Book Reveals." *Chicago Tribune,* July 28, 1991. https://www.chicagotribune.com/news/ct-xpm-1991-07-28-9103230797-story.html.

"Georgia O'Keeffe." *Wikipedia,* last modified December 28, 2018. https://en.wikipedia.org/wiki/Georgia_O%27Keeffe.

Greenough, Sarah, ed. *My Faraway One: Selected Letters of Georgia O'Keeffe and Alfred Stieglitz.* New Haven, CT: Yale University Press, 2011.

Lisle, Laurie. *Portrait of an Artist: A Biography of Georgia O'Keeffe.* New York: Washington Square Press, 1997.

Sooke, Alastair. "How Georgia O'Keeffe Left Her Cheating Husband for a Mountain: 'God Told Me If I Painted It Enough, I Could Have It.'" *The Telegraph,* June 30, 2016. https://www.telegraph.co.uk/art/what-to-see/how-georgia-okeeffe-left-her-cheating-husband-for-a-mountain-god.

Stamberg, Susan. "Stieglitz and O'Keeffe: Their Love and Life in Letters." *Morning Edition,* National Public Radio, July 21, 2011. https://www.npr.org/2011/07/21/138467808/stieglitz-and-okeeffe-their-love-and-life-in-letters?t=1531653063198.

REI KAWAKUBO AND ADRIAN JOFFE

Amed, Imran. "Inside Yohji Yamamoto's Fashion Philosophy." *The Business of Fashion,* May 15, 2016. https://www.businessoffashion.com/articles/video/inside-yohji-yamamotos-fashion-philosophy.

Bagley, Christopher. "Behind Comme des Garçons Stands Zen-Loving Contrarian CEO." *Bloomberg Markets,* October 7 2014. https://www.bloomberg.com/news/articles/2014-10-07/behind-comme-des-garcons-stands-zen-loving-contrarian-ceo.

Banks, Grace. "Six Questions With Dover Street Market CEO Adrian Joffe." *Forbes* online, April 12, 2016. https://www.forbes.com/sites/gracebanks/2016/04/12/six-questions-with-dover-street-market-ceo-adrian-joffe/#486c94b27a92.

Bischof, Felix. "Adrian Joffe: How Comme des Garcons Turned Retail Into an Art Form." *The Week,* March 7, 2017. https://www.theweek.co.uk/82267/adrian-joffe-how-comme-des-garcons-turned-retail-into-an-art-form.

Blanks, Tim. "Rei Kawakubo: A Punk's Pain." *The Business of Fashion,* April 24, 2017. https://www.businessoffashion.com/articles/people/rei-kawakubo-interview-commes-des-garcons-metropolitan-museum-of-art.

Blumberg, Naomi. "Rei Kawakubo." *Encyclopædia Britannica,* last modified October 7, 2018. https://www.britannica.com/biography/Rei-Kawakubo.

"BoF 500: Adrian Joffe." *The Business of Fashion,* accessed March 30, 2019. https://www.businessoffashion.com/community/people/adrian-joffe.

Bolton, Andrew. *Rei Kawakubo Comme des Garçons: Art of the In-Between.* New York: Metropolitan Museum of Art, 2017.

Campbell, Thomas P. Foreword to *Rei Kawakubo Comme des Garcons: Art of the In-Between* by Andrew Bolton. New York: Metropolitan Museum of Art, 2017.

"Critical Analysis of Two Japanese Designers." All Answers Ltd. UKessays.com, November 22, 2018. https://www.ukessays.com/essays/cultural-studies/critical-analysis-of-two-japanese-designers-cultural-studies-essay.php.

English, Bonnie. *Japanese Fashion Designers: The Work and Influence of Issey Miyake, Yohji Yamamoto, and Rei Kawakubo.* London: Berg, 2011.

Frankel, Susannah. "Rei Kawakubo: Fashion's Great Iconoclast." *Dazed,* September 2004. Republished on *Dazed Digital,* October 3, 2015. www.dazeddigital.com/fashion/article/26740/1/rei-kawakubo-fashion-s-great-iconoclast.

Frankel, Susannah. "Your First Look at the New Dover Street Market London." *AnOther Magazine* online, March 11, 2016. http://www.anothermag.com/fashion-beauty/8465/your-first-look-at-the-new-dover-street-market-london.

Friedman, Vanessa. "Lunch With the FT: Adrian Joffe." *Financial Times,* January 17, 2014. https://www.ft.com/content/4ce0c520-7d35-11e3-a579-00144feabdc0.

Gonsalves, Rebecca. "The Y Still Has It: The Masterful Japanese Designer Yohji Yamamoto Shows No Signs of Taking a Back Seat in His Fashion Empire." *The Independent,* February 1, 2014. https://www.independent.co.uk/life-style/fashion/features/the-y-still-has-it-the-masterful-japanese-designer-yohji-yamamoto-shows-no-signs-of-taking-a-back-9093949.html.

Hyzagi, Jacques. "Rei Kawakubo's Radical Chic." *The Guardian,* September 20, 2015. https://www.theguardian.com/fashion/2015/sep/20/rei-kawakubo-radical-chic.

[Juma, Beverlyn.] "Newport International Runway Group Tokyo Fashion: Zen-Loving CEO Rewrites the Rules of Retail." *Newport International Group Runway* blog, October 9, 2014. https://newportinternationalgrouprunway.wordpress.com/2014/10/09/newport-international-runway-group-tokyo-fashion-zen-loving-ceo-rewrites-the-rules-of-retail/

Lee, Elaine Y. J. "The Father of CdG and DSM, Adrian Joffe, Talks New Beijing Outpost and Reveals Paris Expansion." *Hypebeast,* April 3, 2018. https://hypebeast.com/2018/4/adrian-joffe-dover-street-market-beijing-interview.

Livingstone, Josephine. "The Passion of Rei Kawakubo." *The New Republic,* May 3, 2017. https://newrepublic.com/article/142457/passion-rei-kawakubo.

Marra-Alvarez, Melissa. "When the West Wore East: Rei Kawakubo, Yohji Yamamoto and the Rise of the Japanese Avant-Garde in Fashion." *DRESSTUDY* 57 (Spring 2010). https://www.kci.or.jp/research/dresstudy/pdf/D57_Marra_Alvarez_e_When_the_West_Wore_East.pdf.

"Odeur 53." Comme des Garçons Parfums online product page, accessed March 30, 2019. https://www.comme-des-garcons-parfum.com/perfumes/odeur-53.

Schneier, Matthew. "Rei Kawakubo, the Nearly Silent Oracle of Fashion." *New York Times,* May 1, 2017. https://www.nytimes.com/2017/05/01/fashion/rei-kawakubos-commes-de-garcons.html.

Thurman, Judith. "The Misfit." *The New Yorker,* July 4, 2005. www.newyorker.com/magazine/2005/07/04/the-misfit-3.

LOU REED AND LAURIE ANDERSON

Anderson, Laurie. "Laurie Anderson's Farewell to Lou Reed: A *Rolling Stone* Exclusive." *Rolling Stone,* November 6, 2013. https://www.rollingstone.com/music/music-news/laurie-andersons-farewell-to-lou-reed-a-rolling-stone-exclusive-243792.

Bono. "Bono Remembers Lou Reed's 'Perfect Noise.'" *Rolling Stone,* November 6, 2013. https://www.rollingstone.com/music/music-news/bono-remembers-lou-reeds-perfect-noise-243596.

Brighton Festival website. *Lou Reed Drones* installation description, accessed March 23, 2019. https://brightonfestival.org/event/8407/lou_reed_drones.

DeCurtis, Anthony. *Lou Reed: A Life.* New York: Little, Brown, and Company, 2017.

Diamond, Jamie. "Laurie Anderson." *People,* May 7, 1990. https://people.com/archive/laurie-anderson-vol-33-no-18.

Dolan, Jon. "Lou Reed, Velvet Underground Leader and Rock Pioneer, Dead at 71." *Rolling Stone* online, October 27, 2013. https://www.rollingstone.com/music/music-news/lou-reed-velvet-underground-leader-and-rock-pioneer-dead-at-71-100874.

Fricke, David. "Inside Lou Reed's Revelatory New Public Archive." *Rolling Stone,* March 2, 2017. https://www.rollingstone.com/music/music-features/inside-lou-reeds-revelatory-new-public-archive-193112.

Fricke, David. "Q&A: Lou Reed." *Rolling Stone,* November 5, 1987. https://www.rollingstone.com/music/music-news/qa-lou-reed-87827.

Holpuch, Amanda. "Lou Reed's Sister: Singer's Electroshock Therapy Wasn't for Homosexuality." *The Guardian,* April 15, 2015. https://www.theguardian.com/music/2015/apr/15/lou-reed-sister-mental-health-homosexuality-rumors.

Homes, A. M. "Laurie Anderson." *Interview,* November 2, 2015. https://www.interviewmagazine.com/culture/laurie-anderson-1.

Januszczak, Waldemar. "Laurie Anderson: 'Boy, This Is It. This Is All We Have.'" *The Sunday Times,* April 17, 2016. https://www.thetimes.co.uk/article/boy-this-is-it-this-is-all-we-have-mhbgzxwz7.

Jones, Josh. "Lou Reed and Laurie Anderson: Buddhist Power Couple." *Engage!,* June 30, 2016. https://engagedharma.net/2016/06/30/lou-reed-laurie-anderson-buddhist-power-couple.

Jones, Josh. "Lou Reed and Laurie Anderson's Three Rules for Living Well: A Short and Succinct Life Philosophy." *Open Culture,* June 30, 2016. http://www.openculture.com/2016/06/lou-reed-and-laurie-andersons-three-rules-for-living-well.html.

Laurie Anderson. Interview by John Papageorge. Silicon Valley Radio, Web Networks, Inc. Transcript accessed March 23, 2019. http://www.transmitmedia.com/svr/vault/anderson/ander_transcript.html.

"Laurie Anderson and Lou Reed Interviewed by Charlie Rose (2003) - Part Two." YouTube video, from an interview televised by CNN on July 8, 2003, posted by "Mneme Mnemosyne," April 19, 2011. https://www.youtube.com/watch?v=iQWiyKtMemo.

"Laurie Anderson (feat. Lou Reed) - In Our Sleep." YouTube video, posted by "EM B," September 14, 2011. https://www.youtube.com/watch?v=F2lOx2TqT60.

"Laurie Anderson: 'My Dog's Character Was Pure Empathy. I Tried to Express That.'" Interview by Jonathan Romney. *The Guardian,* March 27, 2016. https://www.theguardian.com/music/2016/mar/27/laurie-anderson-interview-q-and-a-heart-dog-lolabelle-terrier-brighton-festival-lou-reed-o-superman.

Leland, John. "Laurie Anderson's Glorious, Chaotic New York." *New York Times,* April 21, 2017. https://www.nytimes.com/2017/04/21/nyregion/laurie-anderson-new-york.html.

"Lou Reed, 1942–2013: Inside the New Issue of *Rolling Stone.*" *Rolling Stone* online, November 6, 2013. https://www.rollingstone.com/music/music-news/lou-reed-1942-2013-inside-the-new-issue-of-rolling-stone-243339.

"Lou Reed and Laurie Anderson Vivid 2010 Press Conference Un-Edited in Full Sydney, Australia." YouTube video, posted by James DeWeaver, November 10, 2013. https://www.youtube.com/watch?v=pLeOHReBC08.

"Lou Reed Memorial 16 Laurie Anderson Talking: Personal/Artistic Relationship With Lou." YouTube video, posted by Jim Fouratt, December 17, 2013. https://www.youtube.com/watch?v=ZpgPLlFo73o.

"Lou Reed's Last Words: Watch His Final Interview." Interview by Farida Khelfa, posted by *Rolling Stone* online, November 8, 2013. https://www.rollingstone.com/music/music-news/lou-reeds-last-words-watch-his-final-interview-41310.

Palmer, Robert. "The Pop Life." *New York Times,* March 10, 1982. https://www.nytimes.com/1982/03/10/arts/the-pop-life-239009.html.

Prois, Jessica. "Lou Reed Was More Influential Than You Realized." *HuffPost,* October 28, 2013. https://www.huffingtonpost.com/2013/10/28/lou-reed_n_4171241.html.

"Read Laurie Anderson's Moving Rock Hall Speech for Lou Reed." *Rolling Stone* online, April 19, 2015. https://www.rollingstone.com/music/music-news/read-laurie-andersons-moving-rock-hall-speech-for-lou-reed-98794.

Ring, Trudy. "Performance Artist Laurie Anderson Marries a Woman in Impromptu San Francisco Wedding." *Pride,* November 12, 2015. https://www.pride.com/entertainment/2015/11/12/performance-artist-laurie-anderson-marries-sophie-calle-impromptu-san.

Sisario, Ben. "Laurie Anderson on Lou Reed's Love, Work, and Retirement Plan." *New York Times,* March 3, 2017. https://www.nytimes.com/2017/03/03/arts/music/laurie-anderson-on-lou-reeds-love-work-and-retirement-plan.html.

Stern, Mark Joseph. "Was Lou Reed the First Out Rock Star?" *Slate,* October 27, 2013. https://slate.com/human-interest/2013/10/lou-reed-bisexual-was-he-the-first-out-rock-star.html.

Wall, Mick. *Lou Reed: The Life.* London: Orion Publishing Group, 2013.

Weiner, Merrill Reed. "A Family in Peril: Lou Reed's Sister Sets the Record Straight About His Childhood." *Cuepoint,* April 13, 2015. https://medium.com/cuepoint/a-family-in-peril-lou-reed-s-sister-sets-the-record-straight-about-his-childhood-20e8399f84a3.

Weiner, Sue. "Performance Artist Laurie Anderson Opens Up on Late Husband Lou Reed, Love for Dogs." *Patch,* August 5, 2016. https://patch.com/new-york/easthampton/performance-artist-laurie-anderson-opens-late-husband-lou-reed-love-dogs.

ALEJANDRO AND PASCALE JODOROWSKY

Alejandro and Pascale Jodorowsky. Interview by Angella M. Nazarian. E-mail, September 11, 2018.

Benson, Eric. "The Psychomagical Realism of Alejandro Jodorowsky." *New York Times Magazine,* March 14, 2014. https://www.nytimes.com/2014/03/16/magazine/the-psychomagical-realism-of-alejandro-jodorowsky.html.

Brady, Tara. "Alejandro Jodorowsky: 'I Never Seek Money. I Make Films to Lose Money.'" *Irish Times,* December 16, 2016. https://www.irishtimes.com/culture/film/alejandro-jodorowsky-i-never-seek-money-i-make-films-to-lose-money-1.2902873.

Buda, Marilyne. "A Life Ideal: Interview With the Painter Pascale Montandon-Jodorowsky." Translated by Jessica Sequeira. *Ventana Latina,* January 15, 2014. www.ventanalatina.co.uk/2014/01/a-life-ideal-interview-with-the-painter-pascale-montandon-jodorowsky.

Dollar, Steve. "Alejandro Jodorowsky's 'Dance of Reality' Takes a Look at His Painful Childhood in Chile." *Washington Post,* May 23, 2014. https://www.washingtonpost.com/lifestyle/style/alejandro-jodorowskys-dance-of-reality-takes-a-look-at-his-painful-childhood-in-chile/2014/05/22/71954c18-e1c8-11e3-9743-bb9b59cde7b9_story.html.

Gleiberman, Owen. "Film Review: 'Endless Poetry.'" *Variety,* May 14, 2016. https://variety.com/2016/film/festivals/cannes-film-review-jodorowsky-endless-poetry-1201774470.

Grau, Donatien. "PascALEjandro." *Purple,* Spring/Summer 2017. http://purple.fr/magazine/ss-2017-issue-27/pascalejandro.

Grau, Donatien, ed. *PascALEjandro: Alchemical Androgynous.* Arles: Actes Sud, 2017.

Nechvatal, Joseph. "An Artist Couple's Collaborations Have Chemistry, But No Alchemy." *Hyperallergic,* May 24, 2017. https://hyperallergic.com/380975/an-artist-couples-collaborations-have-chemistry-but-no-alchemy.

Yepes, Julia. "The Eternal Search of the Jodorowskys." *Interview,* July 25, 2017. https://www.interviewmagazine.com/film/jodorowsky-endless-poetry.

Zara, Janelle. "Witnessing the Private Spiritual Love of Cult Filmmaker Alejandro Jodorowsky and His Wife Pascale." *W* magazine, June 12, 2017. https://www.wmagazine.com/story/alejandro-jodorowsky-director-movies-wife-pascale-paris-home.

Notes

INTRODUCTION

1. Emily Bazelon, "The Place of Women on the Court," *New York Times Magazine,* July 7, 2009, https://www.nytimes.com/2009/07/12/magazine/12ginsburg-t.html.

LOU ANDREAS-SALOMÉ AND RAINER MARIA RILKE

1. "Rainer Maria Rilke and Lou Andreas-Salomé: The Correspondence," Briefly Noted, *The New Yorker,* July 31, 2006, https://www.newyorker.com/magazine/2006/07/31/rainer-maria-rilke-and-lou-andreas-salome-the-correspondence.
2. Julia Vickers, *Lou von Salomé: A Biography of the Woman Who Inspired Freud, Nietzsche, and Rilke* (Jefferson, NC: McFarland, 2008), 30.
3. Ibid, 60.
4. Ibid, 112.
5. Ibid.
6. Ibid, 142.
7. Rachel Corbett, *You Must Change Your Life: The Story of Rainer Maria Rilke and Auguste Rodin* (New York: W. W. Norton, 2017), 115.
8. Ibid, 192.
9. Vickers, *Lou von Salomé,* 159.
10. Ibid, 157.
11. Ibid, 182.
12. Ibid, 184.
13. Rainer Maria Rilke and Lou Andreas-Salomé, *Rilke and Andreas-Salomé: A Love Story in Letters* (New York: W. W. Norton, 2008), translated by Edward Snow and Michael Winkler, excerpted in "13 December (1926): Rainer Maria Rilke to Lou Andreas Salomé," *The American Reader,* theamericanreader.com/13-december-1926-rainer-maria-rilke-to-lou-andreas-salome.
14. Corbett, *You Must Change Your Life,* 262.
15. Vickers, *Lou von Salomé,* 185.
16. Ibid.
17. Ibid, 190.

TONI WOLFF AND CARL JUNG

1. Nan Savage Healy, *Toni Wolff and C. G. Jung: A Collaboration* (Los Angeles: Tiberius Press, 2017), 7.
2. Ibid, 2.
3. Ibid, 74.
4. Ibid, 79.
5. Ibid, 76.
6. Ibid, 98.
7. Ibid, 95.
8. Ibid, 96.
9. Ibid.
10. Ibid, 116.
11. Ibid.
12. Ibid.
13. Ibid, 151.
14. "The Red Book," W. W. Norton and Company product page, accessed April 25, 2019, https://books.wwnorton.com/books/detail.aspx?ID=12004.
15. Healy, *Toni Wolff and C. G. Jung,* 126.
16. Ibid, 227.
17. Ibid.
18. Deirdre Bair, *Jung: A Biography* (New York: Back Bay Books, 2003), 324.
19. Ibid, 390.
20. Ibid, 559.
21. Ibid, 829.
22. Ibid, 306.

SALVADOR DALÍ AND GALA

1. Salvador Dalí, *The Secret Life of Salvador Dalí* (New York: Dover Publications, 1993. First published 1942 by Dial Press, New York), translated by Haakon M. Chevalier, 1.
2. Salvador Dalí, *50 Secrets of Magic Craftsmanship* (New York: Dover Publications, 1992. First published 1948 by Dial Press, New York), translated by Haakon M. Chevalier, Apple e-book, 198.
3, Tim McGirk, *Wicked Lady: Salvador Dalí's Muse* (London: Hutchinson, 1989), 32.
4. Ibid, 276.
5. Ibid, 60.
6. Dalí, *The Secret Life of Salvador Dalí,* 715.
7. Clifford Thurlow, *Sex, Surrealism, Dalí, and Me: The Memoirs of Carlos Lozano* (London: Yellow Bay Books, 2011), chapter 1.
8. Ian Gibson, *The Shameful Life of Salvador Dalí* (London: Faber and Faber, 1997), 495.
9. Thurlow, *Sex, Surrealism, Dalí, and Me,* chapter 11.
10. Ibid.
11. Gibson, *The Shameful Life of Salvador Dalí,* 546.
12. Thurlow, *Sex, Surrealism, Dalí, and Me,* 217–218.
13. McGirk, *Wicked Lady,* 141.
14. Gibson, *The Shameful Life of Salvador Dalí,* 574.
15. Thurlow, *Sex, Surrealism, Dalí, and Me,* chapter 22.
16. Ibid.

SERGE GAINSBOURG AND JANE BIRKIN

1. Sylvie Simmons, *Serge Gainsbourg: A Fistful of Gitanes: Requiem for a Twister* (London: Helter Skelter, 2001), 58.
2. Ibid.
3. Ibid, 59.
4. Gilles Verlant, *Gainsbourg: The Biography* (Los Angeles: TamTam Books, 2012), translated by Paul Knobloch, 357.
5. Ibid, 358.
6. Ibid, 204.
7. Ibid, 342.
8. Simmons, *Serge Gainsbourg,* 52.
9. Ibid, 93.
10. Verlant, *Gainsbourg,* 186.
11. Ibid, 400.
12. Simmons, *Serge Gainsbourg,* 71.
13. Ibid, 89.
14. Ibid, 96.
15. Ibid, 95.
16. Verlant, *Gainsbourg,* 705.
17. Simmons, *Serge Gainsbourg,* 125.
18. Verlant, *Gainsbourg,* 568.

JEAN-PAUL SARTRE AND SIMONE DE BEAUVOIR

1. Louis Menand, "Stand by Your Man," *The New Yorker,* September 18, 2005, https://www.newyorker.com/magazine/2005/09/26/stand-by-your-man.
2. Hazel Rowley, *Tête à Tête: The Lives and Loves of Simone de Beauvoir and Jean-Paul Sartre* (Chatto and Windus, 2006), e-book, chapter 2.
3. Menand, "Stand by Your Man."
4. Lisa Appignanesi, "Did Simone de Beauvoir's Open 'Marriage' Make Her Happy?" *The Guardian,* June 10, 2005. https://www.theguardian.com/world/2005/jun/10/gender.politicsphilosophyandsociety.
5. Rowley, *Tête à Tête,* chapter 4.
6. Ibid, chapter 6.
7. Ibid, chapter 3.
8. De Beauvoir, Simone, *The Second Sex* (New York: Vantage, 2011. First published 1949 by Éditions Gallimard, Paris), translated by Constance Borde and Sheila Malovany-Chevallier, PDF e-book, chapter 12.
9. Clancy Sigal, "The Torrid Affair Between Nelson Algren and Simone de Beauvoir," *Los Angeles Times,* October 18, 1998, https://www.articles.latimes.com/1998/oct/18/books/bk-33545-story.html.
10. Rowley, *Tête à Tête,* chapter 8.
11. Ibid, chapter 12.
12. Ibid, chapter 11.
13. Ibid.

14. Simone de Beauvoir, *Force of Circumstance* (Harmondsworth, U.K.: Penguin, 1985), translated by Richard Howard, 659.
15. Rowley, *Tête à Tête,* chapter 3.
16. Ibid, chapter 13.
17. Ibid.
18. "Simone de Beauvoir, Author and Intellectual, Dies in Paris at 78," *New York Times,* April 15, 1986, https://www.nytimes.com/1986/04/15/obituaries/simone-de-beauvoir-author-and-intellectual-dies-in-paris-at-78.html.
19. Ibid.
20. Caroline Moorehead, "A Talk With Simone de Beauvoir," *New York Times,* June 2, 1974.
21. Rowley, *Tête à Tête,* chapter 13.

BILL MASTERS AND VIRGINIA JOHNSON

1. Thomas Maier, *Masters of Sex: The Life and Times of William Masters and Virginia Johnson, the Couple Who Taught America How to Love* (New York: Basic Books, 2009), chapter 8.
2. Ibid.
3. Ibid, chapter 9.
4. Ibid, chapter 10.
5. Ibid, 234.
6. Ibid, 266.
7. Ibid, 267.
8. Ibid, 306.
9. Ibid, 316.
10. Ibid, 590.

RUTH BADER AND MARTIN GINSBURG

1. "Ruth Bader Ginsburg on Integrity," video posted on Academy of Achievement website, 46:17, accessed April 21, 2019, https://www.achievement.org/video/gin0-int-020.
2. Katie L. Gibson, *Ruth Bader Ginsburg's Legacy of Dissent: Feminist Rhetoric and the Law* (Tuscaloosa: University of Alabama Press, 2018), 18.
3. Elahe Izadi, "Ruth Bader Ginsburg's Advice on Love and Leaning In," *Washington Post,* July 31, 2014, https://www.washingtonpost.com/news/post-nation/wp/2014/07/31/ruth-bader-ginsburgs-advice-on-love-and-leaning-in.
4. Ruth Bader Ginsburg, with Mary Hartnett and Wendy W. Williams, *My Own Words* (New York: Simon and Schuster, 2018), 17.
5. Nina Totenberg, "Martin Ginsburg's Legacy: Love of Justice (Ginsburg)," *Weekend Edition Saturday,* National Public Radio, July 3, 2010, https://www.npr.org/templates/story/story.php?storyId=128249680.
6. Jay Mathews, "The Spouse of Ruth," *Washington Post,* June 19, 1993, https://www.washingtonpost.com/archive/lifestyle/1993/06/19/the-spouse-of-ruth/a57e6536-3e1b-4c30-8bab-1f2c629cf172/?utm_term=.e790d3aab72c.
7. Irin Carmon and Shana Knizhnik, *Notorious RBG: The Life and Times of Ruth Bader Ginsburg* (New York: Dey Street, 2015), 18.
8. Ruth Bader Ginsburg, "Ruth Bader Ginsburg's Advice for Living," Opinion, *New York Times,* October 1, 2016, https://www.nytimes.com/2016/10/02/opinion/sunday/ruth-bader-ginsburgs-advice-for-living.html.
9. Elizabeth Vrato, *The Counselors: Conversations With 18 Courageous Women Who Have Changed the World* (Philadelphia: Running Press, 2002), 176.
10. Helena Hunt, ed., *Ruth Bader Ginsburg: In Her Own Words* (Evanston, IL: Agate B2, 2018), 89.
11. Ginsburg, *My Own Words,* 16.
12. Totenberg, "Martin Ginsburg's Legacy."
13. Ibid.
14. Carmon and Knizhnik, *Notorious RBG,* 60.
15. Katy Steinmetz, "How Ruth Bader Ginsburg Found Her Voice," *Time* online, accessed April 21, 2019, time.com/ruth-bader-ginsburg-supreme-court.
16. Carmon and Knizhnik, *Notorious RBG,* 99.
17. Jane Sherron De Hart, *Ruth Bader Ginsburg: A Life* (New York: Knopf, 2018), 416.
18. Ruth Bader Ginsburg, e-mail interview by Angella M. Nazarian, August 8, 2017.

QUEEN ELIZABETH II AND PRINCE PHILIP

1. Sally Bedell Smith, *Elizabeth the Queen* (New York: Random House, 2012), preface, xii.
2. Ibid, 44.
3. Ibid, 50.
4. Gyles Brandreth, *Philip and Elizabeth: Portrait of a Royal Marriage* (London: Arrow, 2004), 178.
5. Ibid, 293.
6. Bedell Smith, *Elizabeth the Queen,* 75.
7. Ibid, 76.
8. Ibid, 147.
9. Ibid, 146.
10. Ibid, 147.
11. Brandreth, *Philip and Elizabeth,* 347.
12. Bedell Smith, *Elizabeth the Queen,* 215.
13. Patrick Hennessy and Roya Nikkhah, "Diamond Jubilee: Queen Voted Favourite Monarch of All Time," *The Telegraph,* June 3, 2012.
14. Bedell Smith, *Elizabeth the Queen,* 412.
15. "A Speech by the Queen on Her Golden Wedding Anniversary," royal.uk, November 20, 1997, https://www.royal.uk/golden-wedding-speech.
16. "An Address by the Queen to Parliament, 2012," royal.uk, March 20, 2012, https://www.royal.uk/queens-address-parliament-20-march-2012.

CHARLES AND RAY EAMES

1. Daisy Woodward, "Ten Things You Might Not Know About Charles and Ray Eames," *AnOther Magazine* online, October 23, 2015, http://www.anothermag.com/design-living/7945/ten-things-you-might-not-know-about-charles-and-ray-eames.
2. Ibid.
3. Ibid.
4. *The World of Charles and Ray Eames,* edited by Catherine Ince (London: Barbican Art Gallery, with Thames and Hudson Ltd., 2015), exhibition catalog.
5. Pat Kirkham, *Charles and Ray Eames: Designers of the Twentieth Century* (Cambridge, MA: MIT Press, 1998), 219.
6. Ibid, 89.
7. Ibid, 80.
8. Ibid, 82.
9. Ibid.
10. Ibid, 65.
11. Ibid, 31.
12. Ibid, 87.
13. Office of Charles and Ray Eames, *Powers of Ten* (1977), film, 00:17, from Eames Office website, http://www.eamesoffice.com/education/powers-of-ten-2.
14. Ibid, 00:45.
15. Pascale Richard, "The Beauty of Simplicity: The Films of Charles and Ray Eames," *Images and Views of Alternative Cinema,* 2014, posted by Christopher Zimmerman on the blog *View From the Corner: Reflections on Contemporary Culture,* June 30, 2014, http://cmzimmermann.blogspot.com/2014/06/ivac-2014-beauty-of-simplicity.html.
16. Ibid.
17. "Everything Is Connected," Eames Office website, http://www.eamesoffice.com/scholars-walk/everything-is-connected.

LUCILLE BALL AND DESI ARNAZ

1. Coyne Steven Sanders and Tom Gilbert, *Desilu: The Story of Lucille Ball and Desi Arnaz* (New York: William Morrow and Company, 1993), 17–18.
2. Ibid, 19.
3. Ibid.
4. Ibid.
5. Ibid.
6. Ibid, 22.
7. Ibid, 28.
8. Ibid.
9. Ibid, 35.
10. Michael Percoco, "Remembering Pioneering Comedian Lucille Ball and *I Love Lucy,*" *Geeks of Doom,* April 26, 2014,

https://www.geeksofdoom.com/2014/04/26/remembering-pioneering-comedian-lucille-ball-and-i-love-lucy.
11. Cecil Smith, "They Still Love Lucy 30 Years Later," *San Francisco Examiner,* October 11, 1981.
12. Sanders and Gilbert, *Desilu,* 90.
13. Ibid, 29.
14. Ibid, 180.
15. Ibid.
16. Ibid, 182.
17. Ibid, 92.
18. Ibid, 197.
19. Ibid, 215.
20. Roxane Arnold, "From the Archives: Lucille Ball Dies; TV's Comic Genius was 77," *Los Angeles Times,* April 27, 1989. https://www.latimes.com/local/la-me-lucille-ball-19890427-story.html.
21. Sanders and Gilbert, *Desilu,* 255.
22. Ibid.
23. Ibid.

JOAN DIDION AND JOHN GREGORY DUNNE

1. Tracy Daugherty, *The Last Love Song: A Biography of Joan Didion* (New York: St. Martin's Press, 2016), 363.
2. Joan Didion, "A Problem of Making Connections," *Life,* December 5, 1969
3. Tracy Daugherty, *The Last Love Song,* 139.
4. Ibid.
5. Ibid, 99.
6. Richard Severo, "John Gregory Dunne, Novelist, Screenwriter and Observer of Hollywood, Is Dead at 71," *New York Times,* January 1, 2004, https://www.nytimes.com/2004/01/01/arts/john-gregory-dunne-novelist-screenwriter-and-observer-of-hollywood-is-dead-at-71.html.
7. Leslie Garis, "Didion and Dunne: The Rewards of a Literary Marriage," *New York Times,* February 8, 1987, https://www.nytimes.com/1987/02/08/magazine/didion-dunne-the-rewards-of-a-literary-marriage.html.
8. Daugherty, *The Last Love Song,* 109.
9. Griffin Dunne, *The Center Will Not Hold,* documentary film, Netflix, 2017.
10. Daugherty, *The Last Love Song,* 97.
11. Ibid, 167.
12. Ibid, 270.
13. Lili Anolik, "How Joan Didion the Writer Became Joan Didion the Legend," *Vanity Fair,* February 2016, https://www.vanityfair.com/culture/2016/02/joan-didion-writer-los-angeles.
14. Daugherty, *The Last Love Song,* 320.
15. Ibid, 391.
16. Ibid, 194.
17. Ibid, 624.
18. John Gregory Dunne, *Quintana and Friends* (New York: Dutton, 1978), 6.
19. Daugherty, *The Last Love Song,* 330.
20. Ibid.
21. Ibid, 92.
22. Joan Didion, *The Year of Magical Thinking* (New York: Knopf, 2005), 23.
23. Daugherty, *The Last Love Song,* 544.
24. Ibid, 564.
25. Didion, *The Year of Magical Thinking,* 166.
26. Daugherty, *The Last Love Song,* 550.
27. Ibid, 585.
28. Ibid, 563.
29. Hermione Hoby, "From Literary Heavyweight to Lifestyle Brand: Exploring the Cult of Joan Didion," *The Guardian,* August 17, 2015, https://www.theguardian.com/lifeandstyle/2015/aug/17/joan-didion-literary-heavyweight-lifestyle-brand-celine.
30. Joan Didion, *The White Album* (New York: Simon and Schuster, 1979), 11.

GEORGIA O'KEEFFE AND ALFRED STIEGLITZ

1. Laurie Lisle, *Portrait of an Artist: A Biography of Georgia O'Keeffe* (New York: Washington Square Press, 1997), 83.
2. Joan Didion, "Georgia O'Keeffe," third essay in section 3 of *The White Album* (New York: Simon and Schuster, 1979), excerpted in "In Praise of Hard Women: Joan Didion on Georgia O'Keeffe," *Reading Is Therapy,* February 15, 2018, http://www.readingistherapy.com/praise-hard-women-joan-didion-georgia-okeeffe.
3. Ibid.
4. Lisle, *Portrait of an Artist,* 80.
5. Sarah Greenough, ed., *My Faraway One: Selected Letters of Georgia O'Keeffe and Alfred Stieglitz* (New Haven, CT: Yale University Press, 2011), letter dated September 18, 1923.
6. Ibid, letter dated October 26, 1916.
7. Ibid, letter dated June 10, 1917.
8. Ibid, letter dated November 22, 1916.
9. Lisle, *Portrait of an Artist,* 129.
10. Benita Eisler, *O'Keeffe and Stieglitz: An American Romance* (New York: Doubleday, 1991), 479.
11. Lisle, *Portrait of an Artist,* 136.
12. Ibid.
13. Greenough, ed., *My Faraway One,* introduction.
14. Lisle, *Portrait of an Artist,* 173.
15. Didion, "Georgia O'Keeffe."
16. Greenough, ed., *My Faraway One,* letter dated July 27, 1928.
17. Ibid, letter dated July 13, 1928.
18. Ibid, chapter titled "The Kiss That Is My Life: 1919–1928."
19. Ibid, letter dated September 21, 1926.
20. Ibid, chapter titled "A Terrible Rightness: 1929–1933."
21. Ibid, letter dated July 14, 1929.
22. Ibid, letter dated July 15, 1929.
23. Ibid, letter dated July 21, 1929.
24. Laurie Lisle, *Portrait of an Artist: A Biography of Georgia O'Keeffe* (New York: Washington Square Press, 1997), Apple eBook, 660.
25. Simone de Beauvoir, *The Second Sex,* trans. Constance Borde and Sheila Malovany-Chevallier (New York: Vintage Books, 2011), 152.
26. Eisler, *O'Keeffe and Stieglitz,* 477.
27. Ibid, 478.
28. Ibid, 479.

REI KAWAKUBO AND ADRIAN JOFFE

1. Thomas P. Campbell, foreword to *Rei Kawakubo Comme des Garçons: Art of the In-Between,* by Andrew Bolton (New York: Metropolitan Museum of Art, 2017).
2. Ibid.
3. Andrew Bolton, *Rei Kawakubo Comme des Garçons: Art of the In-Between* (New York: Metropolitan Museum of Art, 2017), 8.
4. Judith Thurman, "The Misfit," *The New Yorker,* July 4, 2005, www.newyorker.com/magazine/2005/07/04/the-misfit-3.
5. Vanessa Friedman, "Lunch With the FT: Adrian Joffe," *Financial Times,* January 17, 2014, https://www.ft.com/content/4ce0c520-7d35-11e3-a579-00144feabdc0.
6. Thurman, "The Misfit."
7. Jacques Hyzagi, "Rei Kawakubo's Radical Chic," *The Guardian,* September 20, 2015, https://www.theguardian.com/fashion/2015/sep/20/rei-kawakubo-radical-chic.
8. Thurman, "The Misfit."
9. J. D. Kidd, "Comme des Garçons: The Woman Behind the Boys," *Daily News Record,* May 9, 1983, quoted in Bolton, *Rei Kawakubo Comme des Garçons,* 229.
10. Christopher Bagley, "Behind Comme des Garçons Stands Zen-Loving Contrarian CEO," *Bloomberg Markets,* October 7 2014, https://www.bloomberg.com/news/articles/2014-10-07/behind-comme-des-garcons-stands-zen-loving-contrarian-ceo.
11. Friedman, "Lunch With the FT: Adrian Joffe."
12. Thurman, "The Misfit."
13. Friedman, "Lunch With the FT: Adrian Joffe."
14. Matthew Schneier, "Rei Kawakubo, the Nearly Silent Oracle of Fashion," *New York Times,* May 1, 2017, https://www.nytimes.com/2017/05/01/fashion/rei-kawakubos-commes-de-garcons.html.
15. Bolton, *Rei Kawakubo Comme des Garçons,* 29.
16. Ibid, 112.
17. Friedman, "Lunch With the FT: Adrian Joffe."
18. Susannah Frankel, "Your First Look at the New Dover Street Market London," *AnOther Magazine* online, March 11, 2016, http://www.anothermag.com/fashion-beauty/8465/your-first-look-at-the-new-dover-street-market-london.

19. [Whitney Vargas, ed.], "Rei Kawakubo," *WSJ Magazine,* September 2011, quoted in Bolton, *Rei Kawakubo Comme des Garçons,* 232.
20. Bagley, "Behind Comme des Garçons Stands Zen-Loving Contrarian CEO."
21. "Odeur 53," Comme des Garçons Parfums online product page, accessed March 30, 2019, https://www.comme-des-garcons-parfum.com/perfumes/odeur-53.
22. Susannah Frankel, "Rei Kawakubo: Fashion's Great Iconoclast," *Dazed,* September 2004, republished on *Dazed Digital,* October 3, 2015, www.dazeddigital.com/fashion/article/26740/1/rei-kawakubo-fashion-s-great-iconoclast.
23. Elaine Y. J. Lee, "The Father of CdG and DSM, Adrian Joffe, Talks New Beijing Outpost and Reveals Paris Expansion," *Hypebeast,* April 3, 2018, https://hypebeast.com/2018/4/adrian-joffe-dover-street-market-beijing-interview.

LOU REED AND LAURIE ANDERSON

1. Anthony DeCurtis, *Lou Reed: A Life* (New York: Little, Brown, and Company, 2017), 148.
2. "Lou Reed's Last Words: Watch His Final Interview," interview by Farida Khelfa, posted by *Rolling Stone* online, November 8, 2013, https://www.rollingstone.com/music/music-news/lou-reeds-last-words-watch-his-final-interview-41310.
3. Ibid.
4. Ben Sisario, "Laurie Anderson on Lou Reed's Love, Work, and Retirement Plan," *New York Times,* March 3, 2017, https://www.nytimes.com/2017/03/03/arts/music/laurie-anderson-on-lou-reeds-love-work-and-retirement-plan.html.
5. David Fricke, "Q&A: Lou Reed," *Rolling Stone,* November 5, 1987, https://www.rollingstone.com/music/music-news/qa-lou-reed-87827.
6. Jamie Diamond, "Laurie Anderson," *People,* May 7, 1990, https://people.com/archive/laurie-anderson-vol-33-no-18.
7. John Leland, "Laurie Anderson's Glorious, Chaotic New York," *New York Times,* April 21, 2017, https://www.nytimes.com/2017/04/21/nyregion/laurie-anderson-new-york.html.
8. Laurie Anderson, "Laurie Anderson's Farewell to Lou Reed: A *Rolling Stone* Exclusive," *Rolling Stone,* November 6, 2013, https://www.rollingstone.com/music/music-news/laurie-andersons-farewell-to-lou-reed-a-rolling-stone-exclusive-243792.
9. Ibid.
10. Ibid.
11. "Lou Reed Memorial 16 Laurie Anderson Talking: Personal/Artistic Relationship With Lou," YouTube video, 2:10, posted by Jim Fouratt, December 17, 2013, https://www.youtube.com/watch?v=ZpgPLlFo73o.
12. Ibid.
13. DeCurtis, *Lou Reed,* 391.
14. "Laurie Anderson and Lou Reed Interviewed by Charlie Rose (2003) - Part Two," YouTube video, 11:36, from an interview televised by CNN on July 8, 2003, posted by "Mneme Mnemosyne," April 19, 2011, https://www.youtube.com/watch?v=iQWiyKtMemo.
15. DeCurtis, *Lou Reed,* chapter 7.
16. Ibid, 216.
17. Robert Palmer, "The Pop Life," *New York Times,* March 10, 1982, https://www.nytimes.com/1982/03/10/arts/the-pop-life-239009.html.
18. DeCurtis, *Lou Reed,* 306.
19. "Lou Reed Memorial," 7:43.
20. DeCurtis, *Lou Reed,* 439.
21. Josh Jones, "Lou Reed and Laurie Anderson's Three Rules for Living Well: A Short and Succinct Life Philosophy," *Open Culture,* June 30, 2016, http://www.openculture.com/2016/06/lou-reed-and-laurie-andersons-three-rules-for-living-well.html.
22. "Lou Reed Memorial," 7:14.
23. "Lou Reed and Laurie Anderson Vivid 2010 Press Conference Un-Edited in Full Sydney, Australia," YouTube video, 15:42, posted by James DeWeaver, November 10, 2013, https://www.youtube.com/watch?v=pLeOHReBC08.
24. DeCurtis, *Lou Reed,* 414.
25. David Fricke, "Lou Reed: The *Rolling Stone* Interview," *Rolling Stone,* May 4, 1989, https://www.rollingstone.com/music/music-news/lou-reed-the-rolling-stone-interview-2-174015.
26. DeCurtis, *Lou Reed,* 458.
27. Sisario, "Laurie Anderson on Lou Reed's Love, Work, and Retirement Plan."
28. Anderson, "Laurie Anderson's Farewell to Lou Reed."
29. "Lou Reed Memorial," 9:42.
30. Leland, "Laurie Anderson's Glorious, Chaotic New York."
31. Waldemar Januszczak, "Laurie Anderson: 'Boy, This Is It. This Is All We Have,'" *The Sunday Times,* April 17, 2016, https://www.thetimes.co.uk/article/boy-this-is-it-this-is-all-we-have-mhbgzxwz7.
32. Sisario, "Laurie Anderson on Lou Reed's Love, Work, and Retirement Plan."
33. Ibid.
34. "Lou Reed Memorial," 12:13.

ALEJANDRO AND PASCALE JODOROWSKY

1. Donatien Grau, ed., *PascALEjandro: Alchemical Androgynous* (Arles: Actes Sud, 2017), 7.
2. Janelle Zara, "Witnessing the Private Spiritual Love of Cult Filmmaker Alejandro Jodorowsky and His Wife Pascale," *W* magazine, June 12, 2017, https://www.wmagazine.com/story/alejandro-jodorowsky-director-movies-wife-pascale-paris-home.
3. Alejandro and Pascale Jodorowsky, interview by Angella M. Nazarian, e-mail, September 11, 2018.
4. Ibid.
5. Ibid.
6. Ibid.
7. Idid.
8. Ibid.
9. Tara Brady, "Alejandro Jodorowsky: 'I Never Seek Money. I Make Films to Lose Money,'" *Irish Times,* December 16, 2016, https://www.irishtimes.com/culture/film/alejandro-jodorowsky-i-never-seek-money-i-make-films-to-lose-money-1.2902873.
10. Ibid.
11. Ibid.
12. Alejandro and Pascale Jodorowsky, interview by Angella M. Nazarian.
13. Steve Dollar, "Alejandro Jodorowsky's 'Dance of Reality' Takes a Look at His Painful Childhood in Chile," *Washington Post,* May 23, 2014, https://www.washingtonpost.com/lifestyle/style/alejandro-jodorowskys-dance-of-reality-takes-a-look-at-his-painful-childhood-in-chile/2014/05/22/71954c18-e1c8-11e3-9743-bb9b59cde7b9_story.html.
14. Eric Benson, "The Psychomagical Realism of Alejandro Jodorowsky," *New York Times Magazine,* March 14, 2014, https://www.nytimes.com/2014/03/16/magazine/the-psychomagical-realism-of-alejandro-jodorowsky.html.
15. Dollar, "Alejandro Jodorowsky's 'Dance of Reality' Takes a Look at His Painful Childhood in Chile."
16. Benson, "The Psychomagical Realism of Alejandro Jodorowsky."
17. Julia Yepes, "The Eternal Search of the Jodorowskys," *Interview,* July 25, 2017, https://www.interviewmagazine.com/film/jodorowsky-endless-poetry.
18. Ibid.
19. Ibid.
20. Ibid.
21. Zara, "Witnessing the Private Spiritual Love of Cult Filmmaker Alejandro Jodorowsky and His Wife Pascale."
22. Ibid.
23. Ibid.
24. Donatien Grau, "PascALEjandro," *Purple,* Spring/Summer 2017, http://purple.fr/magazine/ss-2017-issue-27/pascalejandro.
25. Alejandro and Pascale Jodorowsky, interview by Angella M. Nazarian.
26. Marilyne Buda, "A Life Ideal: Interview With the Painter Pascale Montandon-Jodorowsky," translated by Jessica Sequeira, *Ventana Latina,* January 15, 2014, www.ventanalatina.co.uk/2014/01/a-life-ideal-interview-with-the-painter-pascale-montandon-jodorowsky.
27. Alejandro and Pascale Jodorowsky, interview by Angella M. Nazarian.
28. Grau, ed., *PascALEjandro,* 253.

Acknowledgments

I am deeply grateful to Martine and Prosper Assouline—the creative couple and extraordinary husband-and-wife team behind the beautiful, well-crafted books at their publishing company. I am proud of the partnership and the work we do together. It has been a great privilege to work with such a talented and wholehearted team at Assouline publishers. Thank you to my editors, Esther Kremer and Haley Crawford, and to Cécilia Maurin, Lindsey Tulloch, Hannah Belken, and Jihyun Kim.

I am grateful to Justice Ruth Bader Ginsburg and Pascale and Alejandro Jodorowsky for their insightful stories and responses to my interview questions—it added another layer of richness to the chapters. Thank you, Caroline Dar, for keeping me on track and organized with the mountain of notes and books I had at hand.

I would like to thank David, Phillip, and Eli—you are my heart. A special thanks to Elizabeth and Lili for your never-ending support and love. Throughout the writing of this book, I was constantly reminded of my parents, Maryam and Nasser Maddahi and Soraya and Younes Nazarian. They have been living examples of thriving partnerships.

Credits

p. 13: Fine Art Images/Heritage Images/Getty Images; p. 15 (from left): Sueddeutsche Zeitung Photo/Alamy Stock Photo, ullstein bild via Getty Images; p. 23: Jane Cabot Reid Archive; p. 25 (left): Douglas Glass/Paul Popper/Popperfoto/Getty Images; (right): Fine Art Images/Heritage Images/Getty Images; p. 35: Image Rights of Salvador Dalí reserved. Fundació Gala-Salvador Dalí, Figueres, 2019; p. 36 (clockwise from top left): Patrice Picot/Gamma-Rapho via Getty Images, Philippe Halsman/Toronto Star via Getty Images, Hansel Mieth/The LIFE Picture Collection/Getty Images, Pictorial Press Ltd/Alamy Stock Photo; Photo 12/Alamy Stock Photo; p. 41: Pictorial Press Ltd/Alamy Stock Photo; p. 49: © Roger Picard; p. 51 (from left): United Archives GmbH/Alamy Stock Photo, Courtesy of Cult Epics; p. 58: Giancarlo Botti/Contributor; p. 61: Ullstein bild/ullstein bild via Getty Images; p. 64 (clockwise from top left): Gerard Gery/Paris Match via Getty Images, Bettmann/Contributor, Robert DOISNEAU/Gamma-Rapho/Getty Images; p. 69: Bettmann/Contributor; p. 73: Leonard Mccombe/The LIFE Picture Collection/Getty Images; p. 77 (clockwise from top): Paul Slade/Paris Match via Getty Images, Bettmann/Contributor, Leonard Mccombe/The LIFE Picture Collection/Getty Images; p. 83: Collection of the Supreme Court of the United States; p. 87 (clockwise from top left): The Washington Post/Contributor, Dirck Halstead/The LIFE Images Collection/Getty Images, © Stephen Crowley; p. 91: Credit: dpa picture alliance/Alamy Stock Photo; p. 93: Frank Jurkoski/Contributor; p. 97 (clockwise from top): The Asahi Shimbun/Contributor, The Asahi Shimbun/Contributor, picture alliance/Contributor; p. 103: John Bryson/Contributor; p. 105 (clockwise from top left): © Eames Office, LLC (eamesoffice.com), Allan Grant/The LIFE Picture Collection/Getty Images, Los Angeles Examiner/USC Libraries/Corbis via Getty Images; pp. 108-109: Ken Lubas/Los Angeles Times via Getty Images; pp. 114-115: Bettmann/Contributor; p. 118 (from left): Bettmann/Contributor, John Rawlings/Contributor; p. 121: United Archives GmbH/Alamy Stock Photo; p. 125: © Denis Piel; p. 127 (clockwise from top left): Henry Clarke/Condé Nast via Getty Images, Frank Leonardo/New York Post Archives/© NYP Holdings Inc. via Getty Images, Photo by Frank Edwards/Fotos International/Getty Images; p. 131: Henry Clarke/Condé Nast via Getty Images; p. 137: Everett Collection Inc/Alamy Stock Photo; p. 140: Bettmann/Contributor; p. 149: Vladimir Weinstein/BFA.com, Timothy Greenfield-Sanders/Contributor/Getty Images; p. 151 (from left): Jemal Countess/Getty Images, David X Prutting/BFA.com; p. 159: Guido Harari/Contrasto/Redux; p. 161 (clockwise from top): Gudio Harari/ Contrasto /Redux, Richard Corkery/NY Daily News via Getty Images, Will Ragozzino/Patrick McMullan via Getty Images; p. 165: JOSEP LAGO/AFP/Getty Images; p. 169: Aya Yamamoto; p. 171: © pascALEjandro; p. 175: LOIC VENANCE/AFP/Getty Images; p. 177: Bertrand Rindoff Petroff/Getty Images.

Cover: Ken Lubas/Los Angeles Times via Getty Images.

3 Park Ave, 27th Floor
New York, NY 10016, USA
Tel.: 212-989-6769 Fax: 212-647-0005
www.assouline.com

Editorial direction: Esther Kremer
Creative direction: Jihyun Kim
Art direction: Hannah Belken
Editor: Haley Crawford
Photo editor: Elizabeth Eames
Printed in Turkey
ISBN: 9781614288527

cre·a·tive (krē-'ā-tiv, 'krē)
or power to create: given
2. having the quality of so
imitated: *imaginative* [the ~
esp: one involved in the
2. creative activity or the
in advertisting.

cou·ple ('kə-pəl) *n.* [ME,
married, engaged or oth
b. two persons paired tog
something that joins or lin